AN ORGANIC ARCHITECTURE

■ GROWTH IS A PROCESS OF BECOMING—DECAY IS SO NO LESS. ONLY GROWTH NEEDS OR EVER FINDS EXPRESSION.

■ DEATH IS A CRISIS OF GROWTH.

■ FROM THE GROUND UP IS GOOD SENSE FOR BUILDING. BEWARE OF FROM THE TOP DOWN.

■ BUILDINGS LIKE TREES ARE BROTHERS TO THE MAN. BUILDINGS TREES AND MAN ALL ARE OUT OF THE GROUND INTO THE LIGHT.

■ GOOD FORM IS GOOD SENSE PUT INTO SOME EFFECTIVE SHAPE APPROPRIATE TO SOME MATERIAL.

■ FORM IS MADE BY FUNCTION BUT QUALIFIED BY USE. THEREFORE FORM CHANGES WITH CHANGING CONDITIONS. THE LAST ANALYSIS IS NEVER MADE.

■ WHAT WE UNDERSTAND AND APPRECIATE WE OWN ... WE MAY BE JANITORS OR POLICEMEN OF MORE—BUT THAT IS ALL.

■ CHEWING-GUM THE ROCKING-CHAIR AND PICTURIZING ARE ALL HABITS EQUALLY VALUABLE TO MODERN ART.

■ A MATTER OF TASTE IS USUALLY A MATTER OF IGNORANCE.

■ GENUINE EXPRESSIONS OF PRINCIPLE-AT-WORK AS FORM WILL ALWAYS BE VALUABLE ACHIEVEMENTS OF GROWTH, AND SHOULD BE THROWN AWAY NO MORE THAN BOOKS WHICH EMBODIED TRUTH IN ANY AGE.

■ ALL FORMS STAND PROPHETIC BEAUTIFUL AND FOREVER INSOFAR AS THEY WERE IN THEMSELVES TRUTH EMBODIED. THEY BECOME UGLY AND USELESS ONLY WHEN FORCED TO SEEM AND BE WHAT THEY ARE NOT AND CANNOT BE. LIFE HAS GONE BY SUCCESSION INTO FOLLOWING FORMS.

■ CREATION NEVER IMITATES. CREATION ASSIMILATES ... THE CREATURE IMITATES AND SIMULATES.

■ TRUTH IS PRINCIPLE INVIOLATE ... BUT IN BUILDING FINDS INFINITIVE VARIETY OF EXPRESSION.

■ THE SENSE OF ROMANCE IN ALL HUMAN SENSE OF RHYTHM .... THE HUMAN SPIRIT IS ATTRACTED BY IT AS THE ANIMAL SENSES OF TASTE OR SMELL ARE ATTRACTED BY SWEETS OR PERFUMES ... STYLE.

MODERN ARCHITECTURE

FRANK LLOYD WRIGHT

PRINCETON MONOGRAPHS IN ART AND ARCHAEOLOGY

MODERN ARCHITECTURE
BEING THE KAHN LECTURES FOR 1930
BY FRANK LLOYD WRIGHT

WITH A NEW INTRODUCTION BY NEIL LEVINE

PUBLISHED FOR THE DEPARTMENT OF
ART AND ARCHAEOLOGY OF PRINCETON
UNIVERSITY
PRINCETON UNIVERSITY PRESS
PRINCETON AND OXFORD

Requests for permission to reproduce material from this work
should be sent to Permissions, Princeton University Press

Published by Princeton University Press,
41 William Street, Princeton, New Jersey 08540
In the United Kingdom: Princeton University Press,
3 Market Place, Woodstock, Oxfordshire OX20 1SY

First published, 1931
Facsimile edition, with a new introduction by Neil Levine, 2008

Library of Congress Control Number 2007940601

ISBN 978-0-691-12937-2

British Library Cataloging-in-Publication Data is available

Printed on acid-free paper. ∞

press.princeton.edu

Printed in the United States of America

10 9 8 7 6 5 4 3 2 1

DEDICATED TO YOUNG MEN IN ARCHITECTURE—F.L.W.

CONTENTS

INTRODUCTION

NEIL LEVINE

In a review in the *New Republic* in July 1931, just three months after Frank Lloyd Wright's *Modern Architecture: Being the Kahn Lectures for 1930* was originally published, the brilliant young critic and early devotee of European modern architecture Catherine Bauer described it as "the very best book on modern architecture that exists."[1] A future leader in social housing and community planning, Bauer wrote this neither out of ignorance of the field nor out of personal sympathy with the author's position in it. She had spent the year 1926–27 and the summer and early fall of 1930 in Europe, where she met many of the important figures in the modern movement and studied the work being done. Ernst May and J.J.P. Oud, both deeply engaged in the area of housing, along with her mentor and lover Lewis Mumford, whom she met in 1928, were particularly instrumental in shaping her thinking on the social and collective purposes of architecture.

Bauer began her review of the Wright book affirming her belief that "architecture is intrinsically an unsatisfactory field of expression for the individual poet-genius." "A new architecture," she continued, "depends primarily on the careful establishment and strict acceptance of an idiom that has its roots in the social and economic structure of the time." Acknowledging that Wright was "without doubt the most brilliant individual architect of our time," she deplored the fact that he "only wants to express his own personality" and thus concluded in the review's preamble that his way was not the way of the future. "The future," she stated, "lay in the hands of men like Oud in Holland, Gropius and Stam and May in Germany," who have worked "to strip architecture to its essentials, [and] who have suppressed their differences in the interests of the unit and the whole."[2]

At this point, Bauer stopped and declared: "So much for the convictions of the reviewer. . . . [Bauer's ellipses]" and then went on to exclaim: "Exuberant, confessedly romantic, insistently individualistic, at times even florid and rhetorical, [this book] is still (and I say it, who fought my rising enthusiasm at every turn of a page) the very best book on modern architecture that exists." After summarizing and analyzing its contents, she finally concluded:

I am, still, in active disagreement with about a third of the book. I still would really rather live in a workingman's house in Frankfurt [by Ernst May] than in one of Mr.

ix

Wright's handsome prairie mansions. I still believe that symbolic variations cannot be invented cold on a drafting board, that they must evolve *in time* out of the functional forms themselves or not at all. But, fundamental as this criticism may sound, it detracts very little from my perplexing enthusiasm. . . . [Parts of this book are] so rich in sound observation, trenchant comment and philosophic purity that architecture itself takes on a new dignity, a fresh social importance. And Frank Lloyd Wright emerges as one of the most interesting figures that America has yet produced.[3]

In its exceedingly direct and honest assessment, Bauer's review reveals both the enormous significance of Wright's book as well as the complex and ambiguous status it bears in relation to the evolving history of modern architecture in what is usually considered to be its heroic stage.

Culminating a period of intense development and radical change since the beginning of the century, four books were published in English between 1929 and 1932 under the general title *Modern Architecture*. The one by the German architect Bruno Taut attempted to explain the "principles of the new movement" mainly through its production on the European continent and under the influence of the new material, social, and economic conditions of the industrial age.[4] The other three texts all carried subtitles. The young architectural historian Henry-Russell Hitchcock's *Modern Architecture: Romanticism and Reintegration*, which also came out in 1929, was the first comprehensive historical account and analysis in English of the movement, locating its origins in the breakdown of the classical system in the later eighteenth century and the ensuing eclecticism and technological advances of the following one.[5]

Hitchcock was also directly involved, along with Philip Johnson, Alfred Barr, and Lewis Mumford (who was assisted by Bauer) in the last of these books to appear, *Modern Architecture: International Exhibition*, which served as the catalogue for the show at the Museum of Modern Art in New York that took place in the early months of 1932 and that introduced the American audience to the architecture that the authors referred to as the International Style. Intending neither to trace the history of the movement nor to outline its social and industrial sources or implications, the exhibition catalogue focused on the formal characteristics that defined modern architecture as a "genuinely new style." One of the architects given a featured place in the exhibition, along with Oud, Ludwig Mies van der Rohe, and Le Corbusier, was their architectural "uncle" Frank Lloyd Wright. This was "not," as Barr wrote, because he is "intimately related to the Style" nor merely a "pioneer ancestor," but because, as "a passionately independent genius whose career is a history of original discovery and contradiction," his work had to be seen as "the embodiment of the romantic principle of individualism" that "remains a challenge to the classical austerity of the style of his younger contemporaries."[6]

Wright's *Modern Architecture* appeared the year before the International Style exhibition. In its focus on the role of the individual in the creation of a spiritually liberated form of modern, democratic design along with its opposition of the idea of "an organic architecture" to one based on a collective "machine aesthetic," Wright's book stands as his first major public pronouncement on the subject of how his architecture fits into the development of the modern movement. It is the first actual book he ever published and thus represents the beginning of a determined effort on his part to bring his views on modern architecture into the public domain, an effort that soon saw the appearance of *An Autobiography* and *The Disappearing City* (both 1932) followed by numerous other books over the next twenty-seven years.[7] While laying out the groundwork for a conception of a modern architecture grounded in nature and eschewing the mechanistic and functionalistic stereotypes of the "machine aesthetic," Wright's *Modern Architecture* also foreshadows the new world of decentralized living the architect was soon to call Broadacre City, a world that was to offer all the advantages of modern technology without any of the disadvantages of the urban congestion and blight that many recognized at the time as a major consequence of modernity.

THE PRINCETON KAHN LECTURES

As its subtitle indicates, Wright's *Modern Architecture* was based on a series of public lectures. The fact that these lectures took place at Princeton University in the spring of 1930 is quite extraordinary, considering the conservative character of architectural education at American institutions of higher learning at the time. Walter Gropius would not begin his career at Harvard until 1937 and Mies would not begin his at the Armour (later Illinois) Institute of Technology until the following year.[8] But the invitation to Wright to lecture at Princeton was not offered by the university's School of Architecture as such. Rather, it came from its art history department, then as now known as the Department of Art and Archaeology and under whose aegis the School of Architecture functioned as a fully integrated entity from the time of its establishment in 1919–20 until the early 1950s.[9]

Princeton's Department of Art and Archaeology was the oldest in the country, dat-

INTRODUCTION

ing from 1883–85.[10] It was also one of the largest and certainly one of the most prominent. Among its distinguished faculty in 1930 were Frank Jewett Mather, Charles Rufus Morey, Earl Baldwin Smith, and Theodore Leslie Shear, almost all specialists in medieval and ancient art or architecture. Sherley W. Morgan, an associate professor in the department, served as director of the School of Architecture. Morey, whose main interest lay in medieval iconography, was the prime mover of the department as well as one of the leading figures in the development of art history as a discipline in the United States. He served as department chair from the early 1920s through the mid-1940s, during which time he proved to be a highly successful fundraiser, with special emphasis on the department's publications program.

One of the persons Morey was able to attract as a major donor to the department was the New York banker and philanthropist Otto H. Kahn. Born in Germany, where he got his start in banking, Kahn emigrated to the United States in 1893, first working in New York with Speyer & Company and then with Kuhn, Loeb & Company, where he eventually became a chief partner and the firm's expert in the financing of railroads. His great love was music, and he began his support of New York's Metropolitan Opera Company in 1903, becoming chair in 1911 and president in 1918. He also gave a significant amount of money to underwrite the restoration of the Parthenon in Athens. In the area of higher education, he served as a trustee of the Carnegie Institute of Technology, the Massachusetts Institute of Technology, and Rutgers University.

Morey began corresponding with Kahn in 1923 soon after the financier's son entered Princeton as an undergraduate. By the spring of 1924, Kahn had agreed to give the Department of Art and Archaeology $1,500 a year for two years (subsequently increased to three) in part to bring lecturers from Europe for extended stays.[11] Over the next three years, the scholars brought to Princeton through Kahn's gift included Michael Ivanovitch Rostovzeff, the social and economic historian of the ancient world; the French Byzantinist and professor of aesthetics at the Collège de France Gabriel Millet; and the British Middle Eastern archaeologist John Garstang, who lectured on Hittite art and archaeology.[12]

In 1927 Kahn joined the art history department's Visiting Committee (on which he remained until his death in 1934) and promptly agreed to the "continuation" of his support for a lecture series. The "Kahn Lectures," as they came to be officially called, were to run for a five-year period, beginning in the academic year 1928–29. Out of the $1,500 to be spent annually, half was to go for the lecturer's fee and half for publication costs either for the lectures or for any other books in the Princeton Monographs in Art and Archaeology series. The annual "course" of lectures was "to be eight in number with two evening seminars for graduate students and members of the faculty at which the research problems in the subject will be discussed."[13]

In its deliberations over who should be the first invitee, the department considered Arthur Pillans Laurie, a British authority on the technical processes of painting from antiquity through the seventeenth century, and Eugénie Sellers Strong, the classical archaeologist and art historian noted particularly for her work on Greek and Roman art. Without mentioning any names, it also considered the options of "a lecturer on American [meaning Precolumbian] Archaeology . . . and a lecturer on Architecture."[14] In the end, Johnny Roosval, a respected Swedish medievalist and the first professor of art history at Stockholm University, was invited to speak in the spring of 1929 on the history of Swedish art. Despite the fact that he had no expertise in the field, he was asked to make "particular reference to Swedish architecture, including some of the modern developments."[15] Roosval's lectures, which were apparently not very exciting, were published in 1932 by Princeton University Press in the Princeton Monographs series under the title *Swedish Art: Being the Kahn Lectures for 1929.*[16]

One senses that there were those in the department lobbying for a speaker on architecture, and particularly modern architecture, since that is precisely the field that was targeted for the Kahn Lectures for 1929–30. In his talk on "Frank Lloyd Wright and Princeton," given at Princeton University in the spring of 1980 in the colloquium "Frank Lloyd Wright and the Princeton Lectures of 1930" celebrating the fiftieth anniversary of the event, Robert Judson Clark, upon whose research and insights I have relied heavily for this history, states that a major source for the push for architecture was the request by one of the younger members of the faculty, the medieval architectural historian George Forsyth who was then teaching the required Modern Architecture course, to have "practicing architects be brought in to augment this course."[17] Indeed, the reason given by Morey to the architect eventually chosen by the department for holding the lectures at the end of April or the beginning of May was so that they would "coincide with the closing part of our Modern Architecture course."[18]

Frank Lloyd Wright was not the department's initial choice for the second round of Kahn Lectures. Rather, it was Oud, who at the time was the chief architect of the Municipal Housing Authority of Rotterdam and one of the recognized leaders of the modern movement in Europe. Morey wrote to Oud in early January 1929 asking him if he would "consent to deliver a course of lectures . . . on the modern architecture of Europe or of Holland, or any aspect of the latest movements in architecture which you would prefer to treat." "We feel that no one could speak with more authority than yourself" on "the modernist movement in architecture." Morey also promised that a publication of the lectures in the Princeton Monographs in Art and Archaeology would be part of the deal.[19]

It is unclear precisely who suggested Oud to Morey and his colleagues. Though certainly not a household name by then, Oud had become a star in the rising pantheon of younger European architects. Still, you had to be in the know. Henry-Russell Hitchcock, the most serious and trusted young critic and historian of the movement in the United States, wrote an important article in *The Arts* magazine in February 1928, a year before the invitation, praising Oud's work "as of a quality equal to any which the new manner has achieved in France or Germany" and asserting, in his final sentence, that Oud's work had to be viewed alongside that of Le Corbusier to appreciate its true merit. "Oud and Le Corbusier," Hitchcock wrote, "are as different one from the other as Iktinos [the architect of the Parthenon] and the architect of the temple of Concord [at Agrigento] or the master of Laon and he of Paris."[20] In other words, each is a master in his own right, equal to those who designed the greatest monuments of antiquity and the Middle Ages. Philip Johnson was blown away by this piece and later claimed that his "conversion" to "modern architecture" "came in 1929 when I read [the] article by Henry-Russell Hitchcock on the architecture of J. J. P. Oud."[21] In addition to the purely artistic merits of the work, not to speak of its profound social values, Oud impressed his young American admirers, whether it be Hitchcock, Johnson, or Bauer, with his straightforwardness, his informality, and his openness to discourse.[22]

In his letter of invitation to Oud, Morey stated that "from my friend, Mr. Henry [-]Russell Hitchcock, I have learned that there might be some prospect of obtaining your consent" to give the Kahn Lectures.[23] Can one assume from this that it was Hitchcock who recommended Oud in the first place, or was he just the intermediary? Nothing that we know so far can help answer this question.[24] What we do know is that Oud responded positively, although he requested an additional $250 for his honorarium and wondered whether the lectures could be scheduled for "final [sic] May or early June."[25] Morey agreed to the first but not the second request, remarking, as noted above, that the talks were planned to "coincide" with the last two weeks of the department's "Modern Architecture course."[26]

Everything seemed to proceed according to schedule through the summer and early fall. Morey wrote enthusiastically to Kahn in June of Oud's impending visit:

We expect a rather fine series from Oud, and one that will make something of a sensation in Princeton, which needs waking up to modern architecture very much, so far as the University outside of the Department is concerned. The students in the School of Architecture are drawing a la moderne more and more, and to my mind extremely well, under the guidance of [Jean] Labatut [the School's chief design critic]. Labatut is a Beaux-Arts man and not a modernist in any sense of the word, but he is an exponent of sound architectural principles and does not care at all how they are applied. Consequently, he puts no impediment in the way of the natural trend of the students toward the modernistic style, but his criticism makes them do modern buildings in a sound way.[27]

Morey was certainly correct in assuming that Oud's lectures would create a "sensation," although he clearly underestimated how large and widespread the sensation would have been. He also clearly showed that he had very little idea of what modern architecture was as Oud, Hitchcock, or Bauer understood the term.

Morey wrote the above letter to Kahn on the same day he received one from Oud's wife containing material about the architect to be used for publicity purposes. More ominously, the letter also mentioned that the architect was having health problems, leading Morey to respond that "I shall assume unless I hear to the contrary that Mr. Oud will be able to deliver the lectures in the first two weeks of May, 1930."[28] Oud was suffering from frequent periods of depression, which ultimately led him to cancel his visit. Word did not come to Morey, however, until late December or early January. In a handwritten P.S. to a letter to Kahn of 21 January 1930, Morey said that "Oud has written that he can't come over, on account of illness." Interestingly he then added that "we are asking [the Precolumbian scholar Herbert Joseph] Spinden to give the course on 'Central American Art and Archaeology,' this being something we have wanted for a long time."[29]

Spinden was among those considered for the first Kahn Lectureship. He was the leading Precolumbianist at the time and was recently appointed Curator of Ethnology at the Brooklyn Institute (later Museum). It is unclear, however, whether he was actually ever contacted by Morey, who was about to sail for Europe in two weeks for a leave of absence that would last through September. Spinden eventually gave the third

INTRODUCTION

Kahn Lectures, in January 1931, once Morey returned. Whether he deferred the offer or was not made the offer, Frank Lloyd Wright surfaced as the department's nominee for the second round of Kahn Lectures at the very beginning of February 1930, when Baldwin Smith replaced Morey as acting chair.

Unlike Morey, who was a specialist in painting and sculpture, Smith was a historian of architecture, both ancient and medieval, who began teaching courses in the School of Architecture upon its establishment by Howard Crosby Butler, whose literary executor Smith became on the latter's death in 1922. Smith refocused the search for a replacement for Oud on finding a contemporary architect engaged in the theory and practice of modern architecture. How Wright came to be the person chosen is not known for sure. Robert Clark suggested that George Forsyth, who was from Chicago, first brought up the architect's name, although Sherley Morgan claimed to have had a role in the decision. In any event, given Wright's historical stature and the short lead-time before the lectures were to be given, the decision to invite him seems quite logical in retrospect.[30]

Wright, of course, was most well known at the time for his work in and around Chicago in the period 1893–1909, when, according to Hitchcock, "he created by an imaginative analysis at once intellectual and instinctive most of the aesthetic resources developed by the modern architects of Europe since the War," to wit, "the open planning, the free plastic composition, the grouped fenestration, and the horizontality" all evident in the architect's early Prairie Style. "He was also the first," Hitchcock stated, "to conceive of architectural design in terms of planes existing freely in three dimensions rather than in terms of enclosed blocks."[31] Oud himself had written about Wright's "flawless work" in an important article, "The Influence of Frank Lloyd Wright on the Architecture of Europe," published in English in the Dutch journal *Wendingen* in 1925 and reprinted the following year in German in Oud's *Holländische Architektur*, which came out in Gropius's and Laszlo Moholy-Nagy's Bauhausbücher series.[32]

But the interest in Wright's work tended to remain limited to what he had produced prior to 1910. And while he had done important buildings after that date, namely, his own country house and studio Taliesin in Hillside, Wisconsin (begun 1911), Midway Gardens in Chicago (1913–14), the Imperial Hotel in Tokyo (1913–23), and Hollyhock House in Los Angeles (1919–21), these did not seem to most knowledgeable observers to be as forward-looking as the earlier work. In fact, much of it seemed positively regressive in terms of its massing, its symmetry, and, especially, its decorative elaboration. Furthermore, since returning from the nearly four years he spent in Tokyo working on the Imperial Hotel, which he no doubt thought would take his career onto a new plane of operations, Wright built next to nothing during the 1920s—four private houses in Los Angeles between 1923 and 1925, a rather conservative summer house for a return client on the shore of Lake Erie (1926–28), a house for a cousin in Tulsa, Oklahoma (1928–31), and a temporary camp of canvas and wood for himself in the Arizona desert (1929).

Yet Wright continued to attract European modern architects to work for him and to visit him. These included Heinrich (Henry) Klumb, Erich Mendelsohn, Werner Moser, and Richard Neutra. More importantly, he turned his hand to writing and began publishing a series of articles in the mainstream professional journal *Architectural Record* that brought him and his theories back into public focus. Between May 1927 and December 1928, he published fourteen pieces under the general title "In the Cause of Architecture," ranging in subject matter from the role of the machine and standardization in modern design to the issues of style, meaning, use, and the expression of materials. These articles, which predicted much that Wright would talk about at Princeton, also included illustrations of recent projects.[33] Moreover, Wright directly entered the current debate with a review of Le Corbusier's *Towards a New Architecture* that came out in September 1928, shortly after the book's appearance in English translation (1927), and an attack on Hitchcock and the critic Douglas Haskell following their characterization of his architecture as simply an outmoded prelude to current European practices.[34] But the fact remains that Wright's work was still being discussed and the very same year Hitchcock wrote his 1928 article on Oud, he also published a small book on Wright in France in the Masters of Contemporary Architecture series of the avant-garde house Cahiers d'Art.[35]

In his capacity as acting chair of the department as well as acting director of the School of Architecture, Smith wrote to Wright on 3 February 1930 to invite him to give the Kahn Lectures "between May 5th and May 16th."[36] Smith's letter is interesting on a number of counts, none of which, of course, would have been discernible to Wright. First, it was written on School of Architecture stationary. Second, the invitation was extended on behalf of both the department and the school. And third, the Kahn Lectures were described as a series devoted to "problems of contemporary and artistic interest," a statement that was fundamentally untrue. Wright was then asked "if you could give this series of eight lectures on Modern Architecture in America and Europe, with emphasis as you see fit upon both the theory and the practice." Smith added that he hoped "to get the University to publish the course lectures as a book or monograph" and ended by saying: "I can assure you that you will have a very enthusiastic and intelligent audience, and that the School of Architecture will be very pleased at having your assistance in putting across the ideas of modern building."[37]

Wright had almost no work in the office at the time and, due in large part to the stock market crash the previous October, chances looked extremely dim, if not already entirely out of the question, for his ongoing projects for the San Marcos in the Desert Hotel in the South Phoenix Mountains, Arizona (1928–30), St. Mark's Towers in New York (1929–30), and the Elizabeth Noble Apartments in Los Angeles (1929–30). Wright must have answered Smith the moment he received the letter, for his positive response is dated 8 February. But his acceptance of the offer was not, as some have suggested, based on the prospect of immediate financial gain. The fee of $125 per lecture was "less than merely nominal," as the architect later told Smith. For the 1927–28 "In the Cause of Architecture" series for the *Architectural Record*, he received $500 per article.[38] Rather, Wright's reasons for jumping at the opportunity to give the Kahn Lectures was the prestige of the venue and the bully pulpit it would afford him.

Appreciating "the invitation to help Princeton get her ideas on modern building somewhat nearer the source than other universities have succeeded in doing, so far" and noting that he would be "busy in New York about the time you mention," Wright informed Smith that he would gladly accept, but with one caveat: "I do not know," he wrote, "how well able I may be to sustain interest,—either mine or my hearers,—in a series of eight lectures." "But why eight lectures?" he asked, adding charmingly though cunningly: "In six days the world was made, on the seventh the work was visible and the maker no doubt viewing it,—let us assume with 'the modest assurance of con[s]cious worth!![']'" "Could we not make it six?" he asked, "a seventh to consist of an exhibition I could appropriately arrange, of my own recent work illustrating the ideas and principles involved in the 'course.'"[39]

Wright also included in his response the titles and sequence of the six lectures almost exactly as they would be three months later:

1 Materials and the Machine

2 Style in Industry

3 The Passing of the Cornice

4 The Tyrrany [*sic*] of the Skyscraper

5 The Cardboard House.

6 The City.

7 Exhibition.[40]

Wright never, at this time or later, gave a general title for the series, and certainly not that of "Modern Architecture," which became the title of the book based on the lectures.[41]

Smith responded to Wright immediately, saying a series of six rather than eight lectures, accompanied by an exhibition, would be perfectly satisfactory and that, based on the list of "suggested topics," he was "sure that the course is going to be a treat and an inspiration to our architects." "Having just returned from Europe," he added, "I realize both how conservative our architectural schools are and how far we all have to go in order to digest the modern demands."[42] A week later, Wright wrote back to Smith, amending slightly the titles and sequence of the lectures and suggesting dates both for the lectures and the exhibition.[43] He also alluded to the fact that he already had plans for a traveling exhibition of his work. After "starting at Princeton it may go on to the Architectural League of New York and then at various universities and institutions on the way west," although he assured Smith that "the preview will be Princeton's."[44]

At the same time, Wright pushed to have the lectures be more informal, discussion-type sessions than was expected, claiming inexperience as well as personal inclination for such a format. "Whenever I have attempted lectures, which is not often," Wright told Smith, "I have found it far more interesting to myself and to my audience to let them consist of questions being asked and answered, provoking as many questions as possible. I think you can get the best out of me by some such method as this," tellingly adding, "inasmuch as the best work I have ever done was the result of provocation of this sort." To "record the discussions," he asked if Princeton might provide a stenographer.[45]

In a very polite and elegant though resolute way, Smith responded that he would make sure "a stenographer is present to record the discussions" but that formal lectures were the order of the day. "My own feeling," Smith wrote, "is that your lectures will be so popular, and the attendance so large, that there will not be much 'give and take' during the actual lectures themselves, but that afterwards on the one or two

INTRODUCTION

evenings when you have an informal discussion with the men [i.e., graduate students and faculty], you will get as many questions as you may possibly care to answer." His only query to Wright was whether the architect would use lantern slides to "illustrate" his lectures.[46]

Wright bowed to Smith's insistence on formal lectures and worked extremely fast to produce them. On 1 April, which is to say less than two months after receiving the invitation, he wrote back to Smith to say that "the lectures are now finished, and I must say I have enjoyed writing them." As for slides, however, he said that he thought the lectures "had better be discourses uninterrupted by pictures," adding that he "never cared much for illustrated lectures."[47] Smith, again politely but resolutely, disagreed with Wright on the issue of slides and said that, with the texts of the lectures in hand, he and his staff would choose the appropriate "illustrative material," which would be shown at the end of each lecture. Wright accepted Smith's suggestions, and slides were apparently shown not only at the end of each lecture but sometimes at appropriate moments during the lectures themselves.[48]

Wright sent all six lectures to Smith on 1 May, with the final titles and sequence as follows: "Machinery, Materials and Men," "Style in Industry," "The Passing of the Cornice," "The Cardboard House," "The Tyranny of the Skyscraper," and "The City." He also sent copies of a publication of "short sayings gleaned from the Princeton lectures" that he hoped could be handed out at the beginning of the first lecture (these would become the "Modern Concepts Concerning an Organic Architecture" printed on the endpapers of the book).[49] By now, it was the exhibition that was preoccupying Wright. He noted its significance in terms of his career, telling Smith that "this will be the first time that I have made any effort in the direction of an exhibit since 1907 [he should have said 1914]," and that "this is the real performance that you may look forward to at Princeton." Set up as a "self-contained unit for travel," it was to be comprised of drawings and models plus "several hundred photographs."[50]

The lectures took place on 6, 7, 8, 9, 13, and 14 May and without a hitch, except for the fact that the announcement in the university's *Weekly Bulletin* reversed the order of the third and fourth talks, the ones on 8 and 9 May, and listed the title of the second talk incorrectly, adding the subtitle that was included in Wright's letter of 17 February.[51] Also, a general title for the entire series, "The Problems of Modern Architecture," preceded each individual lecture title despite the fact Wright never supplied one nor was asked for one.[52] The lectures received extensive coverage in the student newspaper, the *Daily Princetonian*, where each was summarized and quoted at some length.[53] The exhibition, which opened on 12 May, was reported on two separate occasions.[54]

According to all accounts, the lectures were a great success. Attendance never fell off, as so often happens in such series, and the audience found Wright to be an inspiring, "almost hypnotic" speaker, who "lectured as though preaching, but not pontificating."[55] Wright apparently stuck closely to his written texts, either reading them or speaking from memory. Both Forsyth and Martin Beck, a recently appointed member of the design faculty, commented on the seriousness with which he approached the task and how well prepared he was. According to Robert Judson Clark, Beck, who was one of those responsible for looking after Wright while he was on campus, recalled that "the night before each lecture [Wright] stayed in, preparing it" to the point that it was "semi-memorized" when he delivered it the next day.[56] Smith reported to Kahn soon after the event that "everyone in the Department feels that it has been our most successful Kahn lecture. He [Wright] has inspired the architectural students and interested a very large public in the whole question of modern architecture in its relation to modern life."[57]

The presentation of the Kahn Lectures gave Wright an experience he had never had before, that of speaking to a sophisticated academic audience over a period of two weeks and having discussions with students and faculty every day during that time. Wright wrote to Smith saying, "I think I enjoyed my Princeton experience more than anybody else could have enjoyed it and probably learned more, too."[58] In a sense, the Princeton lectures opened a new career path for Wright. In the year following those May talks, he lectured at universities, museums, and other institutions in Chicago, Denver, New York, Ann Arbor, Minneapolis, Eugene, Oregon, and Seattle.[59] The exhibition first seen at Princeton proved to be equally important for his reputation and career. After opening on 29 May for a two-week run at the Architectural League in New York, it traveled to the Art Institute of Chicago, and then to Madison, Wisconsin, Milwaukee, the University of Oregon at Eugene, and the University of Washington in Seattle, before touring Europe for six months, where it opened on 9 May 1931 for a three-week run at the Stedelijk Museum in Amsterdam, followed by stops in Berlin, Stuttgart, Antwerp, and Brussels.[60]

The continuing series of Kahn Lectures, by contrast, had a less dramatic and less long-lasting effect on the history of art and architecture. Following Morey's resumption of the position of chair of the art history department, H. J. Spinden gave the third Kahn Lectures on Central American Art and Archaeology in January 1931, at the same time the publication of Wright's talks was in its final stages of production. The fourth, and last, Kahn Lectures were given by the British Orientalist Edward Denison Ross, professor of Persian at the University of London and founding director of the School of Oriental (and later African) Studies in London. His lectures on Persian art, delivered in the fall of 1931, were described by Smith to Wright as "rather flat, as the Englishman thought he could chat along pleasantly on most anything to an American audience."[61] Neither Spinden's nor Ross's lectures were published.

The department's choice for the fifth round, to take place in the fall of 1932, was the leading French medieval architectural historian Marcel Aubert. Due to a scheduling conflict with his teaching duties at Yale, where he was to be a visiting professor, he had to cancel the Princeton engagement. Rather than look for someone else, and in light of the financial crunch graduate students were experiencing, Morey suggested to Kahn that the lecture fee be given as a fellowship to a needy student in 1932–33.[62] Kahn, who had himself suffered serious financial losses in the preceding few years, decided he could not renew his gift for another five years, and the Kahn Lectureship thus came to an untimely and rather undramatic end.

FROM "PRINCETON LECTURES" TO *MODERN ARCHITECTURE* BOOK

The book *Modern Architecture* that records Wright's Kahn Lectures is without a doubt the most historically significant outcome of the entire lecture series as well as being a signal event in the history of Wright's career and its engagement with the modern movement in architecture. The editing, design, and production of the volume that appeared in April 1931 as the fifteenth publication in the Princeton Monographs in Art and Archaeology series proceeded in an atmosphere of mutual respect and collegiality. One might have expected otherwise given the initial reactions to the text of the lectures expressed to Wright by Smith, who was to serve as editor.[63] Two months after the lectures, and basing his remarks solely on his memory of them, he wrote to say that in beginning to think about the "preparation of your manuscript for publication" and "if you are not too busy, I would like to suggest a chapter on your methods of designing, and the introduction of more concrete points based upon your own work and experience." Granting the "great literary quality" of the lectures, Smith further noted that they were clearly written "to be delivered and not read," which led him to suggest to Wright that it might be best "to condense some of the paragraphs and sentences."

Smith ended, however, by saying that "this letter is only a preliminary one" and any final thoughts would have to wait until he had a chance to reread the manuscript.[64]

Smith was perfectly on target in his criticisms, especially the lack of reference by Wright to specific aspects of his own design methods and work. While the architect ultimately did nothing to alter the text in this regard, nor did Smith finally ever ask him to, Wright's response to Smith's letter quoted above was entirely friendly, even accommodating.[65] "The publication of the 'Lectures' can only gain by your interest in them, so do read them again and put marginal notes wherever you conceive a suggestion. Your suggestions will all be sympathetic as well as practical, I know. . . . I am sure your perspective would be invaluable." Wright even invited Smith and his wife to come to Taliesin for a week to work together on the project.[66]

Just recently remarried and in the process of moving, Smith said he had to decline the offer to visit Wright. But having reread most of the manuscript following his previous letter, he stated that he had changed his mind quite decidedly on what needed to be done to get the lectures into shape. "Impressed by their appeal and . . . most anxious to get them to the printer," he told Wright that he now had "no suggestions of any importance . . . to make in regard to changes."[67] This change of mind was elaborated on in the preface Smith wrote for the book, where he said: "I, at first, made the mistake of wishing that he [Wright] had been more explicit, had told more about his methods and less about his theory of life. As I listened to his lectures and talked with the man I saw my mistake, and realized that Wright did not want to give to his public merely his particular forms, developed by him to meet specific conditions. Instead, fearful lest his buildings be copied and repeated as an easy ritual for unimaginative moderns, he wanted only to stir others with his dreams of the possibilities open to architecture in our present age."[68] Smith had obviously been entirely won over to Wright's way of thinking.

Rather than attempting to alter Wright's text in any significant way, Smith focused on issues of layout and design, thus taking the initial steps on that score. He said that he thought the book would have "a very wide sale" and, no doubt thinking of the typically staid design of the Princeton Monographs series, wanted the book to be given "an artistic form." His first suggestion was "to bring out the lectures in a cardboard binding with one of your own decorative color designs for the cover and your precepts [the 'short sayings' handed out at the first lecture] arranged [as endpapers] . . . in the front and back where everyone will see them." He appended a drawing to illustrate his ideas, which Wright obviously liked, for the final design of the book followed Smith's suggestions for both the cover and the endpapers. Smith's final suggestion at this point was to have a photograph of Wright "in the front of the book . . . and then spread through the book examples of his work."[69] Both of these wishes were fulfilled, although the second one much less amply and in a much less up-to-date fashion than he had hoped for.

Wright agreed to Smith's suggestions for the endpapers and for the cover. He had an assistant, Henry Klumb, rework the design "Sahuaro Forms and Cactus Flowers" that he had produced in 1927–28 for one of the covers for *Liberty* magazine that never saw the light of day. He sent a sketch of it to Smith sometime around the middle of August, saying that "a cover of this type puts a different face on 'lectures.' Something ought to take the curse off them." He added that, although it will probably be expensive to produce "if it is executed as I have designed it," "many people will buy the book just for the sake of the cover." As part of the cover design, Wright also suggested "a simple title lettered on back and front." From all we can tell, he assumed the title would be *The Princeton Lectures.* [70]

As for the suggestion regarding illustrations, Wright took issue with Smith, saying they should be "limited in number and [simply] cover a few entire pages in the rear of the book, keeping the typography of the book uninterrupted." And instead of his own image appearing at the front of the book, Wright thought it, too, could be at the rear, "to preface" the others. Finally he asked Smith if he would be willing to write a "prefatory page." Since he had "introduced the lectures," this would, in Wright's mind, "be appropriate and maintain the style and substance of the occasion," celebrated, as the architect thought it would be, in the title of the book.[71]

In early September, Smith confirmed to Wright that he had "no suggestions to make in regard to the text of the lectures." Having entirely read them over during the summer, he was "more and more impressed with their unity and force" and felt that the "words [written] to be spoken still retain their force as words to be read." On the other hand, he had serious concerns regarding Wright's ideas for the title and for the illustrations. Although he said he would have liked "to keep the title 'The Princeton Lectures,'" he had to "agree with the [Princeton University] Press that the book will sell many more copies if the copies have the title, 'Modern Architecture,' by Frank Lloyd Wright."[72] He decorously left the decision up to Wright, but when the architect sent the final design for the cover in mid-October with the title unchanged, Smith wrote back saying that "the Publication Committee insists that the title on the cover should be 'Modern Architecture.'"[73] (Wright had to be satisfied with the spine, which would say "Frank Lloyd Wright Lectures.") As for the illustrations, Smith continued to push for a photograph of the author at the beginning of the book and suggested "one full page halftone of his work at the beginning of each lecture." He was also more than willing to add extra illustrations "at the back of the book."[74]

Page proofs were ready by mid-September and sent on to Wright. Estimates for color for the cover came in quite high and Smith asked Wright if they could go to black and white, but did not insist. Wright naturally preferred the color, as did Smith, and the department and Press ultimately decided to cover the extra cost. After seeing Wright's idea for the placement of the illustrations to precede each lecture, Smith countered with his own, which in fact was the one that was followed. Where Smith wanted (and got) the illustrations to face the opening page of text of each lecture, Wright had thought to have them printed on the recto of the preceding page in order "to accentuate the lectures as well as the illustrations by giving each a blank context."[75]

With everything else apparently settled, Smith returned to the issue of the illustrations. He wanted to know precisely which works of Wright's would be chosen. Five were in question for him since he assumed that a photograph of the architect would serve as the illustration to the first lecture. Photographs had been made of work in the exhibition and, of these, Smith thought that one of the model of St. Mark's Tower for New York and a perspective of the project for the National Life Insurance Company Building in Chicago (1924–25) would be good. Aside from these, he said he would like to see "an example of architectural decoration . . . and then anything else that you can suggest."[76]

Wright had entirely different ideas about the illustrations, and his response to Smith on this question represents one of the few real disagreements they had—and one of the few cases where Wright insisted and got his way (arguably to the detriment of the final product). Wright wanted only examples of his earlier work to be used, and these in the form of radically redrawn images of the original designs but with the original dates next to his signature square. He used both the word "graph" and the German *graf* to describe these stark, highly stylized perspectives in which the subtleties of shading are reduced to flat, black-on-white planes, corresponding, at least in the German émigré Henry Klumb's view, to the type of "graphic presentations that modern architects were addicted to."[77]

In sending his "counter suggestion" to Smith, Wright was clearly quite conscious of the effect he was after in terms of the rewriting of his own history and using the publication of the Princeton lectures to do so. "Why not use the graphs I am sending of the work fundamental to the new movement instead of any photographs of recent work?" he asked. His reason he stated bluntly and shamelessly: "It will make the 'lectures' [a] historical document and 'build in' to our literature something not yet there." In other words, it would make the buildings he designed between 1893 and 1909 look as if they had predicted everything about the architecture of the twenties down to its techniques of representation. By not revealing that the drawings had been redrawn, the Princeton publication would make them part of the historical record and thus give them a totally fabricated historical genealogy. This rewriting of history—placing himself at the origin of the modern movement—supported the larger purpose of the text itself, as Wright unabashedly explained: "It will be appropriate, too, to the purpose of the book."[78]

Whether Smith understood what Wright was up to is unclear, although he certainly let Wright have his way. Some changes were made to the architect's initial scheme, but the main idea of it was followed through in the publication. Whether it actually ever had the effect Wright hoped for is another story. In his initial presentation of the scheme, Wright returned to his thought that the photograph of himself be at the end of the text. He suggested that it "be balanced by one at the beginning" showing a view of the Princeton exhibition paired with the model of St. Mark's Tower on opposite pages. Then would follow the "graphs" (or *grafs*) of the Larkin Building in Buffalo (1902–6), facing lecture 1; the Winslow House in River Forest, Illinois (1893–94), facing lecture 2; Unity Temple in Oak Park, Illinois (1905–8), facing lecture 3; the Robie House in Chicago (1908–10), facing lecture 4; the Bock House and Studio project for Maywood, Illinois (1906), facing lecture 5; and the so-called Yahara River Boathouse project, for the University of Wisconsin, in Madison (1905), facing lecture 6. At the end of the text, opposite one another, would be a perspective of a 1915–16 project for a "small city house," or Town House, from the so-called American Ready-Cut or System-Built Houses on the left and the photograph of the architect on the right.[79] In the end, Wright's suggestions were followed except for the photograph of himself, which was placed opposite the title page as Smith had wanted, and the replacement of the Yahara Boat Club with the "small city house" project. Why the image of the St. Mark's Tower was eliminated is not known, although one can assume it was Wright's decision since Smith was the one who suggested it in the first place.[80]

The final part of the story has to do with the preface by Smith. This is where one might have expected real fireworks and yet, again, everything went quite smoothly. Smith finished it by early February 1931 and thought best to send it to Wright for approval. In the letter accompanying the short text, he offered explanations for certain statements that the architect might take as too critical, claiming that everything he had written was out of "sympathy with your ideals and my enthusiasm for your work" and that any expression of difference was simply in order to preempt negative criticism from others. Smith felt he had to deal with Wright's writing style, which he thought might put off many. In the next to last paragraph of the preface, he wrote:

> His [Wright's] style in writing is as individual as the man himself. Some critics may overemphasize his unconscious disregard of usage and, at times, his disregard of logic; they may dwell unfairly . . . upon his lack of a simple, functional directness in words and his tendency to overdecorate ideas with verbiage; but such critics will have missed the appeal of his imagery and the sincerity of his effort.[81]

To Wright, he explained:

> You are a distinguished man with a marked individuality, and therefore have the right to write as you see fit. On the other hand, your literary style was formed in a period when writing and speaking were much more flowery and decorative than they are today. Style today has in a sense tended to follow the simplification of architecture and insist upon direct, functional simplicity. Therefore some critics may say that you, an advocate of functional line and surface simplicity in architecture, use a decorative verbiage in writing. This to me seems to be entirely beside the point, because it is the content and not the form in which we are interested. But in my introduction I have taken the words out of their mouths, in order to point out the sincerity of your ideal and the fact that your vehicle of expression is architecture and not words, but that even in your words, which follow a now outworn style, there are fire, feeling, and ideals.[82]

Wright's response not just to this aspect of the preface but to the text as a whole was positive, though not without a certain defensiveness. He started by saying that he thought it was "excellently written,—I wish I wrote as well. But it struck on my heart somewhat as though someone was a little ashamed of me having come in from the country on a load of poles—with my heart in the right place—but—certainly out of style, which I dare say is quite right enough." He then went on to explain, perhaps after the fact, perhaps not, why the lectures were written as they were and, in the process, revealed something important about his intentions:

The preface, perhaps is the place to explain that so called "functionalist" writing is as easy for me as for anybody.—

But I came to Princeton to preach. I chose the guise of the preacher as pleasant and heretical at the moment. That guise was the old sermon form as I had listened to it as a boy. My fathers [*sic*] sermons in his church at Weymouth.— There was the preamble—or leisurely amble in the direction of the subject—then came the "text" or the reference to Authority (Which I invented for the occasion.) The threshing out of the body of the subject follows. Finally the summary—gathering up the grain in both hands and directly handing it to the audience—cleaned up.

I enjoyed it. And I believe the boys did—. Here's hoping more may catch the entirely faithful seriousness of it all no less—for the twinkle in the eye. Art must have its logic straight. But deny the Artist his whimsey? Never. Unless you would lose him.[83]

Smith also criticized a lack of logic in Wright's discussion of the relation between materials and forms in the architectures of Egypt, Greece, and Japan, but claimed that, not being a historian, it mattered little "that he [Wright] is not strictly logical in his artistic convictions." He justified this by asking, rhetorically: "Whose likes and dislikes are logical?"[84] Here Wright became more serious, saying that this phrase "strikes me as subversive of any message organic Architecture has. Logic it must have." Provoked, he countered by asking: "And are you not yourself a little illogical when you admit my writing over-decorated with verbiage and then say I require no more apologies for my ideas and buildings? Or do you mean by that that they are over-done?" He would not pursue this with Smith, nor would Smith come back in response.

The final point Wright had to make related to the last sentence in the preface, which he asked Smith to eliminate and which Smith did not. Wright said he was "grateful" for the preface, which "shows your good feeling in every line." But the last one, "the 'I think I will,'" seemed to him to be "a 'let down'" that "weakened the whole." "Just why," Wright could not "say clearly enough." Smith had ended his text in the following way: "This book, as he [Wright] referred to it in a letter, is 'his garden'; in it he nobly believes that others will see the beauty and the possibilities of beauty which have stirred him. I think they will."[85] Did Wright not want Smith to have the last word? Did he not want to allow for the possibility of an unresponsive reader? Or did he not want for there to be any suggestion of a question regarding the ultimate truth and power of his thought?

Not hearing back from Smith for over a month and a half, Wright wrote a note to him at the end of March that must have arrived just about when the book appeared in print. In it, Wright asked: "What has happened to our book? I hope I didn't hurt your feelings? It is hard to wait."[86] Having received a copy a few days later, he telegrammed Smith saying: "The book is swell my dear Smith glad your preface is unchanged. I like it and would have spoiled it."[87] And two days after that, he wrote to Smith again: "The book is charming and splendidly edited. I can't be grateful enough. Princeton sounds and seems to me—princely. I feel this makes her my alma mater."[88]

With that ends the story of Wright's "Princeton Lectures" and the publication of *Modern Architecture*, except for questions regarding sales, financial matters, and the like, which do not interest us here and have little to do with the larger questions posed by a book meant at once to preach the cause of "organic architecture" and to write— or rather to rewrite—the history of modern architecture as a subset of that.[89]

MODERN ARCHITECTURE ACCORDING TO FRANK LLOYD WRIGHT

The six chapters of *Modern Architecture* follow the same sequence as the lectures and are, as far as one can tell, substantively the same in content and form.[90] The subjects treated move from a general statement of the constitutive conditions of modern culture to their particular applications in the fields of architecture and urbanism at ever broadening scales. The main themes that direct Wright's thought and interlace the text devolve from the initial proposition regarding the significance of the machine and its necessary antithesis to the use of the historical "styles." The inauthentic application of forms inherited from the past is equated by Wright with any type of surface-oriented, planar design, which is how he interprets the contemporary European architecture of Le Corbusier and others. In opposition to such pictorialism, or "picture-making," Wright advances the three-dimensionality and structural-ornamental integrity of his own conception of an "organic architecture," which he constantly describes as being the full-bodied source from which the reductive modernism of recent work in Europe evolved. This self-promotion as fountainhead involves not just a critique of European modernism and an assertion of his own priority but also an equation of the truly modern with the concepts of romanticism, imagination, beauty, and nature, all usually spelled with capital letters and placed in opposition to the scientific, the philosophically rational, and the collective. The vision of an American democratic freedom and individualism, averse to any form of commercial exploitation and corruption, ultimately connects all these strands and gives powerful voice to what Smith describes in the book's preface as the author's "faith."

The image facing the first page of "Machinery, Materials and Men" is the most dramatic and telling of the six Wright chose to illustrate the book. It is a partial plan and raking perspective of the Larkin Building, based on a photograph published in 1908 in the retrospective of the architect's work in *Architectural Record* accompanying his article "In the Cause of Architecture," in which he laid out his design principles for the first time.[91] Drawn in 1930 in highly contrasted black-and-white lines and planes, though bearing the date 1903, the image of this early industrial work by Wright that European architects beginning with H. P. Berlage had singled out as an extraordinarily precocious example of the application of a machine aesthetic to architectural design was clearly meant to indicate the author's originary role in reconceptualizing architectural design in terms of the machine.[92] Indeed, in the 1908 publication, Wright began his description of the building by saying that "it was built to house the commercial engine of the Larkin Company." After specifying that "most of the critic's 'architecture' had been left out," he ended with the prophetic phrase: "Therefore the work may have the same claim to consideration as a 'work of art' as an ocean liner, a locomotive or a battleship."[93]

The date of 1903 on the drawing sets the historical stage for the main ploy of the text, which is the incorporation of a lecture within the lecture, which Wright claimed to have given in Chicago in the same year as the fictitious date on the drawing and which he believed incontrovertibly established him as the first to fully realize the significance of the machine for modern architecture. "The Art and Craft of the Machine" was indeed an early and very important talk given by Wright at Chicago's Hull House as a critique of the backward-looking practices of the Arts and Crafts Movement and in favor of the machine. But it was given in 1901, not 1903, and the lecture incorporated in the Kahn Lectures, and in *Modern Architecture*, is a different one, probably dating from several years later. Furthermore, whatever its original date, it was, like the Larkin drawing, heavily edited for the Princeton volume—updated in many places and recontextualized in others to make it appear both more like what it was supposed to be and more prophetic than it originally was.[94] And the ploy worked. In her review of the book, Bauer, the most aware of European modernism of all the reviewers, made a major point of saying that "the transcription of Wright's famous Hull House speech, of 1903, positively establishes him as the instigator of the articulate modern movement."[95]

Wright's intention right at the beginning of the book, as it would be throughout, was not merely to prove his paternity. It was, even more importantly, to foreclose the possibility that the recent modern architecture of Europe, and in particular that of Le Corbusier, might be taken as the source of the idea that the machine was the fundamental new element in the creation of modern architecture. In his 1928 review of *Towards a New Architecture*, Wright asserted that "all Le Corbusier says or means was at home here in architecture in America in the work of Louis Sullivan and myself—more than twenty-five years ago."[96] But he did not, for that reason, devalue Le Corbusier's text or its theoretical consequences either for modern architecture in general or for his own work in particular. Wright was clearly impressed by it to the extent of recommending that "everyone engaged in making or breaking [architecture in] these United States . . . read the Le Corbusier book," and those in "universities especially."[97]

For his own part, Wright included *Towards a New Architecture* as one of only four writings mentioned by name for the library of the new Hillside Home School of Allied Arts, soon to become the Taliesin Fellowship, that he proposed in December 1928 and discussed in chapter 2 of *Modern Architecture* (more on this later). He characterized Le Corbusier's volume in the school's brochure as "of a similar portent" to his own "In the Cause of Architecture" series and of "a similar spirit" to the writings of Viollet-le-Duc, Owen Jones, and Louis Sullivan, all well-known heroes of his. In addition, Wright listed Le Corbusier as one of the architects he hoped would serve on the school's visiting faculty. *Towards a New Architecture* clearly weighed heavily on Wright's mind and would make its mark on his *Modern Architecture* from beginning to end.

By way of introduction to the "transcription" of the "Art and Craft of the Machine," Wright stated that "long ago, . . . I passionately swore that the Machine was no less, rather more, an artist's tool than any he had ever had or heard of" and "today, twenty-seven years later, the heresy is become truism." Coyly veiling a reference to Le Corbusier's belated though effective awareness in a characterization that few if any in the audience at Princeton, and perhaps not even many today in reading the book, would immediately be able to decode, Wright added: "And yet, a Pompeian [Le Corbusier] recently come back and struggling for nourishment on French soil has reiterated one-quarter of the matter, made more stark, with signs of success right here in our own country."[98]

This "reiteration" was dangerous as Wright saw it. It was reductive and "superficial" in producing buildings defined simply by "Surface and Mass," as Le Corbusier, in Wright's view, had done, indeed, to such a degree that "surface and mass" design became Wright's code word for Le Corbusier and the European modernism associated with him.[99] Appearing to be "Machine-made," and even "resembling Machinery," such buildings entirely lacked the three all-important components of a truly modern, that is to say, organic architecture. These were: (1) an expression of the "Nature of Materials"; (2) an engagement with the "Third Dimension"; and (3) a development of "Integral Ornament."[100] Wright would come back time and again in the succeeding chapters to these ideas and ultimately even name Le Corbusier, but for openers he apparently thought it best to refrain from direct attack and to use the insinuation of his early lecture on "The Art and Craft of the Machine" as unimpeachable evidence of his authority. As the redrawn images of the early buildings were meant to "build in" to the literature on him "something not yet there," the device of transcribing the "1903" lecture allowed it, as he said, to be "read into the record, once more."[101]

The lecture within the lecture begins by defining the modern age as "the Machine Age—wherein locomotive engines, engines of industry, engines of light or engines of war or steamships take the place works of Art took in previous history." The definition echoes Wright's earlier commentary on the Larkin Building but does not really prepare us for the line of argument he will take. Rather than looking at machines, or engines, as analogous to, metaphors for, or even models for buildings, as Le Corbusier would powerfully suggest in the text and especially the illustrations of *Towards a New Architecture*, Wright focuses almost entirely on machines as simply "substitutes for tools," updated "implements" that the human being must learn to master and exploit and, at all costs, to avoid being mastered by.[102]

Wright bemoaned and decried the misuse of machinery to imitate the work of earlier handicraft. Describing the eclectic architecture and interior decoration of the turn of the century as monstrous "abominations," "butchered forms," a "nostalgic masquerade" thoroughly "prostituting" the sources, Wright predicted the protest against kitsch that was to form the basis of so much of the avant-garde literature of the 1920s, including the writings of Le Corbusier, Taut, Walter Curt Behrendt, and others.[103] In contrast to the crass and utter "degradation" the machine had produced so far, Wright maintained that an intelligent use of it in terms of its inherent capabilities could lead the modern architect to the creation of "simple forms" and "plastic" results "consistent with Nature and impossible to handicraft."[104]

In one of the most powerful and stirring sections of the chapter, Wright describes the modern city, in this case Chicago, as a vast machine—the "great Machine"—the home to "automatons working day and night in every line of industry." Wondering aloud "if this power must be uprooted that civilization may live," he answers, "then civilization is already doomed."[105] The need to confront and overcome the debilitating, dehumanizing, "relentless force" of the machine that has already "lacerated hands everywhere" brings him in the end, almost full circle, to a kind of neo-Ruskinianism, where education is offered as the panacea for humanizing the machine, offering instruction to the individual in how to master it and not be mastered by it, and thus finally making the machine "a peerless tool for him to use to put foundations beneath a genuine Democracy."[106]

Wright pursued the issue of education in the following chapter, "Style in Industry," but reserved the main discussion of the subject until the last few pages, where he proposed an idea for a new kind of "experimental" school combining training in the arts with training in industrial design that closely followed the model of the Bauhaus in Germany, founded by Walter Gropius in 1919 and established in the building he designed for it in Dessau in 1925–26. Wright's idea, like Gropius's, was that architecture would be the umbrella, "the broad essential background of the whole endeavor," and that the artists and architects serving as instructors would educate "the needed designer for Industry now."[107] The vexing and extremely timely question of style served Wright as a way to introduce his educational venture.

Repeating almost word for word Le Corbusier's famous line from *Towards a New Architecture* that "architecture has nothing to do with the 'styles,'"—meaning the historical styles that formed the basis of nineteenth-century eclecticism—Wright stated that you could "be sure of one thing," that "STYLE *has nothing to do with 'the' Styles!*"[108] And also like Le Corbusier, he defined style as the organic, coherent, integral, and spontaneous expression of a particular culture, thus inimitable outside its original context. To give body to this concept, especially as it related to his own work, Wright turned to the premodern, preindustrial culture of Japan. Following a cultural, even religious, program of "cleanliness," "simplicity," and "standardizing," Japanese art and architecture achieved an "organic" style that served as a model for the modern, equally important to Wright, as he states, as it was to the Secessionists, the Arts and Crafts, and the Wiener Werkstätte.[109]

Clearly aware of the more recent development in Europe of what was about to be christened the International Style, Wright then warned about the tendency to eliminate human imagination and feeling from the equation. This would result in a "hard" and "mechanical," even "mechanistic" type of design, postulating that a "house or a chair or a child is a machine" as if "our own hearts are suction pumps."[110] Obviously referencing Le Corbusier, the author of the phrase "a house is a machine for living in," Wright went on to heap scorn on the so-called machine style, predicting that "our Architecture," if it falls under its sway, "would become a poor, flat-faced thing of steel-bones, box-outlines, gas-pipe and hand-rail fittings . . . without this essential *heart* beating in it." "There is no good reason," he declared, "why Objects of Art in Industry, because they are made by Machines in the Machine Age, should resemble the machines that made them, or any other machinery whatsoever."[111]

Between the nostalgia for "the Art and Craft of Old Japan" and the invective against the modern movement in Europe, there are some extraordinary passages about the concept of "plasticity," the bane of the "pictorial," and especially about the use of new materials. Glass, which Wright describes as the modern material par excellence, lets the architect "now work with light, light diffused, light reflected, light refracted" to make entirely unprecedented "prismatic buildings."[112] The application of industrial processes to the use of materials finally leads Wright to his concluding remarks on education. As a "means to grow our own STYLE IN INDUSTRY," Wright offered what he called "a practical suggestion," perhaps even thinking that he might interest Princeton in taking part in it.[113]

In 1928, as already mentioned, Wright had proposed the establishment of a Hillside Home School of Allied Arts on the land where he would create the Taliesin Fellowship four years later. Its purpose was "to harmonize the spirit of art and the spirit of the machine" in an "uncompromisingly modern" educational environment that would function concurrently as a "farm school" where the students would "get their own living as far as possible from the ground itself." In this ruralized Bauhaus, training in the fine arts would be combined with training in the industrial arts under the umbrella of architecture and under the aegis of the University of Wisconsin. Students would design and produce objects for use, ranging from glassware to textiles to plans for buildings, which would not only ideally be marketable but would also serve as examples for "all the design-forms of American industrial production now characterizing our homes and our lives."[114]

In recycling this idea for the Princeton lectures, Wright expanded the scope of the project to create numerous campuses and thus open up the possibility for involvement of not just the University of Wisconsin but of "our universities" around the country. He referred to these new "Art Schools" as "Industrial 'STYLE' Centers" and "Experiment Stations." They would be "endowed" and furnished with machinery and per-

sonnel by the "industries themselves." As a return on their investment, the partici-
pating companies would "share in benefit of designs or presently in designers themselves." Small in size (each no more than forty students) and situated in rural locations, the centers would include "physical work on the soil" for self-subsistence and
include activities in all areas of the arts and culture, from music and theater to land
conservation and town planning. Wright acknowledged that, while "creative Art cannot be taught," his ideal educational establishment held the promise of "cultivating
the creative quality in Man" that might help grow the desired "quality of STYLE IN IN-
DUSTRY" and exhorted "any great institution" within earshot to help "initiate" the
venture.[115] Needless to say, Princeton did not take the bait.

I have said nothing about the drawing of the Winslow House used to illustrate the
second chapter, and that is because the reason for its choice is not very clear. The
house was Wright's first building and he always considered it extremely important to
his career. Looking back on it in 1936, he described it as "the first 'prairie house.' "[116]
The drawing is based on the opening image in the so-called Wasmuth portfolio of 1910,
the Berlin publication entitled *Ausgeführte Bauten und Entwürfe von Frank Lloyd
Wright* that introduced his work to the European audience.[117] But what does it have
to do with the issue of style? My guess is that it represented for Wright the initial
statement by him of a homegrown style native to the Midwest—the Prairie Style—and
thus the prime example in his view of how a modern style could develop out of contemporary conditions and without resort to "the styles" inherited from the past. By
contrast, the reason for the choice of Unity Temple to keynote the following chapter
seems quite clear. With its flat roofs articulated by cantilevered reinforced-concrete
slabs, the church bears direct witness to "The Passing of the Cornice" in Wright's
early work and thought.[118]

On first reading, the chapter "The Passing of the Cornice" might seem just as simple and as transparent as the relationship between text and image it is built on. Moving from his teenage home of Madison, Wisconsin, to the site of the Acropolis in
Athens, Wright narrates a story rich in anecdote and personal feeling of classical imitation in architecture and its ultimate demise in the "sham" products of turn-of-the-
century America.[119] It is a story of death and exorcism, of undisguised repugnance for
the classical tradition and a complete lack of regret for its "passing," indeed, a cele-
bration of it. The stage is set for this emotional tirade by the minidrama of the collapse
of the State Capitol in Madison during its construction in the mid-1880s, where Wright
witnessed workers maimed and even killed by the crumbling classical elements of the

building and one worker, in particular, hanging out of a window, dripping blood, with a loose piece of the cornice above threatening to fall and decapitate him.

Wright does not look at these classical elements in purely abstract and formal terms. He sees them as symbolic and meaningful of the cultures of which they were a part and which they express. They are related to the manners, the clothing, the music, even the food of their time. "Cornices were extravagant hats for buildings"; the other "pretentious" features of classical architecture are compared with the "hoop-skirt" and the "bustle," "puffed sleeves, frizzes, furbelows and flounces."[120] More importantly, at least in architectural terms, is their deceitfulness. Instead of being the direct expression of a structural principle or functional purpose, as his theoretical models Viollet-le-Duc and Sullivan would have had it, these classical forms are used purely for appearance sake—"in order to preserve 'appearances,'" as it were—more often than not in violation of the underlying structure they "hang on."[121]

To exorcise this ghost of appearance, Wright finally leaves the "cornice" he first came to despise in Madison to track it down "at the source from which it came to us." And here is where the story gets more interesting and much more complicated. "Of course I visited Athens," Wright declares, although when that may have been is entirely unrecorded and unmentioned in any document or any other writing by the architect prior to 1930 that has yet come to light:

> [I] held up my hand in the clean Mediterranean air against the sun and saw the skeleton of my hand through its covering of pink flesh—saw the same translucence in the marble pillars of the aged Parthenon, and realized what "color" must have been in such light. I saw the yellow stained rocks of the barren terrain. I saw the ancient temples, barren, broken, yellow stained too, standing now magnificent in their crumbling state, more a part of that background than ever they were when born—more stoic now than allowed to be when those whose record they were had built them. . . . Like all who stand there, I tried to re-create the scene as it existed when pagan love of color made it come ablaze. . . . And gradually I saw the whole as a great painted, wooden temple. Though now crumbling to original shapes of stone, so far as intelligence went at that time there were no stone forms whatever. The forms were only derived from wood! I could not make them stone, hard as I might try. Nor had the Greeks cared for that stone quality in their buildings.[122]

On one level, this is simply a reiteration of the theory that the classical forms of Greek architecture were derived from wooden prototypes. It gave Wright license to claim that the Parthenon "was no organic stone building" but "only a wooden temple embalmed." "In the hands of the impeccable Greeks here was noble, beautiful stone insulted and forced to do duty as an imitation enslaved to wood." A "philosophic" and "sophisticated abstraction" (words Wright otherwise reserved for Le Corbusier), even a "pagan poison," the original source of the Madison cornice could now be seen as the representation of a foreign body on American soil, one contrary to the "ideal of Organic Architecture" that grows out of the inherent characteristics of materials and "*un*folds" from within its own cultural and natural conditions.[123]

But why go to the Acropolis to make the point he had already made numerous times already in the book, and why resort to a replay of the academic chestnut of the wood origins of classical architectural forms? The answer lies in the subtext of the chapter, which involves, once again, Wright's response to and competition with Le Corbusier. In *Towards a New Architecture*, Le Corbusier devoted one of his most powerful and memorable chapters to the Acropolis and the Parthenon. Characterizing the temple as a "pure creation of the mind," an expression of "emotion . . . born of unity of aim; of that unperturbed resolution that wrought its marble with the firm intention of achieving all that is most pure, most clarified, most economical," the author denied the theory that "the Doric column was inspired by a tree" in order to show that, out of the precise and demanding manipulation of stone itself, "*the Greeks created a plastic system directly and forcibly affecting our senses*," a "plastic machinery . . . realized in marble with the rigour that we have learned to apply in the machine." Far from painted wood now turned to "broken, yellow stained" stone as Wright described it, "the impression" Le Corbusier had, and conveyed, of the Parthenon was "of naked polished steel."[124]

The confrontation with Le Corbusier reaches a climax on the final page of the chapter, where Wright approaches Le Corbusier's model of the machine on firmer and more home grounds. "We begin to glimpse this great adversary as the instrument of a New Order," he begins. "We are willing to believe there is a common sense," he continues, "a sense common to our time directed toward specific purpose." And then Wright goes off on a description of the "New Order" of the "Machine Age" that can be read as a gloss on his much earlier commentary on the Larkin Building through the images of modern conveyances that Le Corbusier famously displayed in page after page of photographs in *Towards a New Architecture* for those philistine "Eyes Which Do Not See."[125] "We see," Wright wrote in rhythms echoing those of his nemesis, "an aeroplane clean and light-winged—the lines expressing power and purpose; we see the

INTRODUCTION

ocean-liner, stream-lined, clean and swift—expressing power and purpose. The loco-motive, too—power and purpose. Some automobiles begin to look the part. Why not buildings, too, indicative of their special purpose? The forms of things that are per-fectly adapted to their function, we now observe, have a superior beauty of their own."[126]

Then, as if coming back to his senses, and to his own way of thinking and writing, he speaks of the realization of the "new value in freedom" that arises from this "new value in individuality," a democratic "Ideal" that ultimately allows him to see his way through and beyond Le Corbusier. "The plane is a plane;" Wright remarks, "the steamship is a steamship; the motor-car is a motor-car, and the more they are and *look* just that thing the more beautiful we find them. Buildings, too—why not? Men too? Why not?" Appearance thus returns in the end to define freedom and individuality through difference and within an idealist, humanist framework.

The title of the following chapter, "The Cardboard House," is even catchier than "The Passing of the Cornice."[127] It is also decidedly more polemical, as the chapter demonstrates from its opening pages and with great humor and irony throughout. After fairly uncharacteristically defining the house in terms of the biological body ("electric wiring for nervous system, plumbing for bowels, heating system and fire-places for arteries and heart," etc., etc.), Wright turns the scientific analogy on its head by saying that a house should be "a noble consort to man and the trees"—"com-plementary to its nature-environment"—and should not "outrage the Machine by try-ing to . . . [be] too complementary to Machinery."[128]

In defiance of the "humane purposes" he claims for the modern house, Wright ridicules the "cardboard houses" deriving from the " 'Surface-and-Mass' Aesthetic [read Le Corbusier]" of the European modern movement as looking "as though cut from cardboard with scissors, the sheets of cardboard folded or bent in rectangles with an occasional curved cardboard surface added to get relief. The cardboard forms thus made are glued together in box-like forms—in a childish attempt to make buildings resemble steamships, flying machines or locomotives."[129] Differentiating these works from the "bad surface-decoration" designs of the Art Déco type (referred to as "Art and Decoration" throughout the text), Wright allows that they are "to be preferred"—but not by a lot! Their simplicity "is too easily read," their "construction . . . complicated or confused, merely to arrive at [the effect] of exterior simplicity" and the false and misleading appearance of "a Machine."[130]

To the "cardboard house," Wright offers his own architecture as a badly needed

xxxviii

"antidote." But instead of referring to the present and dealing with his recent work in the area of domestic design, Wright returns to his beginnings, just as he did in revisiting "The Art and Craft of the Machine" in chapter 1. This no doubt explains the choice of the Robie House, the most famous of his early houses among Europeans, to serve as the illustration for the chapter.[131] And by indicating how his ideas on domestic design as they were developed between 1893 and 1909 predicted current work in Europe, the decision to focus exclusively on his own past was also surely meant to prove, as he wrote in his review of Le Corbusier's *Towards a New Architecture* two years before, that "all Le Corbusier says or means was at home here in architecture in America in the work of Louis Sullivan and myself—more than twenty-five years ago."[132]

Wright describes the characteristic Victorian house of the turn of the century and how he worked to develop a modern paradigm to replace it, the domestic type commonly referred to since as his Prairie House. While his description of his goals and methods issues from the initial statement of this effort as it appeared in 1908 in the article "In the Cause of Architecture," there is much that is new.[133] Much of what is new is simply the result of reflection upon a period and a body of work by then a quarter of a century old; but a lot is also the result of an appropriation of ideas, words, and concepts learned over the previous decade from the very European architects Wright was claiming to be his heirs. The new description of the Prairie House is the one that Wright used as the basis for the section "Building the New House," and the following one "Simplicity," in *An Autobiography* (1932).[134]

The major new additions to his description of the house type he developed between 1893 and the first years of the twentieth century relate to the recent discourses on architectural space, as that evolved in the 1920s, and the new classicism, as that became evident in the work of Oud, Le Corbusier, and Mies, among others. Wright's remarks in the 1908 text regarding the interior planning of the Prairie House were limited to saying that a building should no longer be "cut up into box-like compartments" and that it "should contain as few rooms" as necessary. The living room could be expanded to become the "one room" on the ground floor with the kitchen, dining room, and library "otherwise sequestered from it or screened within it by means of architectural contrivances."[135] In "The Cardboard House," Wright went well beyond this rather limited and tentative statement. He now said that, in his Prairie House, he "declared the whole lower floor as one room" with the effect that "the house became more free as 'space'" and "interior spaciousness began to dawn."[136] He went on to describe these early houses as "true *enclosure of interior space*," a definition that implied a newly minted explanation of the relationship between interior and exterior that paralleled Le Corbusier's pronouncement that "the plan proceeds from within to without; the exterior is the result of an interior." Or as Wright put it: "the *outside* of the house . . . was there chiefly because of what had happened *inside*."[137]

No mention, however, was now made of the fact, of which Wright seemed to have been very proud earlier in his career, that "in laying out the ground plans for even the more insignificant of these buildings a simple axial law and order . . . is practiced . . . and, although the symmetry may not be obvious always the balance is usually maintained." "The plans," he earlier stated, completely unapologetically, "are as a rule much more articulate than is the school product of the Beaux-Arts."[138] In eliminating this critical but conservative sounding aspect of his design methodology, it would appear that Wright was trying both to establish his own modernity and, at the same time, to distance himself from the European modern movement. In 1925, in an article about Wright and his growing irrelevance, Oud described the negative reaction of the younger Europeans to Wright's romanticism and their positive move away from his "influence" by means of "a new—an unhistorical!—classicism."[139]

In searching for a term to characterize his own architecture in contradistinction to the association of the "modern" with the purist, neoclassical "cardboard houses" of the younger Europeans, Wright now, for the first time in any consistent and programmatic way, began to refer to his own brand of modernism as "organic architecture," a term that appeared here and there in earlier chapters as well as in a short piece he published in 1929 criticizing the new European architecture and, especially, its supporters in the United States.[140] While Wright had used the adjective "organic" to characterize aspects of his work from quite early on, and continued to do so throughout the teens and twenties, the only previous time the architect used the expression "organic architecture" as a self-defining term of nomenclature was in 1914, when he was faced with a situation analogous to the one in 1930. Then, as in 1930, he was looking for a way to differentiate himself from followers he thought had misinterpreted and degraded his ideas and forms (the so-called New School of the Middle West he referred to disparagingly earlier in the chapter).[141] All this certainly helps to explain Wright's resistance to the use of the title *Modern Architecture* for the book. The phrase "Modern Concepts Concerning an Organic Architecture" that was prominently displayed as the heading of the front endpapers served to undermine and demote the word "modern" to the status of a mere qualifier.

The "Organic Architecture" that Wright now declared as his own defined itself in opposition to the reductive simplicity of the "cardboard house." "A home *is* a machine to live in" as "a tree *is* a machine to bear fruit." This Wright would not deny. But such statements, while being true, were not enough, just as the "surface and mass" simplicities of the "cardboard house" were not enough to satisfy the profound "humane purposes" at the heart of the domestic program. "To eliminate expressive words that intensify or vivify meaning in speaking or writing is not simplicity," Wright said, just as "in Architecture, expressive changes of surface, emphasis of line and especially textures of materials, may go to make facts eloquent, forms more significant." "Organic Architecture" recognized that "the Simplicity of the Universe is very different from the Simplicity of a Machine." In total contrast to the plane surfaces and hard lines of the "modern" buildings of the younger Europeans, Wright foresaw an "organic architecture" in Blakean terms, wherein "exuberance is *beauty*."[142]

The final two chapters, "The Tyranny of the Skyscraper" and "The City," form a close-knit pair. They deal with some of the most pressing problems of the period and were especially cited by contemporary critics for their important contributions to the discourse. More than any of the other four, they are grounded in the economic, social, and political events of the period and can be read in relation to the crisis of capitalism exposed by the stock market crash and the onset of the Great Depression. Bauer stated in her review that "the problem of the skyscraper has never been better summarized"; while the New York architect, architectural historian, and critic Talbot Hamlin described Wright's "trenchant analysis of the skyscraper and the modern city" as a "brilliant presentation of the problem [for which] all architects and laymen alike, who are hoping and working for a future that is not slavery, may be deeply grateful."[143] The significance of the subjects of these two chapters led the *New York Times Book Review* to give Wright's volume a front-page article by the cultural critic and urban historian R. L. Duffus in its Sunday edition of 31 May 1931 under the headline " 'Tyranny of the Skyscraper': Frank Lloyd Wright Attacks Its Dominion of Our Architecture," accompanied by a large etching of a construction scene in New York.[144]

In contrast to the previous chapters, the last two also deal with issues in which the architect himself was deeply engaged at the time and in relation to which he had either recently done projects or was in the process of doing so. These highly innovative, inventive, and sometimes visionary designs included the thirty-two-story National Life Insurance Company Building for Water Tower Square in Chicago (1924–25); the six-block multitower Skyscraper Regulation scheme, probably also for Chicago (1926);

the four-building St. Mark's Towers project for downtown Manhattan (1927–30); the twenty-four-story block-long slab of Grouped Apartments for a site between Water Tower Square and Lake Michigan in Chicago (1930); and the decentralist plan for the urbanization of the entire United States called Broadacre City (1929–35).

Curiously, even amazingly so, one would have no idea about this work from reading "The Tyranny of the Skyscraper." In fact, one might actually assume from the vehemence of the critique of the building-type that the author had no connection to or even interest in designing such urban structures. The disconnect between theory and practice rears its face with the opening illustration. It is a redrawing of the plan and garden perspective of the house and studio Wright designed in 1906 (not 1902 as the caption states) for the sculptor Richard Bock, a sometime collaborator, for a site in an undistinguished residential suburb ten miles west of Chicago.[145] As we remember, Baldwin Smith had urged Wright to consider illustrations of the St. Mark's Tower and the National Life Insurance Building. Neither was chosen. Why the Bock House and Studio was, instead, is a mystery, except if one assumes the rather fanciful scenario that Wright did not want to appear hypocritical, since he was about to advise architects in the course of the chapter to be "something more than hired men" and decline commissions for urban skyscrapers since nothing good could come of them.[146] Perhaps less fanciful, though still difficult to fathom, is that Wright saw the cubic, step-back shape and clear rectilinear expression of the building's reinforced-concrete structure as foreshadowing an appropriate rational form for the modern skyscraper.[147]

Unlike the previous chapters, however, Wright does not proceed in this one to take any credit for the modern development of the building-type nor even to imply that his work played a role in predicting its course. Also, there is no critique or even mention of recent architecture in Europe, the only invective being reserved for the large commercial firms in America responsible for the bulk of tall office buildings. And finally, what is also different here is that the architect had previously written almost nothing on the subject and was therefore free to approach the subject exclusively from the perspective of the present and in any way he saw fit.[148] The result is a kind of freshness and directness to the argument and a lack of overblown rhetoric.

After setting the stage, through reference to Michelangelo's dome of St. Peter's, for how an architectural type-solution can tyrannize a culture by establishing itself as an authoritative and hegemonic form, Wright goes on to legitimize himself as a critical authority in the case of the skyscraper by noting his own presence in Chicago in the later years of the nineteenth century when the modern building-type first came into being. Even more to the point, he places himself in Louis Sullivan's office at the very moment the Wainwright Building in St. Louis was designed (1890), the building that in Wright's estimation was "the very first . . . expression of a tall steel office-building as Architecture." Deriving its form from the steel frame itself and expressing the nature and purpose of that construction through its "vertical walls" treated as "vertical screens," the "Wainwright Building," according to Wright, "has characterized all skyscrapers since"—or should have, which is where Wright's disappointment with the twentieth-century development of the type comes in.[149]

In several places in the chapter, Wright traces the devolution of the type and its attendant loss of significance and emotional power—the "thrill" one originally got from it "as an individual performance" in the city. After Sullivan came the Beaux-Arts solution modeled on the tripartite division of the classical column, and after that the Gothic Cathedral of Commerce. More recently, and especially in Manhattan, appeared the "plain masonry surfaces and restrained ornament" of the "picturesque" tower or slab based on the "set-back laws" of the 1916 zoning code. But as in all previous versions, the underlying structural steel frame is masked and denied and "the picturesque element in it . . . is false work built over a hollow box." All are "shams." "Today," Wright concluded, "all skyscrapers have been whittled to a point. . . . They whistle, they steam, they moor dirigibles, they wave flags, or they merely aspire, and nevertheless very much resemble each other at all points. . . . Empty of all other significance, . . . they no longer startle or amuse. . . . The light that shone in the Wainwright Building as a promise, flickered feebly and is fading away. Skyscraper architecture is a mere matter of a clumsy imitation masonry envelope for a steel skeleton."[150]

Wright offered little in the way of advice on how such buildings could be made better architecture despite his own recent efforts in the field. He described the main purpose of the skyscraper as merely "space-manufacturing-for-rent," which simply proved to him that the entire undertaking was an intractable, inconsequential, and even unethical one. The skyscraper, he wrote "is a commercial exploit or a mere expedient" and nothing more. "It has no higher ideal of unity than commercial success."[151] In the end, the problem of the skyscraper was not an architectural one but rather a social, economic, cultural, and, especially, an urban one. The "tyranny" it exercised over the city had brought "congestion," "super-concentration," "the traffic problem," and inflated "fictitious land-values," not to speak of physical and psychological health problems as well. The building-type had become merely a form of advertising and a way for landlords and speculators to get rich. The development was entirely "haphazard" and involved no thought of "spacious city planning."[152] Any attempt to deal with the issue in architectural terms was by definition merely a palliative, what Wright continually referred to as a temporary and ultimately ineffectual "expedient."

Wright did, however, offer a couple of proposals aimed at the urban aspects of the problem based on two recent projects of his, although he did not identify either by name or claim any actuality for them. They dealt with the issues of traffic and congestion. One solution, which Wright acknowledged was in no way original to him, was the construction of multilevel streets and sidewalks, separating vehicular from pedestrian movement. This was a popular alternative in the 1920s and one that Wright himself exploited in his 1926 Skyscraper Regulation project. Curiously he made no mention of one of the most innovative aspects of his scheme, which was the inclusion of enclosed parking garages topped by garden courts in the center of each block, whose buildings occupied only the perimeter and whose skyscraper elements emerged only at alternating corners.

The other recommendation dealt more specifically with congestion. Directly engaging the relationship between buildings and the street line, and following ideas previously set forth by Le Corbusier and others, Wright suggested that tall buildings be placed in the middle of their parcels in order to receive light on all four sides and to create "park space" out of the unbuilt areas. This concept was given physical shape by Wright just prior to the writing of the lectures in the St. Mark's Towers project, which was aborted shortly after the closing of the exhibition that featured a model of one of the four towers designed for the Manhattan site.[153]

It was in the countryside, however, that Wright believed the skyscraper would ultimately find its home. "The haphazard skyscraper in the rank and file of city streets is doomed," he declared. Any attempt to accommodate it to the city "is no more than an expedient." As the necessity for concentration in urban centers diminishes due to the increased means of mechanical transportation and telecommunications, there will be an "eventual urban exodus" and the "citizen of the near future," Wright predicted, "will gradually abandon the city." And so "the tyranny of the skyscraper" would end while the tall building itself, "in the country" and no longer a congestion-creating "space-maker-for-rent," would become a new symbol of freedom in which the exurban citizen "might take genuine pride."[154] If this sounds utopian, the final chapter fleshes out the picture of the move from the city to the countryside and the transformations such a move would effect in modern society.

Chapter 6, "The City," provides the first description in Wright's published work of the decentralized form of community he would soon call Broadacre City. While this fact has often been correctly noted by historians, it has also been assumed that Wright wrote the text expressly for the Kahn Lectures with the hope that such a distinguished venue would give the proposal a special cachet and perhaps even what we would today call "legs." But unlike the chapter on the skyscraper, the one on the city was an almost complete recycling of an article written more than four months prior to the invitation to give the Princeton lecture series and a year and a half before the publication of *Modern Architecture*. The typescript of "In the Cause of Architecture: The City" is dated 29 September 1929. Possibly written as a continuation of the 1927–28 *Architectural Record* series of the same name, its eleven-page text comprises fully four-fifths of chapter 6 (101–12) and, while heavily edited, it remained essentially unchanged in the published version.[155]

Wright began "The City" by asking a rhetorical question the answer to which underwrote the rest of the discussion. Is the city merely a "necessity," a "hang-over" from the past? The answer was a not unexpected, and resounding, yes. What had once made the concentration of people in cities necessary was now counteracted by the new forms of Machine Age transportation and telecommunication, which allowed what was previously only able to be accomplished in the city to be done by a dispersed population living in a healthier, more spacious, and more wholesome environment. As a result, "the city, as we know it, is to die," Wright stated. The exacerbation of urban problems exposed in the previous chapter on "The Tyranny of the Skyscraper" merely proved that "we are witnessing the acceleration that precedes dissolution."[156]

Any attempt to redress the evils of the city within the framework of the traditional concept of the urban environment was thought by Wright not only to be doomed to failure but also to raise false hopes. He consequently felt it necessary, unlike in the previous chapter, and also perhaps because this was the final one, to attack once again the "new movement" in architecture and specifically "Le Corbusier and his school," whom he now referred to for the first time by name, for their plans to redesign the existing city in the guise of "a machine-made Utopia."[157] Continuing to refer to his Swiss-French nemesis as an abstract thinker rather than an architect, Wright spoke of how "philosophers [read Le Corbusier] draw plans, picture, and prophecy a future city, more desirable, they say, than the pig-pile now in travail, their pictures reducing everything to a mean height—geometrically spaced."

The description clearly fits Le Corbusier's project for a City of Three Million Inhabitants (1922), with its twenty-four cruciform, glass curtain-walled towers, all the same sixty-story height, occupying the central transportation and commercial hub, surrounded by lower ranges of housing blocks, all the same height and laid out on a modified gridiron plan. "In order to preserve air and passage, this future city," Wright continued in a graphic descriptive passage foreshadowing J. G. Ballard's dystopian vision of the modern metropolis (not to speak of Brasilia's realization of Le Corbusier's ideas), "relegates the human individual as a unit or factor to pigeonhole 337611, block F, avenue A, street No. 127. And there is nothing at which to wink an eye that could distinguish No. 337611 from No. 337610 or 27643, bureau D, intersection 118 and 119." It is the expression of "a mechanistic system appropriate to man's extinction."[158]

Perhaps because he was having too much fun, but also because he did not want to limit his criticism to a purely formal analysis, Wright refused to leave the matter of Le Corbusier's projected city just there and returned to it a bit later when talking about the problem of "the poor" and the social dimension of housing. Here, for the first time in the book, he raised the issue of class and money in relation to equality of opportunity in housing. According to Wright, the machine in Le Corbusier's "city of the future" acted as a social leveler to produce and enforce "the common denominator." Not fully understanding the economic and social classification of the housing types in the Corbusian scheme, Wright assumed that "the poor man" was to be treated "just as is the rich man—No. 367222, block 99, shelf 17, entrance K" and thus poverty to be "built in" to the system. "This new scheme for the city is delightfully impartial, extinguishes everyone, distinguishes nothing except by way of the upper stories," where the "routine economies sacred to a business man's civilization" were carried on by the "nominators," the elite of Corbusian technocrats for whom the city was designed and who would run its affairs. Everyone else was reduced "to the ranks—of the poor."[159]

In Wright's counterproject, which is based on no greater but no fewer economic specifics than Le Corbusier's, the common denominator would no longer be the poverty bred by the congestion of the city. The horizons of "all, rich or poor," would be expanded by life in the countryside, just as everyone would be afforded the privacy and the freedom available to no one, except perhaps the superrich or superpowerful, in the existing city or the "machine-made Utopia" of Le Corbusier.[160] Based on the pattern of decentralization he noted as already occurring in metropolises like Chicago and Los Angeles—which were "splitting up . . . into several centers, again to be split up into many more"—as well as the ideas for the "decentralization of industry" put forward by Henry Ford in his plans for Muscle Shoals, Alabama, Wright proposed a radical, multicentered, unbounded, and extensive conception of the city to replace the traditional, hierarchically organized, self-contained urban form. Instead of bringing the "air, space, and greenery" of the countryside to the city, as Le Corbusier proposed, Wright's idea was to take "the city . . . to the country." Clearly setting his own vision in direct opposition to Le Corbusier's *urbanisme*, Wright described his new type of city as a form of "Ruralism as distinguished from Urbanism"—thus characteristically "American, and truly Democratic."[161]

Wright allowed that the move to the countryside might not be total at first, or even in the conceivable future. The natural devolution of the city was toward a purely "utilitarian" state. As such, and Wright gave no terminus ad quem for this, the city would be reduced to a six-hour, three-day-a-week schedule, "invaded at ten o'clock, abandoned at four." The rest of one's time would be lived entirely outside of it. As "the country absorbs the life of the city," it would eventually offer all the cultural as well as commercial opportunities the city once did and become, in Wright's words, "a festival of life." The machine had already made possible the necessary "margin of leisure" for this abandonment of the traditional city, and the infrastructure for such a complete reorganization of human existence was already in place. All that was needed was a realization through design.[162]

The fundamental infrastructural elements allowing for the dispersal of the population from urban centers and their regroupment into new forms of community were the existing highway system and the various new forms of telecommunication, such as telephone, radio, telegraph, and, most recently, television. While never defining a true linear city, as was proposed as early as the 1880s by the Spaniard Arturo Soria y Mata and developed by the Soviet planner Nikolai Miliutin in 1930 and later by Le Corbusier, the highway system served as the underlying, multidirectional, and multifunctional network of Wright's proposal. It was not merely a means of physical movement but also took on the role of place-making that squares or plazas once played in older forms of cities.

The gas station, or "service station along the highway," was to serve as the catalyst of this anamorphic urbanism. As "the future city in embryo," in Wright's words, it would "naturally grow into a neighborhood distribution center, meeting-place,

INTRODUCTION

restaurant, . . . or whatever else is needed." Spread throughout the landscape in every direction, such service stations would form "a thousand centers as city equivalents." "Stores linked to the decentralized chain service stations" would become neighborhood shopping centers, while "temporary lodging" could be had there in what later would be called motels. Perhaps the most significant architectural element that would define these community centers were the "automobile objectives." Based on a design Wright had done for one in 1924–25 for a rural site near Dickerson, Maryland, about an hour's drive from Washington, D.C., for the same real estate developer Gordon Strong he referred to in chapter 5, such automobile-accessible, multiuse structures would house planetariums, concert halls, theaters, museums, and art galleries as well as other outdoor facilities on the "recreation grounds" surrounding them. Affording panoramic views of the landscape from the spiral road encircling the building, such "automobile objectives" were envisioned "from end to end of the country."[163]

While the highway and its centers for shopping, eating, and recreational and cultural activities would amply "gratify," in Wright's words, the "get-together instinct," much of the social and intellectual life of the individual would be focused on the single-family house, "the home of the individual social unit." Predicting the defining, bottom-line condition of Broadacre City, Wright stated that each family would be given "an acre" as "the democratic minimum" of land. While he did not specify how this would be achieved nor how that land was to be used other than for residential purposes, he did make much of the fact that the private house would become in this new "ruralism" an integrated home "entertainment" center complementing and supplementing the ones on the highway. "Soon there will be little not reaching him [the family member] at his own fireside by broadcasting, television and publication." "The 'movies,' 'talkies' and all," he forecast, "will soon be seen and heard better at home than in any hall. Symphony concerts, operas and lectures will eventually be taken more easily to the home than the people can be now be taken to the great halls in old style, and be heard more satisfactorily in congenial company." This domestic environment would provide all sorts of programming, be it for entertainment or education, in the "intimate comfort" of one's own home and with "free individual choice."[164]

Wright had not yet designed the typical house for the minimum acre freehold that would dot the countryside and be referred to by him in the later 1930s as the Usonian House, based on the name for America he began using in 1925 and employed often in the text of *Modern Architecture*.[165] He had, however, already designed the automobile objective, the most significant building in the cultural life of the new city. And he used a spectacular aerial perspective of it to illustrate *Two Lectures on Architecture*, the publication of the talks he gave at the Art Institute of Chicago after the ones at Princeton, which appeared about four months after *Modern Architecture* did.[166] One therefore wonders why, instead of using it to illustrate the final chapter of *Modern Architecture*, he chose a rather minor and idiosyncratic work of the mid-1910s that seems to bear no relationship whatsoever to the subject matter at hand and even to be at odds with it. The project for the "small city house," or urban Town House of 1915–16 (misdated 1912–13 and curiously labeled a "Small Town Hall") was one of a large number of designs for the series of prefabricated American Ready-Cut or American System-Built Houses. It is conceivable that Wright thought its standardized construction along with its verticality and pronounced asymmetry might be interpreted as predicting later European developments—but still . . . one wonders. . . .

There is no doubt that Wright was generally more concerned about the discursive text of the book than about the illustrative material, just as he was in the lectures. But even so, there was something special about the final chapter and its utopian subject matter. Despite the fact that his "ruralist" vision was deeply grounded in the realities of American land-use development and would eventually come to fruition in many of its aspects, the type of new city Wright described in "The City" did not cohere as an image but only as a descriptive text. It was in fact invisible—as indeterminate in shape as it was boundless in scope. Unlike Le Corbusier's projected cities of the 1920s, where the power of the images was undoubtedly greater than the words accompanying them, in Wright's case it was the text that carried the force of the argument and made the imagination work overtime. Even when the proposal adumbrated in chapter 6 was developed in *The Disappearing City* the following year and given the name Broadacre City, there was still no visual representation of it. That only came in 1934–35, when a large sectional model, accompanied by smaller ones of individual structures, was built and exhibited in New York, Madison, Pittsburgh, and Washington, D.C. Wright later often described Broadacre City as being located "nowhere unless everywhere," thereby acknowledging both the shapelessness and fundamental invisibility of the concept as well as its source in the "no place" that the Greek neologism Utopia means.[167]

The literary conceit of time travel that Wright used to end the final chapter, and thus the book as a whole, relates, in general, to the literature of utopia (and its corollary dystopia) and, in particular, to one of the architect's favorite novels in the genre, Edward Bellamy's *Looking Backward: 2000–1887* (1888). At the same time, it also bears comparison with the final chapter in Le Corbusier's *Towards a New Architec-*

ture, where the terms "Architecture or Revolution" are set in opposition to one another in a kind of "do or die" scenario not unlike the doomsday one that activates Wright's final thoughts. Following the last glowing description of his new city as an environment where "architectural beauty related to natural beauty" will transform "the countryside far and near" into "a festival of life," Wright appended a darker, more cautionary note.[168]

What if, Wright asks, America were to follow the "superficial" suggestions of the "machine-made Utopia" of the European modern movement rather than the home-grown, land-based, democratically grounded proposal he is offering? In answer to this question, he asks his reader to follow him into the far-distant future to see what the ruins of modern civilization would look like. There will be nothing left as an authentic reminder of the "experiment in civilization we call Democracy." There would not even be any evidence to help in recreating what might have existed: "The ruin would defy restoration by the historian; it would represent a total loss in human Culture, except as a possible warning."[169] There would be bits of historical details from other civilizations used in eclectic buildings; there would be "a wilderness of wiring, wheels and complex devices of curious ingenuity"; there would be "our plumbing," "the most characteristic relic of all"; and then there would be "the vast confusion of riveted steelwork in various states of collapse and disintegration." "Only our industrial buildings could tell anything worth knowing about us," "but few of these buildings would survive that long." To the question "What Architecture would appear in the ruins?" the answer was none.[170] Unless, that is, America woke up immediately to the architectural and urban ideas that Wright had shown to be organic to its character, its landscape, its ideology, and its historical evolution, in other words, that America looked to itself through his example and became aware of the fact that its "culture itself [was] becoming year by year more plastic."[171]

The message was clear: Architecture or Ruination. This was different from Le Corbusier's message, but not that much. Wright, we have to remember, was writing on the cusp of the Great Depression whereas Le Corbusier had been anticipating with great optimism the major industrial effort being put into the Reconstruction of France after the end of World War I. Instead of looking back at the present from an imaginary future, Le Corbusier "set [the present] against the past," analyzing it not just in relation to the recent past, or even to "the nineteenth century, but to the history of civilizations in general." In that *longue durée*, the architect described the creation of new tools of industry, new methods of business, new methods of construction, and new laws of architecture resulting from the above as denoting, whether one liked it or not, whether one was conscious of it or not, a "Revolution." The problem was that the advantages of this revolution had not filtered down to the individual, especially those in the working class, who saw the benefits of the machine at work but none of those benefits in their increasingly longer leisure-time hours. Le Corbusier's answer to the dilemma was similar to Wright's. "Revolution [read Ruination] can be avoided" through the implementation of his ideas about architecture in all aspects and at all levels of society, in other words, "Architecture or Revolution."[172]

LOOKING BACKWARD AT *MODERN ARCHITECTURE*

As Wright himself told Baldwin Smith at the onset of their discussions about what he would do for the lectures, "the best work I have ever done was the result of provocation." There is no doubt, as is evidenced throughout the book, that Wright felt provoked by almost everyone and everything around him. It was not just "Le Corbusier and his school" but the entire establishment of American professional architecture, the business leaders and real estate developers who gave them jobs, and the mediocrity of the culture of "sham" and kitsch that was ultimately at the source of it all. But there is also no doubt that "Le Corbusier and his school" were the most significant and dangerous of those Wright characterized as his "enemies" because they, for the first time ever in his career, had claim to having produced an architecture and an urbanism that were more advanced and more modern than his own.[173]

In two important articles published in *Architectural Record* in 1928 to which I have already alluded, Hitchcock placed Wright in the camp of the out-of-date New Tradition, along with Berlage, Auguste Perret, and Eliel Saarinen, among others; Le Corbusier, Oud, Mies, and Gropius, by contrast, were lauded as representing the new avant-garde.[174] Hitchcock repeated the same argument in his book *Modern Architecture: Romanticism and Reintegration* (1929), where he maintained that Wright's work "has but a limited sympathy with the spirit of the machine" and therefore little relevance to current avant-garde practices. Le Corbusier, on the other hand, was described as "the type of the new architect," the one "who has succeeded best in destroying the validity of the New Tradition" and "achieved a more advanced demonstration of the possibilities of an new aesthetic than any other architect."[175]

Up until the late 1920s, Wright only had to worry about those who, in his view, stole his ideas and made them more palatable to public consumption; but in the years just preceding the invitation to give the Kahn Lectures, he began to realize that there were ideas in the air newer than his own that he might himself be tempted to appropriate or, at the very least, to feel the need to engage. His review of Le Corbusier's *Towards a New Architecture*, which came out four months after Hitchcock's articles, was the first of his attempts to deal with the unexpected situation. Characterizing Le Corbusier, in extremely positive terms, as "no sentimentalist," Wright criticized "the talented Frenchman" for the focus on " 'surface and mass' effects" and the "stark," reductive form of his machine-inspired designs. Yet he went on to state that Le Corbusier was "right" in his praise for the " 'new' beauty" of machinery, correct in his dismissal of the "styles," and on the mark in "dressing down" the eclectic commercial architecture of New York.[176]

Wright also expressed the thought, almost in passing, that Le Corbusier may not be that distant from his own world after all, and that "the French movement may soon lose its two dimensions, 'surface and mass,' within the three that characterize the American work." Whether such a rapprochement would ever actually occur is not something Wright dwelt on, although it is interesting that he noted the possibility. Finally, after urging "everyone engaged in making or breaking [architecture in] these United States . . . [to] read the Le Corbusier book," he appended a curiously open note of give-and-take, one that could even be read as implying a debt to be repaid: "So welcome Holland, Germany, Austria and France! Had you not taken it [the lessons furnished by Sullivan and himself], we as a Nation might never have been aware of it, never, even, have seen it!"[177]

As Wright's first full-fledged public presentation of his reaction to the new modern architecture of Europe and, especially, that of Le Corbusier, the Kahn Lectures and the book that came out of them reveal not just Wright's antagonism toward the younger Europeans but even more importantly the first stage in his attempt to grapple with their ideas. In many instances this involved, consciously or not, a large degree of appropriation. We saw this already in the many connections that exist on a substantive as well as a structural level between the texts of *Modern Architecture* and *Towards a New Architecture*. Wright could never assume the declarative, analytic, epigrammatic style of writing that Le Corbusier used so effectively, nor could he weave together text and image in the way the latter did to create entirely new and extraordinary connections between buildings and things. All this was foreseen by Baldwin Smith, who at first bemoaned the lack of "functional directness" and "simplicity" in Wright's prose. But, in his own way—as the preacher rather than the logician—

Wright sought to insert his text into the advanced discourse of the period as that was fundamentally and irrevocably shaped by Le Corbusier.

Wright was certainly more articulate and more compelling, indeed, even more poetic, in his buildings than in his words. He was also much more original and creative when it came to designing than writing and yet, even in his design thinking, the confrontation with "Le Corbusier and his school" had a powerful and permanent effect. In the proposal for a new paradigm of the city laid out in chapter 6 of *Modern Architecture*—the first and only self-generated design by Wright for an ideal city—Wright barely veiled the source of his countertype in stating that it was based on "Ruralism as distinguished from Urbanism," urbanism having by that time become the special domain of Le Corbusier.[178] The encounter with the latter's freestanding cruciform skyscrapers raised on *pilotis* above their surrounding parklike space likewise influenced the design of the St. Mark's Towers scheme, which broke with the perimeter-block concept the architect had previously employed in the Skyscraper Regulation project and the National Life Insurance Company Building. Wright, of course, would never openly acknowledge such influence, admitting in the second chapter of *Modern Architecture* that "artists, even great ones, are singularly ungrateful to sources of inspiration," while doing himself little justice by adding that "among lesser artists ingratitude amounts to phobia."[179]

Wright ultimately became phobic about the impact European modernism had on his work and, especially after the 1932 International Style exhibition, was more and more critical of anything the younger Europeans accomplished and more and more unwilling to admit the rapprochement of ideas he previously suggested might occur. It was, in fact, the "propagandist" efforts of the Museum of Modern Art to institutionalize a style, "conceived by the few to be imposed upon all alike," rather than the new architecture itself that really got his ire up and set the ball in motion.[180] He wrote that the exhibition was "trying to head me off."[181] The term "Organic Architecture," which in *Modern Architecture* first became his usual way of distinguishing his work from the "'surface and mass' effects" of European modernism, soon was used as a rallying cry meant to circle the wagons and call into question the significance of any other form of contemporary architectural expression.[182] While intended to define his work in a timeless, transcendent way, it also indicated the centrist role he saw for himself when he spoke in 1932 of working with "an enemy in each eye. Two extremes. The predatory eclectic in the right eye. The predatory 'internationalist' in the left eye."[183]

INTRODUCTION

There is no denying that the very architectural thinking Wright had lauded between 1928 and 1931 as of unusual "portent" and "extremely valuable . . . as an enemy" was about to prove its value as a catalytic agent of great power and subtlety in the designs the architect began producing from the mid-1930s on.[184] This story has often been told and is not worth repeating, except to note that the design of both Fallingwater, the weekend house for the Kaufmann family in Mill Run, Pennsylvania (1934–37), and the Jacobs House in Madison, Wisconsin (1936–37), the first Usonian House, were both profoundly engaged with the formal ideas earlier developed by Le Corbusier, Mies, and others. Both realize the ideal Wright set out in his review of *Towards a New Architecture* in stating that "the third dimension we already have to be added to the two of France is *depth*."[185] Fallingwater and the Jacobs House were almost immediately celebrated as major contributions to the world of modern architecture and as representative works of Wright's resurgent career as that was documented in the January 1938 issue of *Architectural Forum* devoted exclusively to the architect's recent work.[186]

In the later 1930s, 1940s, and 1950s, Wright went on to do extraordinary work, as original, as interesting, and as important as any he had done earlier in his career, so much so that, by 1948, Hitchcock completely reversed his view on Wright's relevance to modern architecture. In an important symposium on the current state of architecture held at New York's Museum of Modern Art in 1948, the critic and historian declared that "it is hard, unless we turn to that extraordinary man, Frank Lloyd Wright, to find much wealth or variety or range of expression in modern architecture at the present time," adding that "a range of expression sufficient for several centuries seems to be concentrated in that man's last few years' projects."[187]

Wright's return to the forefront of modern architecture was as important for the discipline itself as it was for his own career and legacy. In rising to the challenge of the European modern movement and engaging with it as he did, Wright served to make modern architecture itself a more complex, multilayered phenomenon, even if he himself usually preferred to declare his own independence from it. From the later 1930s on, he opened certain new avenues for investigation and thus gave as much as he took. While he would always claim exclusive ownership of the label "organic architecture," others, like Alvar Aalto, and later Jørn Utzon, both strongly influenced by Wright, were included by the historian and critic Sigfried Giedion in a trend "toward the irrational and the organic" that he saw, as early as 1941, as indicating how "European and American architecture together may find a new and common path."[188]

In opposition to the earlier, 1920s conception of the "rational-functional," the "irrational-organic," in Giedion's view, brought into play a new sense of liveliness, individuality, and freedom in the design process as well as a close connection to nature through flexible site planning and the use of natural materials.[189] Wright's centrist position vis-à-vis the radical purism of the "machine aesthetic" also gave him a unique and exemplary place in the post–World War II turn toward what Lewis Mumford described as "a native and humane form of modernism" emphasizing "the 'feeling' elements in design." This "domestication" of modern architecture, as Alfred Barr would describe it, drew much from Wright's work in its goal of "providing," as Barr put it, "'comfortable' houses for ordinary living."[190]

Wright's *Modern Architecture* remains a key text in the development of modern architecture, marking some of the most important changes that occurred in its evolution following the climactic years of the 1920s and the first evidence of its institutionalization in the Museum of Modern Art's International Style exhibition. On the most obvious level, it reveals Wright's engagement with the new movement and prepares us for the unexpected "second career" he would have. But more importantly, it affords us a window into how his interaction with European modernism would ultimately complicate and enrich later developments. At the same time, it helps us to assess more accurately his own role in those events by indicating the centrist—dare one say middle-of-the-road?—position he was led to take by his training, belief system, and way of life, and that he chose to adopt in reaction to the revolutionary changes unfolding around him.

ACKNOWLEDGMENTS AND NOTES

A number of people were instrumental in enabling me to gather the information necessary to putting this story together. Robert Judson Clark was exceedingly generous in making available to me all the pathbreaking research he did in 1980 as well as the notes for a lecture he gave at that time on Wright's Kahn Lectures. Bruce Brooks Pfeiffer and Margo Stipe of the Frank Lloyd Wright Archives were, as always, unstinting in their willingness to provide access to documents and share their lights on the subject with me. In addition, Pfeiffer's publication of Wright's *Collected Writings* proved invaluable in my review of Wright's literary output prior to the Kahn Lectures. Sara Stevens did extraordinary research in the Princeton University archives and provided many thoughts on how to interpret the material she uncovered. Erica Kim did significant bibliographical research at the beginning of the project. Paolo Scrivano provided information about Oud and photocopies of his correspondence in the Netherlands Architectural Institute. Anthony Alofsin, Mardges Bacon, Hilary Ballon, Jean-Louis Cohen, Richard Joncas, Francesco Passanti, and Kathryn Smith all graciously responded to questions

INTRODUCTION

I had. Finally, I should like to thank Susan Jacobs Lockhart for the advice and help she gave in all phases of this project.

A note on typological errors: errors found in the older edition of this book have not been corrected, for historical reasons.

1. Catherine Bauer, "The 'Exuberant and Romantic' Genius of Frank Lloyd Wright," review of *Modern Architecture: Being the Kahn Lectures for 1930*, by Frank Lloyd Wright, *New Republic* 67 (8 July 1931): 214. For other reviews, see List of Reviews and Notices following the notes.

2. Ibid.

3. Ibid., 214–15.

4. Bruno Taut, *Modern Architecture* (London: Studio, 1929), 1. According to the author's foreword, the manuscript was written in English. A German version of the text was published as *Die neue Baukunst in Europa und Amerika*, Bauformen-Bibliothek, no. 26 (Stuttgart: J. Hoffmann, 1929).

5. Henry-Russell Hitchcock Jr., *Modern Architecture: Romanticism and Reintegration* (1929; reprint, New York: Hacker Art Books, 1970).

6. Alfred H. Barr et al., *Modern Architecture: International Exhibition* (New York: Museum of Modern Art, 1932), 13, 15.

7. While Wright wrote on 6 June 1931 to E. Baldwin Smith, the member of Princeton's Department of Art and Archaeology who served as editor of *Modern Architecture* and wrote the preface, that he "appreciate[d] to the full the advantages of first appearing in book form in my own country under the patronage of Princeton," in a follow-up letter of 15 June 1931 to Charles Rufus Morey, the chair of the department, Wright described the recently published book unqualifiedly as "my first book." Frank Lloyd Wright Foundation, Scottsdale, AZ (hereafter FLWF). The Wasmuth publications *Ausgeführte Bauten und Entwürfe von Frank Lloyd Wright* (1910) and *Frank Lloyd Wright: Ausgeführte Bauten* (1911) were pictorial monographs with short texts, respectively, by Wright and C. R. Ashbee. Wright's *The Japanese Print: An Interpretation* (Chicago: Ralph Fletcher Seymour, 1912) was a booklet based on a lecture. Wright's *Two Lectures on Architecture*, based on talks given at the Art Institute of Chicago in October 1930, was published by the museum in July 1931. The books after 1932 include significantly revised and enlarged versions of previously published works as well as jointly authored volumes and collections edited by others.

8. Terence Riley, *The International Style: Exhibition 15 and the Museum of Modern Art*, Columbia Books on Architecture, cat. 3 (New York: Rizzoli/Columbia Books on Architecture, 1992), 205n39, reports that Philip Johnson took the initiative in the fall of 1933 of inviting Oud to lecture for "two months" in the spring term at Columbia University and the Museum of Modern Art. Oud declined as he had the previous year to an earlier invitation by Johnson. According to Mardges Bacon, *Le Corbusier: Travels in the Land of the Timid* (Cambridge, MA, and London: MIT Press, 2001), 27–29, Joseph Hudnut, as acting dean at Columbia, came up with a plan in early 1934 to involve a number of American schools in inviting three European architects from the following list of six: Walter Gropius, Le Corbusier, André Lurçat, Erich Mendelsohn, Oud, and Ivar Tengbom. Nothing came of this. Le Corbusier eventually came on a major lecture circuit in 1935, which included talks at Bowdoin College, Columbia, Cranbrook Academy,

the Massachusetts Institute of Technology, Princeton, Vassar College, Wesleyan University, the University of Wisconsin, and Yale University (ibid., 314).

9. See David Van Zanten, "The 'Princeton System' and the Founding of the School of Architecture, 1915–20," in *The Architecture of Robert Venturi*, ed. Christopher Mead (Albuquerque: University of New Mexico Press, 1989), 34–44.

10. Marilyn Aronberg Lavin, *The Eye of the Tiger: The Founding and Development of the Department of Art and Archaeology, 1883–1923, Princeton University* (Princeton, NJ: Department of Art and Archaeology and the Art Museum, Princeton University, 1983).

11. Kahn also promised another $1,000 annually for five years to support department activities in general and publications in particular.

12. Rostovzeff's lectures were published in 1929 as *The Animal Style in South Russia and China* by Princeton University Press, for the department, in the Princeton Monographs in Art and Archaeology series.

13. Charles Rufus Morey to Otto H. Kahn, 16 April 1928, Box 221, Folder 13, Otto H. Kahn Papers, Department of Rare Books and Special Collections, Princeton University Library, Princeton, NJ (hereafter PUL); and *Bulletin of the Department of Art and Archaeology of Princeton University* (November 1928): 13–14. Initially Kahn said that he preferred the lecture series not to carry his name and suggested, perhaps facetiously, that they be called the "Morey Lectures." Kahn to Morey, 18 April 1928, PUL. But on the insistence of Morey, who wrote to Kahn that "everyone speaks of the lectures as the 'Kahn lectures,'" Kahn eventually agreed to the appellation. Morey to Kahn, 15 May 1929; and Kahn to Morey, 2 June 1929, PUL.

14. Morey to Kahn, 16 April 1928; and Morey to Kahn, 23 April 1928, PUL.

15. Morey to Kahn, 1 June 1928, PUL.

16. Johnny Roosval, *Swedish Art: Being the Kahn Lectures for 1929*, Princeton Monographs in Art and Archaeology, no. 18 (Princeton, NJ: Princeton University Press, 1932), 75–77.

17. Robert Judson Clark, "FLW at Princeton," (lecture, Princeton University, 16 May 1980), 3. Clark based his statement on telephone interviews, on 25 and 27 April 1980, with Forsyth, who went on to a distinguished career at the University of Michigan.

18. Morey to J.J.P. Oud, 12 April 1929, Archief Oud, correspondentie B, Netherlands Architecture Institute, Rotterdam (hereafter NAi).

19. Morey to Oud, 4 January 1929, NAi.

20. Henry-Russell Hitchcock Jr., "The Architectural Work of J. J. P. Oud," *Arts* 13 (February 1928): 103.

21. Philip Johnson, "Afterword," in *Writings* (New York: Oxford University Press, 1979), 268. In preparation for the International Style exhibition, Johnson had his parents commission a vacation house in Pinehurst, North Carolina, from Oud; and in early July 1931 he wrote to Oud saying, "I am only propagating you and Mies van der Rohe." Ed Taverne, Cor Wagenaar, and Martien de Vletter, *J. J. P. Oud, Poetic Functionalist, 1890–1963: The Complete Works* (Rotterdam: NAi Publishers, 2001), 327.

22. According to H. Peter Oberlander and Eva Newbrun, *Houser: The Life and Work of Catherine*

Bauer (Vancouver: UBC Press, 1999), 67, Oud was Bauer's "favourite architect in Europe—both for his direct, informal manner and because he reminded her of Lewis Mumford."

23. Morey to Oud, 4 January 1929, NAi.

24. An unsigned article on the 1980 Princeton colloquium celebrating the fiftieth anniversary of the Wright lectures, "Frank Lloyd Wright and the Princeton Lectures of 1930," *Frank Lloyd Wright Newsletter* 3 (second quarter, 1980): 12, noted that "it has been surmised that Oud's name was put forward by Alfred Barr, who had just become director of the Museum of Modern Art." Barr received his B.A. and M.A. from Princeton in the early 1920s, having worked closely with Morey, with whom he remained in contact over the years, and taught at the university in 1924–25, at the instigation of Morey. Hitchcock, who by 1929 was teaching at Wesleyan, would have met Morey through the work he did as a graduate student at Harvard, where he had originally planned to do his Ph.D. dissertation on aspects of Romanesque architecture. It is interesting to note that in the biography appended to the section on Oud that Hitchcock contributed to MoMA's *Modern Architecture* catalogue, the final entry was "1929 Invited to give the Kahn Lectures at Princeton University" (99).

25. Oud to Morey, 20 February 1929, NAi.

26. Morey to Oud, 28 March 1929 and 12 April 1929, NAi.

27. Morey to Kahn, 4 June 1929, PUL.

28. Morey to Mrs. J.J.P. Oud, 4 June 1929, NAi.

29. Morey to Kahn, 21 January 1930, PUL. Having heard of Oud's invitation to Princeton, Emil Lorch asked the architect on 11 October 1929 if he would give three lectures at the University of Michigan's College of Architecture following the Kahn Lectures. In his response to Lorch of 27 November, Oud said that although he would "like very much to come to Ann Arbor," he has been "ill for months and months and though I am getting better and better I am not yet the old one!" "I hope of course to have regained fully my strength [by] the time I have to part for America but I cannot guarantee for it." "In the circumstances," he concluded, "I am I think not allowed to accept your invitation as I could be obliged to disappoint you by non-appearance!" (NAi).

30. Clark, "FLW at Princeton," 5. The information about Forsyth was based, as noted above, on interviews with him on 25 and 27 April 1980. Sherley Morgan, who was actually on leave that spring term and was being replaced by Smith as acting director of the School of Architecture, told Clark, in an interview on 2 December 1975, that it was he who suggested that an American be invited and that that person should be Wright. Clark, however, made no mention of Morgan in his 1980 lecture and referred exclusively to Forsyth as the instigator.

31. Henry-Russell Hitchcock Jr., "Frank Lloyd Wright," in Barr et al., *Modern Architecture*, 29, 34; H.-R. Hitchcock Jr. and Philip Johnson, *The International Style*, orig. pub. 1932 as *The International Style: Architecture Since 1922* (New York: W. W. Norton & Company, 1966), 25–26.

32. J.J.P. Oud, "The Influence of Frank Lloyd Wright on the Architecture of Europe," *Wendingen* 7 (1925): 85–91; and J.J.P. Oud, *Holländische Architektur* (1926; reprint, Mainz and Berlin: Florian Kupferberg, 1976), 77–83. The article was also reprinted in H. Th. Wijdeveld, *The Life-Work of the American Architect Frank Lloyd Wright* (1925; reprint, New York: Bramhall House, 1965), 85–89.

33. The series is conveniently reprinted in Frederick Gutheim, ed., *In the Cause of Architecture: Frank Lloyd Wright. Essays by Frank Lloyd Wright for* Architectural Record (New York: Architectural Record Books, 1975), 130–230.

34. See Frank Lloyd Wright, "Towards a New Architecture," review of *Towards a New Architecture*, by Le Corbusier, *World Unity* 2 (September 1928): 393–95; reprinted in *Frank Lloyd Wright: Collected Writings*, ed. Bruce Brooks Pfeiffer (hereafter *CW*), vol. 1, *1894–1930* (New York: Rizzoli, in association with the Frank Lloyd Wright Foundation, 1992), 317–18. See also F. L. Wright, "Surface and Mass,—Again!" *Architectural Record* 66 (July 1929), in *CW*, 1:324–28. Wright was responding to Douglas Haskell, "Organic Architecture: Frank Lloyd Wright," *Creative Art* 3 (November 1928): li–lvii; and Henry-Russell Hitchcock Jr., "Modern Architecture. I: The Traditionalists and the New Tradition," *Architectural Record* 63 (April 1928): 337–49.

35. Henry-Russell Hitchcock Jr., *Frank Lloyd Wright*, Les Maîtres de l'architecture contemporaine, no. 1 (Paris: Cahiers d'Art, 1928).

36. E[arl] Baldwin Smith to Frank Lloyd Wright, 3 February 1930, FLWF.

37. Ibid. It almost goes without saying that Smith made no mention to Wright of the fact that he was the department's second (and perhaps even third) choice for the lectureship. If Wright ever discovered this, he was gracious enough, or enough unsure of himself, never to refer to it either privately or publicly. The fact was not kept secret, however. Sherley W. Morgan, "Report on the School of Architecture for the Year 1929–30," *Bulletin of the Department of Art and Archaeology of Princeton University* (September 1930): 17, noted that, "for the departmental lectures this year on the Kahn Foundation," "it had originally been arranged to bring over M. Oud from Holland to discuss the modern European movement. When he was prevented by illness from coming to America, we were particularly fortunate in getting Mr. Frank Lloyd Wright to take his place." As noted above (note 24), the brief "Chronology of Life" of Oud published in Barr et al., *Modern Architecture*, 99, the catalogue of the International Style exhibition, which Wright certainly looked at, listed the invitation by Princeton for the Kahn Lectureship for 1929.

38. Wright to Smith, 6 June 1931, FLWF. The week before, Wright told Smith that he "could have sold the lectures for $3000." Wright to Smith, 26 May 1931, FLWF. This figure matches the per article payment the architect received from the *Architectural Record* according to Bruce Pfeiffer, *CW*, 1:225.

39. Wright to Smith, 8 February 1930, FLWF. While Wright's reference to business in New York probably related to the St. Mark's Towers project, it may also have had to do with the exhibition he was planning for the Architectural League of New York, which would explain his immediate offer to Smith of an exhibition in lieu of two lectures. Wright was apparently contacted by the Architectural League about an exhibition in September 1929. I want to thank Kathryn Smith for sharing with me her information on the precedence of the New York exhibition.

40. Wright to Smith, 8 February 1930, preliminary draft, FLWF. The list of subjects is handwritten on the draft but not included in the final draft cited above. Since Smith referred to it in his response (see below), one has to assume it was included in the correspondence as a separate sheet now lost.

41. The *Princeton University Weekly Bulletin*, 3 May and 10 May 1930, gave as a general title for the lectures "The Problems of Modern Architecture." This may have come from Smith; it certainly did not

come from Wright. The only other place it is mentioned is in the articles covering the lectures published in the student newspaper, the *Daily Princetonian*. See note 53 below.

42. Smith to Wright, 10 February 1930, FLWF. This letter was on department stationary, as were almost all of the later ones from Smith to Wright.

43. Wright to Smith, 17 February 1930, FLWF. Lecture 1 took on its final title; lecture 2 had "The War on Style" added as a subtitle; lectures 3 and 4 remained the same; lectures 5 and 6 were reversed. The dates Wright suggested for the lectures were the ones followed; the exhibition, however, opened three days before his suggested date of 15 May.

44. Ibid.

45. Ibid.

46. Smith to Wright, 20 February 1930, FLWF.

47. Wright to Smith, 1 April 1930, FLWF.

48. Clark, "FLW at Princeton," 6. Clark states that the slides were chosen by Forsyth, Donald Drew Egbert, and "perhaps Martin Beck."

49. They were also published as part of H[einrich] de Fries, "Neue Pläne von Frank Lloyd Wright," *Die Form* 5 (July 1930): 343–49.

50. Wright to Smith, 1 May 1930, FLWF; and Wright to Smith, [1 May 1930], FLWF.

51. Whereas the subtitle in Wright's letter read "The War on Style," in the 3 May 1930 edition of the *Princeton University Weekly Bulletin* it appeared as "The War on 'Styles,'" which actually makes more sense.

52. *Princeton University Weekly Bulletin*, 3 May and 10 May 1930.

53. "Architect to Give Six Lectures Here: Frank Lloyd Wright Who Holds Kahn Lectureship This Year Is Famous in Europe," *Daily Princetonian* (hereafter *DP*), 6 May 1930, 1, 5; "Chicago Architect Gives Initial Talk: Frank L. Wright Opens Lecture Series with Address on 'Machinery, Materials, and Men,'" *DP*, 7 May 1930, 1; "Speaker Lauds Utility in New Building Designs: F. L. Wright, Famous Architect, Praises Simplicity of Style in Address Yesterday," *DP*, 9 May 1930, 3; "Architect Wright Scores Modernism: Speaker Criticizes Freak Designs of Present-Day Dwellings," *DP*, 10 May 1930, 4; "Lecturer Will Discuss Modern Architecture: F. L. Wright Speaks on 'The Tyranny of the Skyscraper' in McCormick 311 at 5 Today," *DP*, 13 May 1930, 1; "Architect Speaks on Modern Trends: F. L. Wright to Continue Discussion Today with a Lecture on 'The City,'" *DP*, 14 May 1930, 1, 4; and "Noted Architect Foresees Depopulation of the City," *DP*, 15 May 1930, 1, 4.

54. "Designer Supplements Lectures by Exhibition of Own Drawings," *DP*, 12 May 1930, 1; and "Drawings of Modern Buildings on Display in McCormick Hall," *DP*, 14 May 1930, 1. Although Wright had initially wanted the exhibition to open the day after the final lecture, as things developed it was decided to have it open at the beginning of the series. In the end, the date was delayed until the beginning of the second week of talks, i.e., 12 May (which was a Monday). It is unclear, however, when the exhibition closed. While it certainly lasted through the second week of the talks, i.e., 15 or 16 May, there is no mention of a closing date in published sources. The *Princeton Alumni Weekly*, 23 May 1930, reported that "during the series of talks, many of his [Wright's] drawings and some of his models were on exhibition," indicating that the show was over by 22 May at the latest. I have Sara Stevens to thank for her help in working this out.

55. Clark, interviews with Forsyth, 25 and 27 April 1980.

56. Clark, interview with Martin L. Beck, 30 April 1980.

57. Smith to Kahn, 16 May 1930, PUL.

58. Wright to Smith, 24 May 1930, FLWF.

59. Only the ones in Chicago were published. See note 7 above.

60. Kathryn Smith, "The Show to End All Shows: Frank Lloyd Wright and the Museum of Modern Art, 1940," in *The Show to End All Shows: Frank Lloyd Wright and the Museum of Modern Art, 1940*, ed. Peter Reed and William Kaizen, Studies in Modern Art, no. 8 (New York: Museum of Modern Art, 2004), 16, 60n11.

61. Smith to Wright, 4 January 1931 [should be 1932], FLWF. Morey to Kahn, 30 November 1931, PUL, said they were more suitable to a "Department of Oriental Languages and Literature" than to an art history audience.

62. Morey to Kahn, 21 April 1932, PUL.

63. It should be pointed out that, although the title page of the Wright volume noted that it was part of the Princeton Monographs in Art and Archaeology series, there was no mention of the volume number (unlike Roosval's and Rostovzeff's contributions, for instance).

64. Smith to Wright, 18 July 1930, FLWF.

65. The Frank Lloyd Wright Archives preserves multiple versions of parts or all of the six lectures. While they give evidence of much editing and rewriting, it appears that most of these changes were done prior to or immediately after the delivery of the lectures. They are: first lecture, "Machinery, Materials and Men," MSS 2401.068 and 2401.008; second lecture, "Style in Industry," MS 2401.069; third lecture, "The Passing of the Cornice," MS 2401.067; fourth lecture, "The Cardboard House," MS 2401.070; fifth lecture, "The Tyranny of the Skyscraper," MS 2401.066; and sixth lecture, "The City," MS 2401.064.

66. Wright to Smith, 24 July 1930, Department of Art and Archaeology Files, Princeton University (hereafter A&A Files).

67. Smith to Wright, 4 August 1930, FLWF.

68. Frank Lloyd Wright, *Modern Architecture: Being the Kahn Lectures for 1930* (hereafter *MA*), Princeton Monographs in Art and Archaeology, [no. 15] (Princeton, NJ: Princeton University Press, for the Department of Art and Archaeology of Princeton University, 1931), n. pag.

69. Smith to Wright, 4 August 1930, FLWF.

70. Wright to Smith, [mid-August 1930], A&A Files; Wright to Smith, [mid-August 1930], FLWF; and Smith to Wright, 3 September 1930, FLWF.

71. Wright to Smith, [mid-August 1930], A&A Files; Wright to Smith, [mid-August 1930], FLWF.

72. Smith to Wright, 3 September 1930, FLWF.

73. [Karl E. Jensen for] Wright to Smith, 17 October 1930, FLWF; and Smith to Jensen, 28 October 1930, A&A Files.

74. Smith to Wright, 3 September 1930, FLWF.

75. Smith to Wright (with notes by Wright to Smith), 23 September 1930, FLWF.

76. Smith to Wright, 7 November 1930, FLWF.

77. Wright to Smith, 13 November 1930, FLWF. The drawings were done by Klumb, Takehiro Okami, and Rudolph Mock. Edgar Tafel, *About Wright: An Album of Recollections by Those Who Knew Frank*

Lloyd Wright (New York: John Wiley & Sons, 1993), 101, quotes Klumb as saying that it was he who "suggested [to Wright] that we might try to reduce his delicate renderings of his best known buildings to two-dimensional black on white graphic presentations that modern architects were addicted to" and that Wright's response was "DO IT." The drawings he lists are the Robie House, Winslow House, Yahara Boathouse, Bock House and Studio, Unity Temple, and Larkin Building (ibid., 101–2). All of these appeared in the Princeton publication except for the Boathouse, which was replaced by a Town House project of 1915–16 (incorrectly dated to 1912–13 in the book and called a Small Town Hall).

Wright's decision to use almost exclusively pre-1910 works as illustrations is in marked contrast to the almost contemporary publication of the *Two Lectures on Architecture*, given at the Art Institute of Chicago. In that much shorter publication, which is really just a booklet, there are nine illustrations, none of which predate the architect's departure from Oak Park. There are four of Taliesin and one each of Midway Gardens, the Ennis House in Los Angeles (1923–24), the Strong Automobile Objective and Planetarium project, near Dickerson, Maryland (1924–25), the National Life Insurance Company Building project, and the St. Mark's Towers project.

78. Wright to Smith, 13 November 1930, FLWF.

79. Wright to Smith, 13 November 1930, A&A Files. Unlike the draft cited immediately above, this version of the letter has numerous emendations in Wright's hand. One regards the switching of the order of Unity Temple and the Robie House, the other the reversal of the final two images. The move of Unity Temple to lecture 3 relates to the subject of "The Passing of the Cornice."

80. And, for whatever reason, the images were not reproduced to bleed off the page as both Wright and Smith had said they should.

81. *MA*, n. pag.

82. Smith to Wright, 12 February 1931, FLWF.

83. Wright to Smith, 19 February 1931, FLWF.

84. *MA*, n. pag.

85. *MA*, n. pag.

86. Wright to Smith, 31 March 1931, FLWF.

87. Wright to Smith, 6 April 1931, FLWF.

88. Wright to Smith, 8 April 1931, FLWF.

89. It should, however, be noted that the sixth lecture, "The City," was reprinted in abridged form in *Architectural Progress* 5 (October 1931): 4–6, 23; and as "O městu budoucnosti" (The City of the Future), in *Styl* (Prague) 16, no. 6 (1931): 93–95, 98. An Italian translation of the book appeared as *Architettura e democrazia* (Milan: Rosa e Ballo, 1945). The book was reprinted in Frank Lloyd Wright, *The Future of Architecture* (New York: Horizon Press, 1953), 67–182; and in *CW*, vol. 2, *1930–1932* (New York: Rizzoli, in association with the Frank Lloyd Wright Foundation, 1992), 19–79.

90. See note 65 above.

91. The angle of the perspective is similar to the one published in Frank Lloyd Wright, *Ausgefürhte Bauten und Entwürfe von Frank Lloyd Wright* (Berlin: Ernst Wasmuth, 1910), pl. 33a; reprinted, with English translation, as F. L. Wright, *Studies and Executed Buildings by Frank Lloyd Wright* (Palos Park, IL: Prairie School Press, 1975). The difference is that the view in the photograph is of the front, main pedestrian entrance of the building and the one in the Wasmuth portfolio shows the rear, or service

entrance side. The photograph published in the 1908 *Architectural Record* was republished in Frank Lloyd Wright, *Frank Lloyd Wright: Ausgeführte Bauten* (Berlin: Ernst Wasmuth, 1911), 129; and in Wijdeveld, *Life-Work*, 6.

92. Berlage wrote: "I was told that Wright's masterwork is the office building of the Larkin Company in Buffalo, New York. I went to see it, and I must confess that . . . [to say masterwork] is not to say enough." Fascinated by the fact that the interior of the building "consists of only one room," Berlage described the interior as a "forceful space" and noted how all the design elements derived from functional considerations and that the brick structure "looks like a warehouse from the outside." "I left convinced that I had seen a great modern work," he concluded, "and I am filled with respect for this master who has been able to create a building which has no equal in Europe." H[endrik] P[etrus] Berlage, "Neuere amerikanische Architektur," orig. pub. 1912; trans. as "The New American Architecture (1912): Travel Impressions of H. P. Berlage, Architect in Amsterdam," in *The Literature of Architecture: The Evolution of Architectural Theory and Practice in Nineteenth-Century America*, ed. Don Gifford (New York: E. P. Dutton, 1966), 614–15.

93. Frank Lloyd Wright, "In the Cause of Architecture," *Architectural Record* 23 (March 1908): 166–67; reprinted in Gutheim, *Cause of Architecture*, 64–65. Europeans would have had easy access to this statement since it was repeated word for word in Wright, *Ausgefürhte Bauten*, caption to pl. 33.

94. The original "Art and Craft of the Machine" was published in the *Catalogue of the Fourteenth Annual Exhibition of the Chicago Architectural Club* [Chicago: Chicago Architectural Club, 1901], n. pag.; reprinted in *CW*, 1:58–69. The manuscript version of the one used in *Modern Architecture*, entitled "The Art and Craft of the Machine by Frank Lloyd Wright," MS 2401.008, carries a later, autograph note at the top, saying "read at Hull House Chicago—1901—Feb. later read at Milwaukee Cincinati [*sic*]—& Chicago Art Institute by F.LLW." It is in no way "blackened and charred by fire," as Wright stated in the book (6). It is typed and heavily edited by hand. The text as it appears in *Modern Architecture* is even further edited, meaning that Wright reworked it in 1930 for the lecture and/or for the publication. Among the many additions to the published text are the date of "A.D. 1903" (*MA*, 11) and the phrase "Now, let us remember in forming this new Arts and Crafts Society at Hull House" (*MA*, 21). Both of these serve to re-"contextualize" the original lecture. Also, the phrase about "space" (*MA*, 20), a word not part of Wright's vocabulary before the later 1920s, was added. It is the *Modern Architecture* version of "The Art and Craft of the Machine" that Lewis Mumford published in his *Roots of Contemporary American Architecture: A Series of Thirty-Seven Essays Dating from the Mid-Nineteenth Century to the Present* (New York: Reinhold, 1952), 169–85.

95. Bauer, "'Exuberant and Romantic' Genius," 214. Wright also referred to the Hull House lecture in the opening of his article "In the Cause of Architecture: The Third Dimension," originally published in *Wendingen* 7 (1925) and immediately reprinted in Wijdeveld, *Life-Work*, 48–65. This article advances many of the same arguments later developed in "Machinery, Materials and Men" and was probably referred to by Wright in drafting the later text. Interestingly, Wright began the 1925 article, which was actually written in 1923, by noting that the first meeting of the nascent Society of Arts and Crafts took place at Hull House "twenty-seven years ago," meaning 1896, and that he presented his talk on the "Art and Craft of the Machine" at the "next meeting." The number of years between the original lecture and its re-

visitings in 1923 and in 1930 was thus claimed to be the same. For the typescript of the 1925 article, see Frank Lloyd Wright, "In the Cause of Architecture: The Third Dimension," 9 February 1923, MS III/2, John Lloyd Wright Collection, Avery Library, Columbia University, New York; MS 2401.022, FLWF, is also apparently another copy of the same typescript, although I have not seen it.

96. Wright, "Towards a New Architecture," in *CW*, 1:317.

97. Frank Lloyd Wright, "The Hillside Home School of Allied Arts," 10 December 1928, 9, 16, Box 5–14, MS 22.8, Frank Lloyd Wright-Darwin D. Martin Papers, University Archives, State University of New York, Buffalo (hereafter SUNY-Buffalo). An edited version of the prospectus, with the same title, was published by Wright at Spring Green, Wisconsin, in October 1931; reprinted in *CW*, vol. 3, *1931–1939* (New York: Rizzoli, in association with the Frank Lloyd Wright Foundation, 1993), 40–49. The books by Viollet-le-Duc and Jones were the former's *Dictionnaire raisonné de l'architecture française du xie au xvie siècle* (1854–68) and the latter's *The Grammar of Ornament* (1856). The "suggested" director of the school was Wijdeveld, "supplemented by Frank Lloyd Wright." The list of visiting studio critics in architecture included: Berlage, Robert Mallet-Stevens, Erich Mendelsohn, Oud, Le Corbusier, Mumford, Harvey Wiley Corbett, Heinrich de Fries, and Claude Bragdon (SUNY-Buffalo, 16). In the 1931 prospectus, the section on the school library, including mention of Le Corbusier's *Towards a New Architecture*, was left out. Le Corbusier was, however, retained on the list of visiting critics, as were all the others except Corbett.

98. *MA*, 5. Wright was no doubt struck by Le Corbusier's lengthy, moving, and very personal descriptions of Pompeian houses in the chapter "The Illusion of Plans."

99. Wright's first reference to the "surface and mass effects" in Le Corbusier's work was in his "Towards a New Architecture," 393. It became the most common, negatively critical phrase by which he characterized Le Corbusier's architecture in *Modern Architecture*. The source is the "Three Reminders to Architects" chapter in the English translation of *Towards a New Architecture*, where the text states that "mass and surface are the elements by which architecture manifests itself." Le Corbusier, *Towards a New Architecture*, orig. pub. 1923; trans. Frederick Etchells, 1927 (reprint, London: Architectural Press; New York: Frederick A. Praeger, 1965), 28. Bacon, *Le Corbusier*, 24, 329n144, points out that Wright's use of the word "mass" is based on Etchells's mistranslation of the French word *volume*.

100. *MA*, 5–6. See, e.g., Walter Curt Behrendt, *The Victory of the New Building Style*, orig. pub. 1927; trans. Harry Francis Mallgrave, Texts & Documents (Los Angeles: Getty Research Institute, 2000), 141–42.

101. *MA*, 7.

102. Ibid., 7–8.

103. Ibid., 11, 15, 20.

104. Ibid., 17, 18.

105. Ibid., 14.

106. Ibid., 15, 21–23.

107. Ibid., 42, 29.

108. Le Corbusier, *Towards a New Architecture*, 45; and *MA*, 31. On pages 27 and 37, Le Corbusier says: "Architecture has nothing to do with the various 'styles.' The styles of Louis XIV, XV, XVI or Gothic, are to architecture what a feather is on a woman's head." The use of the term "styles" in opposi-

tion to "style" was not new in Wright's thinking. Wright stated: "To adopt a 'style' as a motive is to put the cart before the horse and get nowhere beyond the 'Styles'—never to reach *Style*." Frank Lloyd Wright, "In the Cause of Architecture, Second Paper: 'Style, Therefore, Will Be the Man, It Is His. Let His Forms Alone,'" *Architectural Record* 35 (May 1914): 413; reprinted in *CW*, 1:137. Wright more fully echoed the Corbusian diatribe against the "styles" in his "In the Cause of Architecture II: What 'Styles' Mean to the Architect," *Architectural Record* 63 (February 1928): 145–51; reprinted in *CW*, 1:263–68.

109. *MA*, 33, 34.

110. Ibid., 36.

111. Ibid., 39. Wright repeated these sentences almost verbatim in his "The Logic of Contemporary Architecture as an Expression of This Age," *Architectural Forum* 52 (May 1930): 638. Le Corbusier used the phrase "a house is a machine for living in" in *Towards a New Architecture*, 89. If he had read nothing else, Wright would have become aware of the new style in Henry-Russell Hitchcock Jr., "Modern Architecture. II: The New Pioneers," *Architectural Record* 63 (May 1928): 453–60, which we know he read. It was the sequel to "Modern Architecture: Traditionalists and the New Tradition," which dealt in part with his own work.

112. *MA*, 38–39.

113. Ibid., 40. In his letter to Smith of 1 April 1930, Wright said that, while in Princeton, "I should like to meet some people interested as we are in Art and Architecture, especially in the establishment of a new kind of school wherein Art might take the lead in Education and Industry. Such a school is a dream of mine for some years standing" (FLWF). Smith responded on 5 April saying, "I think you would be interested to meet and talk over your idea of an Art School with the members of our Department. We feel we have Art on a very firm and real foundation here in the Princeton scheme of education" (FLWF). There is no evidence that any further discussion took place.

114. Wright, "Hillside Home School of Allied Arts," 6, 12–13; and Ferdinand Schevill, "Summarized Statement of the Project for a School of Allied Arts at Hillside, Wisconsin," 1, SUNY-Buffalo. See note 97 above.

115. *MA*, 41–44.

116. Frank Lloyd Wright, "Recollections: United States, 1893–1920," *Architects' Journal* 84 (16 July 1936): 78.

117. Wright, *Ausgeführte Bauten*, pl. 1. The plan, on which the partial plan was based, was published as part of pl. 3 and the ornamental detail of the entrance was published as a supplement to pl. 1.

118. Except, that is, to some highly critical readers like Harvey M. Watts, who wrote that "when it comes to 'The Passing of the Cornice' one is somewhat flabbergasted in reading the denunciatory passages of cornices to discover that one is faced with, as it were, the old conundrum; for a cornice is a wicked thing when it is put up by somebody else, . . . but when Wright pushes a 'roof edge' over his buildings which for all the world looks like a raking cornice, then everything is lovely and the goose hangs high, and the 'roof edge' just isn't a cornice but a noble piece of functional, necessitated architecture." Harvey M. Watts, "Don Quixote Atilt at His World: The Frank Lloyd Wright Princeton Lectures and Their Message to the Younger Groups," *T-Square Club Journal* 1 (November 1931): 35.

The drawing on which the Unity Temple perspective is based was first published in Rodney F. Johonnot, *The New Edifice of Unity Church, Oak Park, Illinois. Frank Lloyd Wright, Architect* ([Oak Park]:

INTRODUCTION

The New Unity Church Club, 1906), n. pag.; it was republished in Wijdeveld, *Life-Work*, 13. A photograph taken from the same point of view was published in Wright, *Wright: Ausgeführte Bauten*, 14.

119. The word "sham" is used three times on the first three pages of the text. Part of the chapter, roughly corresponding to pages 50–56 in the book, was written about seven months previously, apparently for publication. See Frank Lloyd Wright, "The Passing of the Cornice," 7 October 1929, 1–6, MS 2401.067 B, FLWF. An adumbration of the idea for the theme of the cornice appears in Wright, "In the Cause: What 'Styles' Mean," in *CW*, 1:266.

120. *MA*, 52.

121. Ibid., 54.

122. Ibid., 57.

123. Ibid., 58.

124. Le Corbusier, *Towards a New Architecture*, 190, 192, 201.

125. Ibid., 81–138.

126. *MA*, 62.

127. Wright first used the phrase "the so-called card-board house" in a letter to the editor of April 1929 published as "Surface and Mass,—Again!" in *CW*, 1:328. Many of the ideas and phrases in the fourth chapter of *Modern Architecture* appear already in this article, where Wright criticizes the "dry sophistication" and "asceticism of superficial surface and mass effects" in the buildings of the younger European modernists and, especially, the appreciative response given their work by such critics as Hitchcock and Haskell.

128. *MA*, 65–66.

129. Ibid., 66.

130. Ibid., 66–67.

131. The new drawing is based on a photograph taken when the house was just finished and first published in Wright, *Wright: Ausgeführte Bauten*, 112. Wright predates the house by two years in his caption and also describes the roof as "flat," which it decidedly is not.

132. Wright, "Towards a New Architecture," in *CW*, 1:317.

133. Wright, "In the Cause of Architecture" (1908), in *CW*, 1:86–100.

134. Frank Lloyd Wright, *An Autobiography* (New York, London, and Toronto: Longmans, Green and Company, 1932); reprinted in *CW*, 2:199–206. Since the writing of the *Autobiography* began in 1927 and was an ongoing affair, it is difficult to say whether the part of "The Cardboard House" devoted to the creation of the Prairie House was written for the Kahn Lectures or was adapted from something already in draft.

135. Wright, "In the Cause of Architecture" (1908), in *CW*, 1:87.

136. *MA*, 72. Wright began to suggest a spatial interpretation in his discussion of "depth" in his 1923–25 article "In the Cause: Third Dimension." But it was not until 1928, in the articles "In the Cause: What 'Styles' Mean" and "In the Cause of Architecture, IX: The Terms," *Architectural Record* 64 (December 1928); reprinted in *CW*, 1:310–16, that the actual word "space" is used. In "In the Cause: What 'Styles' Mean," in *CW*, 1:266, Wright states: "The building is no longer a block of building material dealt with, artistically, from the outside. The room within is the great fact about the building—*the room* to be expressed in the exterior as *space enclosed*. This sense of the *room* within, held as the great motif for en-

closure, is the advanced thought of the era in architecture and is now searching for exterior expression." Wright usually attributed his articulation of the concept of space to Kakuzo Okakura's *The Book of Tea* (1906), which he apparently first became aware of in the early 1920s. On the other hand, the very common use in Wright's writings of the later 1920s of the word "room," so obviously related to the German word for space, *raum*, does not indicate a contemporaneous European source.

137. *MA*, 70, 71; and Le Corbusier, *Towards a New Architecture*, 164.

138. Wright, "In the Cause of Architecture" (1908), in *CW*, 1:94.

139. Oud, "Influence of Wright," in Wijdeveld, *Life-Work*, 89. It is interesting to recall in this context the characterization of Wright's work in 1932 in the foreword to Alfred Barr et al.'s *Modern Architecture*, where Barr says: "As the embodiment of the romantic principle of individualism, his [Wright's] work, complex and abundant, remains a challenge to the classical austerity of the style of his best young contemporaries" (15).

140. Wright, "Surface and Mass,—Again!" in *CW*, 1:328. In the article by Haskell, "Organic Architecture," to which Wright took offense, the critic spoke of the architect's "lavish, voluptuous, unnecessarily elaborate" architecture as a counter to the "surge of fierce classicism" in the modern movement of Europe, referring to Wright's work, by contrast, as an "organic architecture" (li, lvii). That Haskell went so far as to use the term to title the article may paradoxically have prompted Wright to return to the phrase.

141. Frank Lloyd Wright, "In the Cause, Second Paper," in *CW*, 1:127–32, 136–37, referred to "the ideal of an organic architecture," "the sense of an organic architecture," "the direction of an organic architecture," "the quality of an organic architecture," "the integrity of an organic architecture," and simply "an organic architecture" at least eleven times according to my count. In a note to its initial use, Wright offered the following definition: "By organic architecture I mean an architecture that *develops* from within outward in harmony with the conditions of its being as distinguished from one that is *applied* from without" (*CW*, 1:127). One might assume that because of its placement in a note, the definition was requested by the editor, which also points to the novelty of the expression at the time.

142. *MA*, 78, 77, 76, 80.

143. Bauer, "'Exuberant and Romantic' Genius," 214; and Talbot Faulkner Hamlin, "Artist and Prophet," review of *Modern Architecture*, by Frank Lloyd Wright, *Saturday Review of Literature* 7 (11 July 1931): 957. Hamlin previously wrote a similar review, "Living for the Beautiful," *Outlook and Independent* 157 (29 April 1931): 598–99.

144. R[obert] L[uther] Duffus, "'Tyranny of the Skyscraper': Frank Lloyd Wright Attacks Its Dominion of Our Architecture," review of *Modern Architecture*, by Frank Lloyd Wright, *New York Times Book Review*, 31 May 1931, sec. 4, 1, 28.

145. The perspective and the plan were both published in Wright, *Ausgeführte Bauten*, pl. 62 and suppl.

146. *MA*, 89. Wright was certainly not averse to acknowledging this commercial work publicly since he published the National Life Insurance Company Building in "In the Cause of Architecture, VIII: Sheet Metal and a Modern Instance," *Architectural Record* 64 (October 1928): 334–42, reprinted in *CW*, 1:305–9; and the St. Mark's Towers project in "St. Mark's Tower: St. Mark's in the Bouwerie, New York City," *Architectural Record* 67 (January 1930): 1–4. Moreover, perspectives of both the National Life Insurance Building

and St. Mark's Tower were used to illustrate Wright's *Two Lectures on Architecture*, which he gave at the Art Institute of Chicago soon after the Kahn Lectures and which were published shortly after *Modern Architecture*. The one of the National Life Insurance Building served as the frontispiece of the book.

147. Had he wanted to use an example of a skyscraper from his earlier work, which would have been consistent with the other illustrations, he could have chosen an image of the San Francisco Call Building, which was designed around 1913 and was included in the 1930–31 traveling exhibition. Two plans and two views of the model were published in Wijdeveld, *Life-Work*, 80–81; and the more dramatic of the views of the model was rendered in a rather crude drawing and published by Adolf Behne as the first plate in his important *Der moderne Zweckbau*, orig. pub. 1926; trans. Michael Robinson as *The Modern Functional Building*, Texts & Documents (Santa Monica, CA: Getty Research Institute for the History of Art and the Humanities, 1996), 151. The drawing reversed the photographic image and misdated the project to 1920.

148. The brochure *Experimenting with Human Lives* (Chicago: Ralph Fletcher Seymour, 1923), that Wright wrote after the Great Kanto Earthquake was less about skyscrapers as an architectural type than about the inadvisability of building them in seismic zones. The article on the National Life Insurance Company Building cited in note 146 above was purely a description and analysis of a single design and not a general consideration of the type or its urban implications.

149. *MA*, 85–86.

150. Ibid., 94–95, 98–99.

151. Ibid., 96, 98.

152. Ibid., 86, 88, 90, 95.

153. See Hilary Ballon, "From New York to Bartlesville: The Pilgrimage of Wright's Skyscraper," in *Prairie Skyscraper: Frank Lloyd Wright's Price Tower*, ed. Anthony Alofsin (New York: Rizzoli; Bartlesville, OK: Price Tower Arts Center, 2005), 100–110.

154. *MA*, 92–93, 89, 91, 96.

155. Frank Lloyd Wright, "~~In the Cause of Architecture:~~ The City," 29 September 1929, MS 2401.064 A, FLWF. The general title of the typescript, as indicated, is crossed out, leaving the subtitle alone. In what may be his first, surely extremely elliptical, reference to the abandonment of the city for the countryside, Frank Lloyd Wright, "In the Cause of Architecture, V: The New World," *Architectural Record* 62 (October 1927): 322; reprinted in *CW*, 1:245, asked the question: "The City?" and gave the answer: "Gone to the surrounding country."

156. *MA*, 101.

157. Ibid., 112, 103, 107. It is not known whether Wright had by this time read or even seen Le Corbusier's *The City of To-morrow and Its Planning*, the translation of *Urbanisme* (1925) published in 1929, which contained a complete exposition in text and images of both the visionary project for a City for Three Million Inhabitants (1922) as well as its application to Paris in the form of the Plan Voisin (1925). If not, Wright could just as well have based his critique of Le Corbusier's urbanism on the drawings and discussion of the subject in *Towards a New Architecture*.

158. *MA*, 101–2. The particular Ballard text I have in mind is the short story "Build-Up," orig. pub. 1957; reprinted in J. G. Ballard, *The Best Short Stories of J. G. Ballard* (New York: Washington Square Press, 1985), 1–24.

lxviii

159. *MA*, 105–7.

160. Ibid., 108, 111.

161. Ibid., 105, 108–9. As if to clarify the reference to Le Corbusier, Wright wrote: "Ruralism as distinguished from 'Urbanisme.'" Wright, *Autobiography*, in *CW*, 2:345.

162. *MA*, 108, 112.

163. Ibid., 109–11.

164. Ibid., 109–10.

165. The first use of the word, which is most probably an acronym for the United States of North America, is in Wright, "In the Cause: Third Dimension," in *CW*, 1:211.

166. Wright, *Two Lectures*, opp. p. 56.

167. Frank Lloyd Wright, *When Democracy Builds* (Chicago: University of Chicago Press, 1945), 58; and F. L. Wright, *The Living City*, orig. pub. 1958; reprinted in *CW*, vol. 5, *1949–1959* (New York: Rizzoli, in association with the Frank Lloyd Wright Foundation, 1995), 295. Prior to settling on this phraseology, Wright used others such as "the city is nowhere or it is everywhere" (F. L. Wright, "'Broadacre City': An Architect's Vision," *New York Times Magazine*, 20 March 1932, 8); or that it is "everywhere or nowhere" (wording on panel of 1935 Broadacre City exhibition). While clearly deriving from the etymological meaning of the word "utopia," Wright's reference to "nowhere" can also be traced to the novels *Erewhon* (1872), by Samuel Butler, and *News from Nowhere* (1890), by William Morris.

168. *MA*, 112. I say appended advisedly, since the unpublished article on which the chapter was based ended just before the scene of time travel and ruination.

169. Wright based the account of the ruin on a previously unpublished manuscript, "The Pictures We Make (Reflection)," 1927, MS 2401.025, FLWF; published in *CW*, 1:219–20. This was written in the spring of 1927 while he was living in Manhattan.

170. *MA*, 113–15.

171. Ibid., 115.

172. Le Corbusier, *Towards a New Architecture*, 250–51, 269.

173. Wright used the word "enemy" to describe "Le Corbusier and his group" in "Highlights [from a talk given to the Michigan Architectural Society]," *Architectural Forum* 55 (October 1931): 409; and to describe both the Art Déco–type modernistic and the International Style modern in "For All May Raise the Flowers Now for All Have Got the Seed," *T-Square* 2 (February 1932); reprinted in *CW*, 3:120.

174. Hitchcock, "Modern Architecture: New Tradition," and "Modern Architecture: New Pioneers." See note 111 above.

175. Hitchcock, *Modern Architecture*, 116–18, 163, 170.

176. Wright, "Towards a New Architecture," in *CW*, 1:317–18.

177. Ibid.

178. All the later versions, in *The Disappearing City* (1932), *When Democracy Builds* (1945), and *The Living City* (1958), are just revisions and amplifications of the 1929–31 text in *Modern Architecture*. The 1912–13 project for a thirty-two-block residential area of Chicago done in the context of the Chicago City Club Competition for a Model Quarter-Section was designed in response to a request from the club's civic secretary, George Hooker, and is in no way an ideal, comprehensive city plan.

179. *MA*, 33.

INTRODUCTION

180. See, esp., Frank Lloyd Wright, "Of Thee I Sing," *Shelter* 2 (April 1932); reprinted in *CW*, 3:113–15. This piece was written after Wright tried to have his work removed from the exhibition at the last moment and was intended by him to be made available to visitors to the exhibition. To emphasize the difference between his feelings about the museum's "propagandist" role and his feelings about the architecture itself, Wright added "An Explanation," or preface, in which he wrote: "I am a sincere admirer of all but several of the men whose work is included in the exhibit" (ibid., 113). We know that Richard Neutra was one of those he did not admire, while Mies, Le Corbusier, and Oud were among those he did.

181. Frank Lloyd Wright, "The International Style," [2], 1933, MS 2401.137, FLWF.

182. Full-blown examples of such rhetoric can be found in Frank Lloyd Wright, "Organic Architecture Looks at Modern Architecture," *Architectural Record* 111 (May 1952); reprinted in *CW*, vol. 5, *1949–1959* (New York: Rizzoli, in association with the Frank Lloyd Wright Foundation, 1995), 45–50; and F. L. Wright, "Frank Lloyd Wright Speaks Up," *House Beautiful* 95 (July 1953); reprinted in *CW*, 5:66–69.

183. Wright, "All May Raise the Flowers," in *CW*, 3:120.

184. Wright, "Hillside Home School of Allied Arts," 9; and Wright, "Highlights," 409.

185. Wright, "Towards a New Architecture," 394.

186. Frank Lloyd Wright, "Frank Lloyd Wright," *Architectural Forum* 68 (January 1938): 1–102.

187. Henry-Russell Hitchcock Jr., remarks in "What Is Happening to Modern Architecture? A Symposium at the Museum of Modern Art," *Museum of Modern Art Bulletin* 15 (Spring 1948): 10.

188. Sigfried Giedion, *Space, Time, and Architecture: The Growth of a New Tradition*, The Charles Eliot Norton Lectures for 1938–1939, orig. pub. 1941; 4th ed., enl. (Cambridge, MA: Harvard University Press, 1962), 412, 415.

189. Ibid., 566–605.

190. Lewis Mumford, "The Sky Line, Status Quo," *New Yorker* 23 (11 October 1947); reprinted in "What Is Happening to Modern Architecture?" 2; and Alfred H. Barr, in ibid., 8.

LIST OF REVIEWS AND NOTICES OF THE ORIGINAL EDITION OF *MODERN ARCHITECTURE*

Anon. Review of *Modern Architecture: Being the Kahn Lectures for 1930*, by Frank Lloyd Wright. *Architectural Forum* 54 (May 1931), suppl. 15.

Bauer, Catherine. "The 'Exuberant and Romantic' Genius of Frank Lloyd Wright." Review of *Modern Architecture: Being the Kahn Lectures for 1930*, by Frank Lloyd Wright. *New Republic* 67 (8 July 1931): 214–15.

Bright, John Irwin. Review of *Modern Architecture: Being the Kahn Lectures for 1930*, by Frank Lloyd Wright. *American Magazine of Art* 23 (August 1931): 170–72.

Duffus, R[obert] L[uther]. "'Tyranny of the Skyscraper': Frank Lloyd Wright Attacks Its Domination of Our Architecture." Review of *Modern Architecture: Being the Kahn Lectures for 1930*, by Frank Lloyd Wright. *New York Times Book Review*, 31 May 1931, sec. 4, 1, 28.

H., T. K. Review of *Modern Architecture: Being the Kahn Lectures for 1930*, by Frank Lloyd Wright. *Landscape Architecture* 22 (October 1931): 77–78.

Hamlin, Talbot Faulkner. "Living for the Beautiful." Review of *Modern Architecture: Being the Kahn Lectures for 1930*, by Frank Lloyd Wright. *Outlook and Independent* 157 (29 April 1931): 598–99.

———. "Artist and Prophet." Review of *Modern Architecture: Being the Kahn Lectures for 1930*, by Frank Lloyd Wright. *Saturday Review of Literature* 7 (11 July 1931): 957.

McMahon, A. Philip. Review of *Modern Architecture: Being the Kahn Lectures for 1930*, by Frank Lloyd Wright. *Parnassus* 3 (May 1931): 38–39.

Morrow, Irving F. "A Modern Prophet." Review of *Modern Architecture: Being the Kahn Lectures for 1930*, by Frank Lloyd Wright. *California Arts and Architecture* 90 (November 1931): 42.

Watts, Harvey M. "Don Quixote Atilt at His World: The Frank Lloyd Wright Princeton Lectures and Their Message to the Younger Groups." Review of *Modern Architecture: Being the Kahn Lectures for 1930*, by Frank Lloyd Wright. *T-Square Club Journal* 1 (November 1931): 5, 34–35. Response by Kuo, Yuan-Hsi. "My Opinion of 'Don Quixote A-Tilt at His World': Replying to an Article Written by Harvey M. Watts on the Frank Lloyd Wright Princeton Lectures." *T-Square* 2 (January 1932): 30–31.

PREFACE

*P*REFACES, *like all introductions, are usually unnecessary but courteous formalities. They are too often a transition between nothing that has gone before and something worthwhile that is to follow. Yet it was not so long ago that Frank Lloyd Wright, a man whom most Europeans consider America's leading architect and designer, a man whose originality has influenced the trend of modern architecture in Europe, needed an introduction to most of his fellow-countrymen. As early as 1903, at Hull House in Chicago, Frank Lloyd Wright challenged all Romantic efforts to escape from the realities of a modern machine world when he objected to the formation of a Society of Arts and Crafts to perpetuate the pseudo-medieval dreams of Morris and Ruskin, and read a paper on "The Art and Craft of the Machine." He was voted down and has continued to be voted down in America, except for a relatively small following, until it has become uncomfortably evident from the books published about him in Europe that his ideas and buildings have raised him to the position of a prophet without honor in his own country.*

When he was invited to deliver the lectures which form the basis of this book before those Princeton undergraduates interested in architecture, I do not believe he felt, as a recent article about him implies, that he was being honored like one already dead. It was neither to honor nor to bury him that the undergraduates, always over-lectured, came in increasing numbers to his lectures, bought illustrations of his work, and sought conferences with him. At first they came because it is youth in America which has discovered to what extent and for how long Wright has been insisting upon the living present against the dead past. They stayed because they were impressed by the pioneer spirit of the man; they felt that something greater than a desire for novelty, an ennui with tradition, and a longing for publicity had impelled him to cut his architectural trail through a new age and a new country. In his lectures and conferences these students found not forms but fire, not formulas but ideas, not formality but vitality.

It is against the tradition of time-honored formalities that Wright has built and preached. Some people may buy this book thinking that it will offer an easy formula for understanding and designing so-called modern architecture. I, at first, made the mistake of wishing that he had been more explicit, had told more about

PREFACE

his methods and less about his theory of life. As I listened to his lectures and talked with the man I saw my mistake, and realized that Wright did not want to give to his public merely his particular forms, developed by him to meet specific conditions. Instead, fearful lest his buildings be copied and repeated as an easy ritual for unimaginative moderns, he wanted only to stir others with his dreams of the possibilities open to architecture in our present age.

His lectures, then, are not didactic rules and architectural short-cuts for making the possibilities of living expression into a new academic tradition. Rather are they the sermons of an engaging, self-confident and enthusiastic artist fired with a faith, not in the machine itself, but in the power of man to master his creation, the machine, and to make it fashion a new manifestation of beauty. It does not matter that long isolation and lack of recognition, to name but a small part of what Wright has suffered, have made him belligerent in his attack on those out-worn architectural conventions whose perfunctory use today retard, in his mind, the creation of a twentieth century American style of architecture. The marvel is that life has not burnt him out and left him bitter and suspicious.

It matters still less that he is not strictly logical in his artistic convictions: that he admires Egyptian temples as the expression of a great stone tradition, and con-demns Greek temples as mere wooden forms translated into stone; that he insists on a modern architecture freed from the whole stereotyped paraphernalia of the past and yet at the same time believes that it should pay unstinted tribute to the wooden forms of Japanese architecture. Whose likes and dislikes are logical? We are now finding that logic, as a convention of human thinking, will not confine within its premises art and life as creative activities. When asked to write on "The Logic of Modern Architecture" Wright replied, "Is the rising sun logical? It is natural and that is better."

In architecture, as in life itself today, we are burdened with our knowledge of and respect for the past; we still think with Aristotelian logic based upon the belief in types and standards of absolute good and beauty. Hence this faith in the natural is perhaps what we need. At least it is what youth wants. Before we can have a thrilling joy in living and can remake our world today so that its realities, like the machine, have beauty and satisfaction for us, we must develop something ap-proaching the naturalness and enthusiastic self-confidence which made the Greek of the fifth century look upon everything non-Greek as barbaric. We are in danger, as moderns, of becoming tolerant to the point of being uninterested in art. In

PREFACE

painting we can tolerate anything from Dutch realism to abstractions, in architecture anything from Egyptian pylons to a smokestack. Therefore there is a stimulating value in Wright's intolerance of the cornice as a symbol of the past. It is an essential part of the naturalness and directness of the man, and fundamental to the faith which he has stated in the following chapters.

His style in writing is as individual as the man himself. Some critics may overemphasize his unconscious disregard of usage and, at times, his disregard of logic; they may dwell unfairly, if they will, upon his lack of a simple, functional directness in words and his tendency to overdecorate ideas with verbiage; but such critics will have missed the appeal of his imagery and the sincerity of his effort. As a creative artist whose ideas have worked not only to shape modern architecture but also to give men a new and hopeful outlook on the Machine, his philosophy of life, with his reactions, ideas and prejudices, will become a document in the history of art. Until it becomes a document it will be a challenge and an appeal.

While Wright says, "I suppose I am to suffer disadvantage, being accustomed to saying things with a hod of mortar and some bricks, or with a concrete mixer and a gang of workmen, rather than by speaking or writing," I think he requires no apologies for his words any more than for his ideas and buildings. They are his, and in them lies something more real than conventions of thought and formulas for building. They embody his faith. This book, as he referred to it in a letter, is "his garden"; in it he nobly believes that others will see the beauty and the possibilities of beauty which have stirred him. I think they will.

E. Baldwin Smith

1: MACHINERY, MATERIALS AND MEN

LARKIN ADMINISTRATION BUILDING
BRICK MASSES. STONE WASHES AND WATER-TABLE.
WROUGHT IRON FENCE.
1903-1905

1903

1: MACHINERY, MATERIALS AND MEN

AN ARCHITECTURE for these United States will be born "Modern," as were all the Architectures of the peoples of all the world. Perhaps this is the deep-seated reason why the young man in Architecture grieves his parents, academic and familiar, by yielding to the fascination of creation, instead of persisting as the creature of ancient circumstance. This, his rational surrender to instinct, is known, I believe, as "rebellion."

I am here to aid and comfort rebellion insofar as rebellion has this honorable instinct—even though purpose may not yet be clearly defined—nor any fruits, but only ists, isms or istics be in sight. Certainly we may now see the dawning of a deeper insight than has for the past thirty years characterized so-called American Architecture. By that length of time American Architecture has been neither American nor Architecture. We have had instead merely a bad form of surface-decoration.

This "dawn" is the essential concern of this moment and the occasion for this series of "lectures." We, here at Princeton, are to guard this dawning insight and help to guide its courage, passion and patience into channels where depth and flow is adequate, instead of allowing youthful adventure to ground in shallows all there beneath the surface in the offing, ready to hinder and betray native progress.

In this effort I suppose I am to suffer disadvantage, being more accustomed to saying things with a hod of mortar and some bricks, or with a concrete mixer and a gang of workmen, than by speaking or writing. I like to write, but always dissatisfied, I, too, find myself often staring at the result with a kind of nausea . . . or is it nostalgia?

I dislike to lecture, feeling something like the rage of impotence. With a small audience hovering over my drawing-board, there would be better feeling on my part and a better chance for the audience. But a lecturer may, in fact must, make his own diversion, indulge his "malice" as he goes along, or get no entertainment at all out of the matter.

So here at my hand I have some gently malicious pamphlets or leaflets issued, as myth has it, by that mythical group to which careless reference is sometimes made, by the thoughtless, as the "New School of the Middle

3

MODERN ARCHITECTURE

West." From these rare, heretical pamphlets, from time to time as I may have occasion, I shall quote. Among them are such titles as: "Palladio turns in his grave and speaks," another, "Groans from Phidias": the author's original title—it would be beside our mark to mention it—was suppressed by the group as just that much too much. One solitary "New School" scholar, himself having, under painful economic pressure, degenerated to the practice of mere Architectural surgery—blaming Vitruvius for his degradation—wrote bitterly and much under the title of "Vitruviolic Disorders."

A number of these leaflets are given over by several and sundry of the "New School" to the ravages of the "Vignola"—an academic epidemic showing itself as a creeping paralysis of the emotional nature—creeping by way of the optic nerve.

During the course of our afternoons, from among these modestly profane references we may have occasion to hear from a rudely awakened Bramante, an indignant Sansovino, a gently aggrieved Brunelleschi, perhaps even from robustious "Duomo" Buonarotti himself, all, plucked even of their shrouds, frowning up from their graves on their pretentious despoilers . . . our own American Classicists. These time-honored Italians in these wayward and flippant leaflets, are made to speak by way of a sort of motor-car Vasari. His name deserves to be lost—and as certainly will be.

Unfortunately and sad to say, because their names and individualities are unknown to us, so close were they, as men, to the soil or to Man,—we shall be unable to hear from the ancient builders of "Le Moyen Âge," those dreamers in cloisters, guild-masters, gardeners, worshipers of the tree, or the noble stone-craftsmen of still earlier Byzantium, who were much like the cathedral builders in spirit. No—we shall hear from them only as we, ourselves, are likewise dreamers, gardeners, or worshipers of the tree and by sympathetic nature, therefore, well qualified to understand the silence of these white men. And those human nature-cultures of the red man, lost in backward stretch of time, almost beyond our horizon—the Maya, the Indian—and of the black man, the African—we may learn mfro them. Last, but not least, come the men of bronze, the Chinese, the Japanese—profound builders of the Orient— imaginative demons, their Art of Earth winging its way to the skies: Dragons with wings—their fitting symbol. Of their Art—much. The ethnic eccentricity of their work makes it safe inspiration for the white man, who now needs,

4

MACHINERY, MATERIALS AND MEN

it seems, aesthetic fodder that he cannot copy nor reproduce. I am not sure but there is more for us in our modern grapple with creation, in their sense of the living thing in Art, than we can find in any other culture. Profundity of feeling the men of bronze could encourage. Their forms we should have to let alone.

• • •   • • •   • • •

In order that we may not foregather here in this dignified atmosphere of Princeton without due reference to authority, we will go far back for our text on this, our first afternoon together. Go so far back that we need fear no contradiction. Go without hesitation, to Rameses the Great, to find that: "All great Architecture"—Rameses might have used the hieroglyph for Art instead of the one for Architecture—"*All great Architecture is true to its Architects' immediate present*," and seal it with the regal symbol. And in this connection comes the title of our discourse—the "MACHINERY, MATERIALS AND MEN" of our immediate present.

Long ago,—yes, so long ago that the memory of it seems to join with recent echoes from Tut-Ank-Amen's ancient tomb,—I passionately swore that the Machine was no less, rather more, an artist's tool than any he had ever had or heard of, if only he would do himself the honor to learn to use it. Twenty-seven years old now, the then offensive heresy has been translated and published, I am told, in seven or more foreign languages, English excepted, which means said in seven or more different ways. But just what the seven different ways each exactly mean, I can have no idea. At the time, I knew no better than to make the declaration—it seemed so sensibly obvious in the vast cinderfield in which I then stood—our enormous industrial Middle West.

Today, twenty-seven years later, the heresy is become truism, at least "truistic," therefore sufficiently trite to arouse no hostility even if said in several or even seven different ways. And yet: a Pompeian recently come back and struggling for nourishment on French soil has reiterated one-quarter of the matter, made more stark, with signs of success right here in our own country. The reiteration reaches us across the Atlantic—more Machine-made than the erstwhile cry in the cinderfield, but with several important omissions—most important, at least, to us. Or perhaps, who knows, they may not really be omissions but evasions. First among these probable evasions is the Nature of Materials; Second, is that characteristic architectural element, the Third

Dimension; and Third, there is Integral Ornament. This neglected Trinity, it seems to me, constitutes the beating heart of the whole matter of Architecture so far as Art is concerned.

Surface and Mass, relatively superficial, however Machine-made or however much resembling Machinery, are subordinate to this great Trinity. Surface and Mass are a by-product, or will be when Architecture arises out of the matter. If proof is needed we shall find it as we go along together. . . .

MACHINERY, MATERIALS AND MEN—yes—these are the stuffs by means of which the so-called American Architect will get his Architecture, if there is any such Architect and America ever gets any Architecture of her own. Only by the strength of his spirit's grasp upon all three—Machinery, Materials and Men—will the Architect be able so to build that his work may be worthy the great name "Architecture." A great Architecture is greatest proof of human greatness.

The difference, to the Architect and his fellow Artists, between our era and others, lies simply enough in the substitution of automatic machinery for tools, and (more confusing), instead of hereditary aristocracy for patron, the Artist now relies upon automatic industrialism, conditioned upon the automatic acquiescence of Men, and conditioned not at all upon their individual handicraftsmanship.

At first blush an appalling difference, and the more it is studied, the more important the difference becomes. And were we now to be left without prophet —that is, without interpretation—and should we among ourselves, be unable to arouse the leadership of supreme human imagination—yes, then we should be at the beginning of the end of all the great qualities we are foregathered here to cherish: namely, the Arts which are those great *qualities* in any civilization. This Republic has already gone far with very little of any single one of these great *saving* qualities, yet it goes further, faster and safer; eats more, and eats more regularly; goes softer, safer, is more comfortable and egotistic in a more universal mediocrity than ever existed on Earth before. But who knows where it is going? In this very connection, among the more flippant references referred to as at hand, there is also heavy matter and I have here serious original matter, saved several years ago from the flames by a miracle. The first pages were blackened and charred by fire, of this original manuscript, first read to a group of professors, artists, architects and manufacturers at Hull House, Chicago. To show you how it all seemed to me, back there, twenty-seven years ago in Chicago, I shall read into the record, once more, from its pages. Should its clumsy earnestness bore you—remember that the young man who wrote, should, in that earlier day, as now, have confined himself to a hod of mortar and some bricks. But passionately he was trying to write—making ready to do battle for the life of the thing he loved. And I would remind you, too, that in consequence he has been engaged in eventually mortal combat ever since.

Here is the manuscript. We will begin, twenty-seven years later, again, at the beginning of—

• • •   • • •   • • •

THE ART AND CRAFT OF THE MACHINE

No one, I hope, has come here tonight for a Sociological prescription for the cure of evils peculiar to this Machine Age. For I come to you as an Architect to say my word for the right use upon such new materials as we have, of our great substitute for tools—Machines. There is no thrift in any craft until the tools are mastered; nor will there be a worthy social order in America until the elements by which America does its work are mastered by American society. Nor can there be an Art worth the man or the name until these elements are grasped and truthfully idealized in whatever we as a people try to make. Although these elemental truths should be commonplace enough by now, as a people we do not understand them nor do we see the way to apply them. We are probably richer in raw materials for our use as workmen, citizens or artists than any other nation,—but outside mechanical genius for mere contrivance we are not good workmen, nor, beyond adventitious or propitious respect for property, are we as good citizens as we should be, nor are we artists at all. We are one and all, consciously or unconsciously, mastered by our fascinating automatic "implements," using them as substitutes for tools. To make this assertion clear I offer you evidence I have found in the field of Architecture. It is still a field in which the pulse of the age throbs beneath much shabby finery and one broad enough (God knows) to represent the errors and possibilities common to our time-serving Time.

Architects in the past have embodied the spirit common to their own life and to the life of the society in which they lived in the most noble of all noble records—Buildings. They wrought these valuable records with the primitive tools at their command and whatever these records have to say to us today would be utterly insignificant if not wholly illegible were tools suited to another and different condition stupidly forced to work upon them; blindly compelled to do work to which they were not fitted, work which they could only spoil.

In this age of steel and steam the tools with which civilization's true record will be written are scientific thoughts made operative in iron and bronze and steel and in the plastic processes which characterize this age, all of which we call Machines. The Electric Lamp is in this sense a Machine. New materials in the man-Machines have made the physical body of this age what it is as distinguished from former ages. They have made our era the Machine Age— wherein locomotive engines, engines of industry, engines of light or engines of war or steamships take the place works of Art took in previous history. Today we have a Scientist or an Inventor in place of a Shakespeare or a Dante. Captains of Industry are modern substitutes, not only for Kings and Potentates, but, I am afraid, for great Artists as well. And yet—man-made environment is the truest, most characteristic of all human records. Let a man build and you have him. You may not have all he is, but certainly he is what you have. Usually you will have his outline. Though the elements may be in him to enable him to grow out of his present self-made characterization, few men are ever belied by self-made environment. Certainly no historical period was ever so misrepresented. Chicago in its ugliness today becomes as true an expression of the *life* lived here as is any center on earth where men come together closely to live it out or fight it out. Man is a selecting principle, gathering his like to him wherever he goes. The intensifying of his existence by close contact, too, flashes out the human record vividly in his background and his surroundings. But somewhere—somehow—in our age, although signs of the times are not wanting, beauty in this expression is forfeited—the record is illegible when not ignoble. We must walk blindfolded through the streets of this, or any great modern American city, to fail to see that all this magnificent resource of machine-power and superior material has brought to us, so far, is degradation. All of the Art forms sacred to The Art of Old are, by us, prostitute.

MACHINERY, MATERIALS AND MEN

On every side we see evidence of inglorious quarrel between things as they were and things as they must be and are. This shame a certain merciful ignorance on our part mistakes for glorious achievement. We believe in our greatness when we have tossed up a Pantheon to the god of money in a night or two, like the Illinois Trust Building or the Chicago National Bank. And it is our glory to get together a mammoth aggregation of Roman monuments, sarcophagi and temples for a Post Office in a year or two. On Michigan Avenue Montgomery Ward presents us with a nondescript Florentine Palace with a grand campanile for a "Farmer Grocery" and it is as common with us as it is elsewhere to find the giant stone Palladian "orders" overhanging plate glass shop fronts. Show windows beneath Gothic office buildings, the office-middle topped by Parthenons, or models of any old sacrificial temple, are a common sight. Every commercial interest in any American town, in fact, is scurrying for respectability by seeking some advertising connection, at least, with the "Classic." A commercial Renaissance is here; the Renaissance of "the ass in the lion's skin." This much, at least, we owe to the late Columbian Fair—that triumph of modern civilization in 1893 will go down in American Architectural history, when it is properly recorded, as a mortgage upon posterity that posterity must repudiate not only as usurious but as forged.

In our so-called "Sky-Scrapers" (latest and most famous business-building triumph), good granite or Bedford stone is cut into the fashion of the Italian followers of Phidias and his Greek slaves. Blocks so cut are cunningly arranged about a structure of steel beams and shafts (which structure secretly robs them of any real meaning), in order to make the finished building resemble the architecture bepictured by Palladio and Vitruvius—in the school-books. It is quite as feasible to begin putting on this Italian trimming at the cornice, and come on down to the base as it is to work, as the less fortunate Italians were forced to do, from the base upward. Yes, "from the top down" is often the actual method employed. The keystone of a Roman or Gothic arch may now be "set"—that is to say "hung"—and the voussoirs stuck alongside or "hung" on downward to the haunches. Finally this mask, completed, takes on the features of the pure "Classic," or any variety of "Renaissance" or whatever catches the fancy or fixes the "convictions" of the designer. Most likely, an education in Art has "fixed" both. Our Chicago University, "a seat of learning," is just as far removed from truth. If environment is significant and indicative, what does this highly reactionary, extensive and expensive scene-painting by means of hybrid Collegiate Gothic signify? Because of Oxford it seems to be generally accepted as "appropriate for scholastic purposes." Yet, why should an American University in a land of Democratic ideals in a Machine Age be characterized by second-hand adaptation of Gothic forms, themselves adapted previously to our own adoption by a feudalistic age with tools to use and conditions to face totally different from anything we can call our own? The Public Library is again Asinine Renaissance, bones sticking through the flesh because the interior was planned by a shrewd Library Board—while an "Art-Architect" (the term is Chicago's, not mine) was "hired" to "put the architecture on it." The "classical" aspect of the sham-front must be preserved at any cost to sense. Nine out of ten public buildings in almost any American city are the same.

On Michigan Avenue, too, we pass another pretentious structure, this time fashioned as inculcated by the École des Beaux Arts after the ideals and methods of a Graeco-Roman, inartistic, grandly brutal civilization, a civilization that borrowed everything but its jurisprudence. Its essential tool was the slave. Here at the top of our Culture is the Chicago Art Institute, and very like other Art Institutes. Between lions—realistic—Kemyss would have them so because Barye did—we come beneath some stone millinery into the grandly useless lobby. Here French's noble statue of the Republic confronts us—she too, Imperial. The grand introduction over, we go further on to find amid plaster casts of antiquity, earnest students patiently gleaning a half-acre or more of archaeological dry-bones, arming here for industrial conquest, in other words to go out and try to make a living by making some valuable impression upon the Machine Age in which they live. Their fundamental tool in this business about which they will know just this much less than nothing, is—the Machine. In this acre or more not one relic has any vital relation to things as they are for these students, except for the blessed circumstance that they are more or less beautiful things in themselves— bodying forth the beauty of "once upon a time." These students at best are to concoct from a study of the aspect of these blind reverences an extract of antiquity suited to modern needs, meanwhile knowing nothing of modern needs, permitted to care nothing for them, and knowing just as little of the needs of the ancients which made the objects they now study. The tyros are

10

taught in the name of John Ruskin and William Morris to shun and despise the essential tool of their Age as a matter commercial and antagonistic to Art. So in time they go forth, each armed with his little Academic extract, applying it as a sticking-plaster from without, wherever it can be made to stick, many helplessly knowing in their hearts that it should be a development from within—but how? And this is an education in Art in these United States, A.D. 1903. Climb now the grand monumental stairway to see the results of this cultural effort—we call it "education"—hanging over the walls of the Exhibition Galleries. You will find there the same empty reverences to the past at cost to the present and of doubtful value to the future, unless a curse is valuable. Here you may see fruits of the lust and pride of the patron-collector but how shamefully little to show by way of encouraging patronage by the Artist of his own day and generation. This is a Temple of the Fine Arts. A sacred place! It should be the heart-center, the emotional inspiration of a great national industrial activity, but here we find Tradition not as an *inspiring* spirit animating progress. No. Now more in the *past* than ever! No more, now, than an ancient mummy, a dead letter. A "precedent" is a "hang over" to copy, the copy to be copied for Machine reproduction, to be shamelessly reproduced until demoralized utterly or unrecognizable.

More unfortunate, however, than all this fiasco, is the Fiasco al Fresco. The suburban house-parade is more servile still. Any popular avenue or suburb will show the polyglot encampment displaying, on the neatly kept little plots, a theatrical desire on the part of fairly respectable people to live in Châteaux, Manor Houses, Venetian Palaces, Feudal Castles, and Queen Anne Cottages. Many with sufficient hardihood abide in abortions of the Carpenter-Architect, our very own General Grant Gothic perhaps, intended to beat all the "lovely periods" at their own game and succeeding. Look within all this typical monotony-in-variety and see there the machine-made copies of handicraft originals; in fact, unless you, the householder, are fortunate indeed, possessed of extraordinary taste and opportunity, all you possess is in some degree a machine-made example of vitiated handicraft, imitation antique furniture made antique by the Machine, itself of all abominations the most abominable. Everything must be curved and carved and carved and turned. The whole mass a tortured sprawl supposed artistic. And the floor-coverings? Probably machine-weavings of Oriental Rug patterns—pattern and texture mechanically perfect; or worse, your walls are papered with paper-imitations of old tapestry, imitation patterns and imitation textures, stamped or printed by the Machine; imitations under foot, imitations overhead and imitations all round about you. You are sunk in "Imitation." Your much-moulded woodwork is stained "antique." Inevitably you have a white-and-gold "reception-room" with a few gilded chairs, an overwrought piano, and withal, about you a general cheap machine-made "profusion" of—copies of copies of original imitations. To you, proud proprietors—do these things thus degraded mean anything aside from vogue and price? Aside from your sense of quantitative ownership, do you perceive in them some fine fitness in form, line and color to the purposes which they serve? Are the chairs to sit in, the tables to use, the couch comfortable, and are all harmoniously related to each other and to your own life? Do many of the furnishings or any of the window-millinery serve any purpose at all of which you can think? Do you enjoy in "things" the least appreciation of truth in beautiful guise? If not, you are a victim of habit, a habit evidence enough of the stagnation of an outgrown Art. Here we have the curse of stupidity—a cheap substitute for ancient Art and Craft which has no vital meaning in your own life or our time. You line the box you live in as a magpie lines its nest. You need not be ashamed to confess your ignorance of the meaning of all this, because not only you, but every one else, is hopelessly ignorant concerning it; it is "impossible." Imitations of imitations, copies of copies, cheap expedients, lack of integrity, some few blind gropings for simplicity to give hope to the picture. That is all.

Why wonder what has become of the grand spirit of Art that made, in times past, man's reflection in his environment a godlike thing. *This* is what has become of it! Of all conditions, this one at home is most deplorable, for to the homes of this country we must look for any beginning of the awakening of an artistic conscience which will change this parasitic condition to independent growth. The homes of the people will change before public buildings can possibly change.

Glance now for a moment behind this adventitious scene-painting passing, at home, for Art in the Nineteenth Century. Try to sense the true conditions underlying all, and which you betray and belie in the name of Culture. Study with me for a moment the engine which produces this wreckage and builds you, thus cheapened and ridiculous, into an ignoble record.

12

MACHINERY, MATERIALS AND MEN

Here is this thing we call the Machine, contrary to the principle of organic growth, but imitating it, working irresistibly the will of Man through the medium of men. All of us are drawn helplessly into its mesh as we tread our daily round. And its offices—call them "services"—have become the commonplace background of modern existence; yes, and sad to say, in too many lives the foreground, middle distance and future. At best we ourselves are already become or are becoming some cooperative part in a vast machinery. It is, with us, as though we were controlled by some great crystallizing principle going on in Nature all around us and going on, in spite of ourselves, even in our very own *natures*. If you would see how interwoven it is, this thing we call the Machine, with the warp and the woof of civilization, if indeed it is not now the very basis of civilization itself, go at nightfall when all is simplified and made suggestive, to the top of our newest Skyscraper, the Masonic Temple. There you may see how in the image of material man, at once his glory and his menace, is this thing we call a City. Beneath you is the monster stretching out into the far distance. High overhead hangs a stagnant pall, its fetid breath reddened with light from myriad eyes endlessly, everywhere blinking. Thousands of acres of cellular tissue outspread, enmeshed by an intricate network of veins and arteries radiating into the gloom. Circulating there with muffled ominous roar is the ceaseless activity to whose necessities it all conforms. This wondrous tissue is knit and knit again and inter-knit with a nervous system, marvellously effective and complete, with delicate filaments for hearing and knowing the pulse of its own organism, acting intelligently upon the ligaments and tendons of motive impulse, and in it all is flowing the impelling electric fluid of man's own life. And the labored breathing, murmur, clangor, and the roar—how the voice of this monstrous force rises to proclaim the marvel of its structure! Near at hand, the ghastly warning boom from the deep throats of vessels heavily seeking inlet to the waterway below, answered by the echoing clangor of the bridge bells. A distant shriek grows nearer, more ominous, as the bells warn the living current from the swinging bridge and a vessel cuts for a moment the flow of the nearer artery. Closing then upon the great vessel's stately passage the double bridge is just in time to receive in a rush of steam the avalanche of blood and metal hurled across it;—a streak of light gone roaring into the night on glittering bands of steel; an avalanche encircled in its flight by slender magic lines, clicking faithfully from station to station—its nervous herald, its warning and its protection.

Nearer, in the building ablaze with midnight activity, a spotless paper band is streaming into the marvel of the multiple-press, receiving indelibly the impression of human hopes and fears, throbbing in the pulse of this great activity, as infallibly as the gray-matter of the human brain receives the impression of the senses. The impressions come forth as millions of neatly folded, perfected news-sheets, teeming with vivid appeals to good and evil passions;—weaving a web of intercommunication so far-reaching that distance becomes as nothing, the thought of one man in one corner of the earth on one day visible on the next to all men. The doings of all the world are reflected here as in a glass—so marvellously sensitive this simple band streaming endlessly from day to day becomes in the grasp of the multiple-press.

If the pulse of this great activity—automatons working night and day in every line of industry, to the power of which the tremor of the mammoth steel skeleton beneath your feet is but an awe-inspiring response—is thrilling, what of the prolific, silent obedience to man's will underlying it all? If this power must be uprooted that civilization may live, then civilization is already doomed. Remain to contemplate this wonder until the twinkling lights perish in groups, or follow one by one, leaving others to live through the gloom;—fires are banked, tumult slowly dies to an echo here and there. Then the darkened pall is gradually lifted and moonlight outlines the shadowy, sullen masses of structure, structure deeply cut here and there by half-luminous channels. Huge patches of shadow in shade and darkness commingle mysteriously in the block-like plan with box-like skylines—contrasting strangely with the broad surface of the lake beside, placid and resplendent with a silver gleam. Remain, I say, to reflect that the texture of the city, this great Machine, is the warp upon which will be woven the woof and pattern of the Democracy we pray for. Realize that it has been deposited here, particle by particle, in blind obedience to law—Law no less organic so far as we are concerned than the laws of the great solar universe. That universe, too, in a sense, is but an obedient machine.

Magnificent power! And it confronts the young Architect and his Artist comrades now, with no other beauty—a lusty material giant without trace of ideality, absurdly disguised by garments long torn to tatters or contemp-

14

tuously tossed aside, outgrown. Within our own recollection we have all been horrified at the bitter cost of this ruthless development—appalled to see this great power driven by Greed over the innocent and defenseless—we have seen bread snatched from the mouths of sober and industrious men, honorable occupations going to the wall with a riot, a feeble strike, or a stifled moan, outclassed, outdone, outlived by the Machine. The workman himself has come to regard this relentless force as his Nemesis and combines against machinery in the trades with a wild despair that dashes itself to pieces, while the Artist blissfully dreaming in the halls we have just visited or walking blindly abroad in the paths of the past, berates his own people for lack-luster senses, rails against industrial conditions that neither afford him his opportunity, nor, he says, can appreciate him as he, panderer to ill-gotten luxury, folding his hands, starves to death. "Innocuous martyr upon the cross of Art!" One by one, tens by tens, soon thousands by thousands, handicraftsmen and parasitic artists succumb to the inevitable as one man at a Machine does the work of from five to fifty men in the same time, with all the Art there is meanwhile prostituting to old methods and misunderstood ideals the far greater new possibilities due to this same Machine, and doing this disgracefully in the name of the Beautiful!

American Society has the essential tool of its own age by the blade, as lacerated hands everywhere testify!

See the magnificent prowess of this unqualified power—strewing our surroundings with the mangled corpses of a happier time. We live amid ghostly relics whose pattern once stood for cultivated luxury and now stands for an ignorant matter of taste. With no regard for first principles of common sense the letter of Tradition is recklessly fed into rapacious maws of machines until the reproduction, reproduced *ad nauseam*, may be had for five, ten or ninety-nine cents although the worthy original cost ages of toil and patient culture. This might seem like progress, were it not for the fact that these butchered forms, the life entirely gone out of them, are now harmful parasites, belittling and falsifying any true perception of normal beauty the Creator may have seen fit to implant in us on our own account. Any idea whatever of fitness to purpose or of harmony between form and use is gone from us. It is lacking in these things one and all, because it is so sadly lacking in us. And as for making the best of our own conditions or repudiating the terms on which this vulgar insult to Tradition is produced, thereby insuring and rectifying the industrial fabric thus wasted or enslaved by base imitation—the mere idea is abnormal, as I myself have found to my sorrow.

And among the Few, the favored chosen Few who love Art by nature and would devote their energies to it so that it may live and let them live— any training they can seek would still be a protest against the Machine as the Creator of all this iniquity, when (God knows) it is no more than the Creature.

But, I say, usurped by Greed and deserted by its natural interpreter, the Artist, the Machine is only the creature, not the Creator of this iniquity! I say the Machine has noble possibilities unwillingly forced to this degradation, degraded by the Arts themselves. Insofar as the true capacity of the Machine is concerned it is itself the crazed victim of Artist-impotence. Why will the American Artist not see that human thought in our age is stripping off its old form and donning another; why is the Artist unable to see that this is his glorious opportunity to create and reap anew?

But let us be practical—let us go now afield for evident instances of Machine abuse or abuse by the Machine. I will show you typical abuses that should serve to suggest to any mind, capable of thought, that the Machine is, to begin with, a marvellous simplifier in no merely negative sense. Come now, with me, and see examples which show that these craft-engines may be the modern emancipator of the creative mind. We may find them to be the regenerator of the creative conscience in our America, as well, so soon as a stultified "Culture" will allow them to be so used.

First—as perhaps wood is most available of home-building materials, naturally then the most abused—let us now glance at wood. Elaborate machinery has been invented for no other purpose than to imitate the wood-carving of early handicraft patterns. Result? No good joinery. None salable without some horrible glued-on botch-work meaning nothing, unless it means that "Art and Craft" (by salesmanship) has fixed in the minds of the masses the elaborate old hand-carved chair as ultimate ideal. The miserable tribute to this perversion yielded by Grand Rapids alone would mar the face of Art beyond repair, to say nothing of the weird or fussy joinery of spindles and jig-sawing, beamed, braced and elaborated to outdo in sentimentality the sentiment of some erstwhile overwrought "antique." The beauty of wood lies in its qualities as wood, strange as this may seem. Why does it take so much imagination—just to see that? Treatments that fail to bring out those qualities, foremost, are not *plastic*, therefore no longer appropriate. The inappropriate cannot be beautiful.

The Machine at work on wood will itself teach us—and we seem so far to have left it to the Machine to do so—that certain simple forms and handling serve to bring out the beauty of wood, and to retain its character, and that certain other forms and handling do not bring out its beauty, but spoil it. All wood-carving is apt to be a forcing of this material likely to destroy the finer possibilities of wood as we may know those possibilities now. In itself wood has beauty of marking, exquisite texture, and delicate nuances of color that carving is likely to destroy. The Machines used in woodwork will show that by unlimited power in cutting, shaping, smoothing, and by the tireless repeat, they have emancipated beauties of wood-nature, making possible, without waste, beautiful surface treatments and clean strong forms that veneers of Sheraton or Chippendale only hinted at with dire extravagance. Beauty unknown even to the Middle Ages. These machines have undoubtedly placed within reach of the designer a technique enabling him to realize the true nature of wood in his designs harmoniously with man's sense of beauty, satisfying his material needs with such extraordinary economy as to put this beauty of wood in use within the reach of every one. But the advantages of the Machines are wasted and we suffer from a riot of aesthetic murder and everywhere live with debased handicraft.

Then, at random, let us take, say, the worker in marbles—his gang-saws, planers, pneumatic-chisels and rubbing-beds have made it possible to reduce blocks ten feet long, six feet deep, and two feet thick to sheets or thin slabs an inch in thickness within a few hours, so it is now possible to use a precious material as ordinary wall covering. The slab may be turned and matched at the edges to develop exquisite pattern, emancipating hundreds of superficial feet of characteristic drawing in pure marble colors that formerly wasted in the heart of a great expensive block in the thickness of the wall. Here again a distinctly new architectural use may bring out a beauty of marbles consistent with Nature and impossible to handicraft. But what happens? The "Artist" persists in taking dishonest advantage of this practice, building up imitations of solid piers with moulded caps and bases, cunningly uniting the slabs at the edge until detection is difficult except to the trained eye. His method does not change to develop the beauty of a new technical possibility; no, the "Artist" is simply enabled to "fake" more architecture, make more piers and column shafts because he can now make them hollow! His architecture becomes no more worthy in itself than the cheap faker that he himself is, for his classical forms not only falsify the method which used to be and belie the method that is, but they cheat progress of its due. For convincing evidence see any Public Library or Art Institute, the Congressional Library at Washington, or the Boston Library.

In the stone-cutting trade the stone-planer has made it possible to cut upon stone any given moulded surface, or to ingrain upon that surface any lovely texture the cunning brain may devise, and do it as it never was possible to do it by hand. What is it doing? Giving us as near an imitation of hand tooth-chiselling as possible, imitating mouldings specially adapted to wood, making possible the lavish use of miles of meaningless moulded string courses, cornices, base courses—the giant power meanwhile sneered at by the "Artist" because it fails to render the wavering delicacy of "touch" resulting from the imperfections of hand-work.

No architect, this man! No—or he would excel that "antique" quality by the design of the contour of his sections, making a telling point of the very perfection he dreads, and so sensibly designing, for the prolific dexterity of the machine, work which it can do so well that hand-work would seem insufferably crude by comparison. The deadly facility this one machine has given "book architecture" is rivalled only by the facility given to it by galvanized iron itself. And if, incontinently, you will still have tracery in stone, you may arrive at acres of it now consistently with the economy of other features of this still fundamental "trade." You may try to imitate the hand-carving of the ancients in this matter, baffled by the craft and tenderness of the originals, or you may give the pneumatic chisel and power-plane suitable work to do which would mean a changed style, a shift in the spiritual center of the ideal now controlling the use of stone in constructing modern stone-buildings.

You will find in studying the group of ancient materials, wood and stone foremost among them, that they have all been rendered fit for *plastic* use by the Machine! The Machine itself steadily making available for economic use the very quality in these things now needed to satisfy its own art equation.

18

MACHINERY, MATERIALS AND MEN

Burned clay—we call it Terra Cotta—is another conspicuous instance of the advantage of the "process." Modern machines (and a process is a machine) have rendered this material as sensitive to the creative brain as a dry plate is to the lens of the camera. A marvellous simplifier, this material, rightly used. The artist is enabled to clothe the steel structure, now becoming characteristic of this era, with modestly beautiful, plastic robes instead of five or more different kinds of material now aggregated in confused features and parts, "composed" and supposedly picturesque, but really a species of cheap millinery to be mocked and warped by the sun, eventually beaten by wind and rain into a variegated heap of trash. But when these great possibilities of simplicity, the gift of the Machine, get to us by way of the Architect, we have only a base imitation of the hand-tooled blocks—pilaster-cap and base, voussoirs and carved spandrils of the laborious man-handled stonecrop of an ancient people's architecture!

The modern processes of casting in metal are modern machines too, approaching perfection, capable of perpetuating the imagery of the most vividly poetic mind without hindrance—putting permanence and grace within reach of every one, heretofore forced to sit supine with the Italians at their Belshazzar-feast of "Renaissance." Yes, without exaggeration, multitudes of processes, many new, more coming, await sympathetic interpretation, such as the galvano-plastic and its electrical brethren—a prolific horde, now cheap fakers imitating "real" bronzes and all manner of metallic antiques, secretly damning all of them in their vitals, if not openly giving them away. And there is electro-glazing, shunned because its straight lines in glasswork are too severely clean and delicate. Straight lines it seems are not so susceptible to the traditional designer's lack of touch. Stream lines and straight lines are to him severely unbeautiful. "Curved is the line of beauty"—says he! As though Nature would not know what to do with its own rectilinear!

The familiar lithograph, too, is the prince of an entire province of new reproductive but unproductive processes. Each and every one have their individualities and therefore have possibilities of their own. See what Whistler made and the Germans are making of the lithograph:—one note sounded in the gamut of its possibilities. But that note rings true to process as the sheen of the butterfly's wing to that wing. Yet, having fallen into disrepute, the most this particular "machine" did for us, until Whistler picked it up,

19

was to give us the cheap imitative effects of painting, mostly for advertising purposes. This is the use made of machinery in the abuse of materials by men. And still more important than all we have yet discussed here is the new element entering industry in this material we call steel. The structural necessity which once shaped Parthenons, Pantheons, Cathedrals, is fast being reduced by the Machine to a skeleton of steel or its equivalent, complete in itself without the Artist-Craftsman's touch. They are now building Gothic Cathedrals in California upon a steel skeleton. Is it not easy to see that the myriad ways of satisfying ancient structural necessities known to us through the books as the art of building, vanish, become History? The mainspring of their physical existence now removed, their spiritual center has shifted and nothing remains but the impassive features of a dead face. Such is our "Classic" architecture.

For centuries this insensate or insane abuse of great opportunity in the name of Culture has made cleanly, strengthy and true simplicity impossible in Art or Architecture, whereas now we might reach the heights of creative Art. Rightly used the very curse Machinery puts upon handicraft should emancipate the artist from temptation to petty structural deceit and end this wearisome struggle to make things seem what they are not and can never be. Then the Machine itself, eventually, will satisfy the simple terms of its modern art equation as the ball of clay in the sculptor's hand yields to his desire—ending forever this nostalgic masquerade led by a stultified Culture in the Name of Art.

Yes—though he does not know it, the Artist is now free to work his rational will with freedom unknown to structural tradition. Units of construction have enlarged, rhythms have been simplified and etherealized, space is more spacious and the sense of it may enter into every building, great or small. The Architect is no longer hampered by the stone arch of the Romans or by the stone beam of the Greeks. Why then does he cling to the grammatical phrases of those ancient methods of construction when such phrases are in his modern work empty lies, and himself an inevitable liar as well.

Already, as we stand today, the Machine has weakened the artist to the point of destruction and antiquated the craftsman altogether. Earlier forms of Art are by abuse all but destroyed. The whole matter has been reduced to mere pose. Instead of joyful creation we have all around about us poisonous tastes—foolish attitudes. With some little of the flame of the old love, and creditable but pitiful enthusiasm, the young artist still keeps on working, making miserable mischief with lofty motives: perhaps, because his heart has not kept in touch or in sympathy with his scientific brother's head, being out of step with the forward marching of his own time.

Now, let us remember in forming this new Arts and Crafts Society at Hull House that every people has done its work, therefore evolved its Art as an expression of its own life, using the best tools; and that means the most economic and effective tools or contrivances it knew: the tools most successful in saving valuable human effort. The chattel slave was the essential tool of Greek civilization, therefore of its Art. We have discarded this tool and would refuse the return of the Art of the Greeks were slavery the terms of its restoration, and slavery, in some form, would be the terms.

But in Grecian Art two flowers did find spiritual expression—the Acanthus and the Honeysuckle. In the Art of Egypt—similarly we see the Papyrus, the Lotus. In Japan the Chrysanthemum and many other flowers. The Art of the Occident has made no such sympathetic interpretation since that time, with due credit given to the English Rose and the French Fleur-de-Lys, and as things are now the West may never make one. But to get from some native plant an expression of its native character in terms of imperishable stone to be fitted perfectly to its place in structure, and without loss of vital significance, is one great phase of great Art. It means that Greek or Egyptian found a revelation of the inmost life and character of the Lotus and Acanthus in terms of Lotus or Acanthus Life. That was what happened when the Art of these people had done with the plants they most loved. This imaginative process is known only to the creative Artist. Conventionalization, it is called. Really it is the dramatizing of an object—truest "drama." To enlarge upon this simple figure, as an Artist, it seems to me that this complex matter of civilization is itself at bottom some such conventionalizing process, or must be so to be successful and endure.

Just as any Artist-Craftsman, wishing to use a beloved flower for the stone capital of a column-shaft in his building must conventionalize the flower, that is, find the pattern of its life-principle in terms of stone as a material before he can rightly use it as a beautiful factor in his building, so education must take the natural man, to "civilize" him. And this great new power of

21

the dangerous Machine we must learn to understand and then learn to use as this valuable, *"conventionalizing"* agent. But in the construction of a Society as in the construction of a great building, the elemental conventionalizing process is dangerous, for without the inspiration or inner light of the true Artist—the quality of the flower—its very life—is lost, leaving a withered husk in the place of living expression.

Therefore, Society, in this conventionalizing process or Culture, has a task even more dangerous than has the Architect in creating his building forms, because instead of having a plant-leaf and a fixed material as ancient architecture had, we have a sentient man with a fluid soul. So without the inner light of a sound philosophy of Art (the Educator too, must now be Artist), the life of the man will be sacrificed and Society gain an automaton or a machine-made moron instead of a noble creative Citizen!

If education is doomed to fail in this process, utterly—then the man slips back to rudimentary animalism or goes on into decay. Society degenerates or has a mere realistic creature instead of the idealistic creator needed. The world will have to record more "great dead cities."

To keep the Artist-figure of the flower *dramatized for human purposes*—the Socialist would bow his neck in altruistic submission to the "Harmonious" whole; his conventionalization or dramatization of the human being would be like a poor stone-craftsman's attempt to conventionalize the beloved plant with the living character of leaf and flower left out. The Anarchist would pluck the flower as it grows and use it as it is for what it is—with essential reality left out.

The Hereditary Aristocrat has always justified his existence by his ability, owing to fortunate propinquity, to appropriate the flower to his own uses after the craftsman has given it life and character, and has kept the craftsman too by promising him his flower back if he behaves himself well. The Plutocrat does virtually the same thing by means of "interests." But the true Democrat will take the human plant as it grows and—in the spirit of using the means at hand to put life into his conventionalization—preserve the individuality of the plant to protect the flower, which is its very life, getting from both a living expression of essential man-character fitted perfectly to a place in Society with no loss of vital significance. Fine Art is this flower of the Man. When Education has become creative and Art again prophetic of the natural means by which we are to grow—we call it "progress"—we will, by means of the Creative Artist, possess this monstrous tool of our civilization as it now possesses us.

Grasp and use the power of scientific automatons in this *creative sense* and their terrible forces are not antagonistic to any fine individualistic quality in man. He will find their collective mechanistic forces capable of bringing to the individual a more adequate life, and the outward expression of the inner man as seen in his environment will be genuine revelation of his inner life and higher purpose. Not until then will America be free!

This new American Liberty is of the sort that declares man free only when he has found his work and effective means to achieve a life of his own. The means once found, he will find his due place. The man of our country will thus make his own way, and *grow* to the natural place thus due him, promised —yes, promised by our charter, the Declaration of Independence. But this place of his is not to be made over to fit him by reform, nor shall it be brought down to him by concession, but will become his by his own use of the means at hand. He must *himself* build a new world. The day of the individual is not over—instead, it is just about to begin. The Machine does not write the doom of Liberty, but is waiting at man's hand as a peerless tool, for him to use to put foundations beneath a genuine Democracy. Then the Machine may conquer human drudgery to some purpose, taking it upon itself to broaden, lengthen, strengthen and deepen the life of the simplest man. What limits do we dare imagine to an Art that is organic fruit of an adequate life for the individual! Although this power is now murderous, chained to botch-work and bunglers' ambitions, the creative Artist will take it surely into his hand and, in the name of Liberty, swiftly undo the deadly mischief it has created.

• • •   • • •   • • •

Here ends the early discourse on the Art and Craft of the Machine.

You may find comfort in the reflection that Truth and Liberty have this invincible excellence, that all man does for them or does against them eventually serves them equally well. That fact has comforted me all the intervening years between the first reading of the foregoing discourse and this reading at Princeton . . . the last reading, for I shall never read it again. Tomorrow afternoon there will be—I am afraid—heavy matter also because the question of qualifying the "Machine-made" in American Industries by human elements of STYLE will be, in detail, our subject. There may be matter more subjective and difficult but I do not know what it may be.

It will be necessary for us all to give close attention and considerable thought to the subject, "STYLE IN INDUSTRY." We shall see that any hope of such style will mean a crusade against *the* STYLES.

2: STYLE IN INDUSTRY

WINSLOW HOUSE
FIRST BUILDING BY FRANK LLOYD WRIGHT.
BRICK WAINSCOTE. MODELLED FRIEZE. TILE
ROOF. STONE WASHES AND WATER TABLE.
1893-1894.

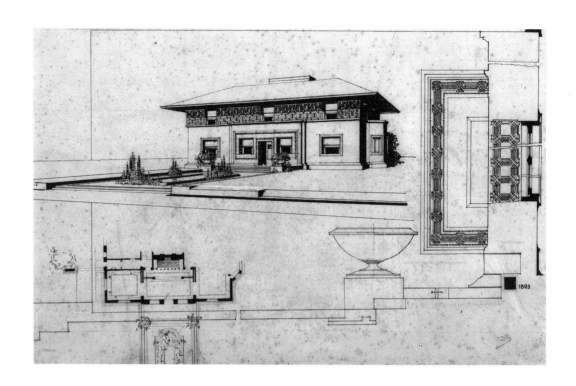

1893

2: STYLE IN INDUSTRY

WHERE certain remarks I have made concern Nature and Romance on the one hand, and the Machine upon the other, I am accused of inconsistency—also in several or seven different languages. But if the word Nature, and the word Romance too, are understood in the sense that each is used we can find little to correct, although the last analysis is never to be made.

THE MACHINE is that mathematical automaton or automatic power contrived in brass and steel by men, not only to take the place of man-power, but to multiply man-power—the brainless craftsman of a new social order.

Primarily the word NATURE means the principle at work in everything that lives and gives to Life its form and character. All lives, so we may refer to the Nature of Two Plus Two Equals Four, if we like, or to the Nature of Tin, or to the Nature of a Disease or of the Chromatic Seventh. The word has nothing to do with realistic or realism, but refers to the essential *Reality* of all things—so far as we may perceive Reality. We cannot conceive Life, we do not know what it is, but we can perceive the Nature of its consequences and effects and so enter into creation with some intelligence. If we have occasion to refer to the visible world we will use the term "External Nature." The word "Organic" too, if taken too biologically, is a stumbling-block. The word applies to "living" structure—a structure or concept wherein features or parts are so organized in form and substance as to be, applied to purpose, *integral*. Everything that "lives" is therefore organic. The inorganic—the "unorganized"—cannot *live*.

While we are at the, perhaps unnecessary, pains of explaining, let us say also what we should understand by ROMANCE. True Romanticism in Art is after all only Liberalism in Art, and is so understood, I believe, by all great Poets. Romance is the essential joy we have in living, as distinguished from mere pleasure; therefore we want no narrow conventions, as preventions, to rise up from small minds and selfish hands, no intolerant "modes" to grow up in the Modern World; it is to be our privilege to build up on new fertile ground. Yes, we are to build in the Arts upon this great ground fertilized *by* the *old* civilizations—a new Liberty.

. . .   .

MODERN ARCHITECTURE

We, so beset by educational advantages as are Americans, cannot say too often to ourselves or others that "Toleration and Liberty are the foundations of this great Republic." We should keep it well in the foreground of our minds and as a hope in our hearts that Liberty in Art as well as Liberty in Society *should* be, and therefore *must* be, the offspring of political liberty.

Then to us all, so-minded, let the Artist come. He has a Public. And as we have already seen in "MACHINERY, MATERIALS AND MEN," the Artist now has both the "Making and the Means." Let him arise in our Industry. For a New People a New Art!

LIBERTY, however, is no friend to License. So, for our text in connection with difficult "STYLE IN INDUSTRY," for due reference to authority suppose we again go far back in history—again to avoid all contradiction—this time to the birth of Old Japan—and there, to safeguard LIBERTY, take for text, simply, "An Artist's Limitations are his best friends," and dedicate that text to JIMMU TENNO.

At least the ancient civilization of his slowly sinking stretch of pendulous island, arising from the sea in the snows of perpetual winter and reaching all the way South to perpetual summer, affords best proof of the text anywhere to be found. "Limitations," in this sense, were, I take it, those of materials, tools and specific purpose.

In JIMMU's Island perfect Style in Industry was supreme and native until "Japan" was discovered within range of our own Commodore Perry's guns. That Western contacts have destroyed this early Style—if not the industry— only enhances the value of that early Style. *Certainly*, the Arts and Crafts, as developed in Nippon during her many centuries of isolation in happy concentration, afford universal object lessons incomparable in STYLE.

INDUSTRY and STYLE there—before the "peaceful" commercial invasion by the West—were supremely natural. Nor in JIMMU TENNO's time was there anywhere to be found separate and contrasted existence between Art and Nature. Nowhere else in the world can we so clearly see this nor so well inform ourselves in considering this matter of STYLE in our own native automatic industries. This notwithstanding the fact that our industries are conditioned upon automatic acquiescence of men instead of upon the craftsmanship of the man. By giving our attention to the ease and naturalness with which things Japanese originally achieved STYLE, we may learn a valuable lesson.

28

STYLE IN INDUSTRY

Our Industry must educate designers instead of making craftsmen—for our Craftsmen are Machines, craftsmen ready-made, efficient and obedient. So far as they go—mechanical power stripped clean. How to get these formidable craft-engines the work to do they may do well? Then, beyond mechanical skill, the cadences of form?

The first answer will seem generalization beyond any immediate mark, for that answer is—by means of Imagination. Imagination superior and supreme. Supreme Imagination is what makes the creative Artist now just as it made one then. And Imagination is what will make the needed designer for Industry now—no less than then or ever before. But, strange to say, it is of the true quality of great Imagination that it can see wood as wood, steel as steel, glass as glass, stone as stone, and make limitations its best friends. This is what Jimmu Tenno's busy people proved so thoroughly well and what may be so useful to us to realize. Our Machine-Age Limitations are more severe and more cruelly enforced than limitations were in this severely disciplined Island-Empire of Japan. Nevertheless, though more difficult in important ways, in other more important directions, we have marvellously more opportunity than ever Japan had.

Principles which made the Art and Craft of Old Japan a living thing—living, that is, for Old Japan—will work as well now as then. The same principles in Art and Craft either of the East or the West, wherever similar truths of being went into effect with some force in the lives of their peoples, need no change now. Secrets of cause and effect in work and materials in relation to Life as lived are the same for the coming designer for Machines as they were for the bygone Craftsman designers. But when a man becomes a part of the machine that he moves—the man is lost.

We Americans, too, *do live*—in a way—do we not? But we differ. We do live and, notwithstanding all differences, our souls yet have much in common with all souls. The principles, therefore, on which we must work our modern style for ourselves will not change the while our interpretation and applications will utterly change. Results in American industry will be simpler, broader, more a matter of texture and sublimated mathematics as music is sublimated mathematics; therefore our designs will be more subjective than before. Our applications will be more generalized but our derivations not more limited than in the days of ancient handicraft.

MODERN ARCHITECTURE

Provided the limitations of any given problem in the Arts do not destroy each other by internal collision and so kill opportunity, limitations are no detriment to Artist endeavor. It is largely the Artist's business—all in his day's work—to see that the limitations do *not* destroy each other. That is to say, it is up to him to get proper tools, proper materials for proper work. Speaking for myself, it would be absurd if not impossible to take advantage of the so-called "free-hand." To "Idealize" in the fanciful sketch is a thing unknown to me. Except as I were given some well defined limitations or requirements—the more specific the better—there would be no problem, nothing to work with, nothing to work out; why then trouble the Artist? Perhaps that is why "Fairs" are so universally uncreative and harmful—the hand is too free, the quality of imagination, therefore, too insignificant.

No,—not until American industrial designers have grown up to the point where they have known and made friends with the limitations characteristic of their job, will America have any STYLE in INDUSTRY. What are these limitations?

Automatic industrial fabrication is not the least of them. But—to reiterate from the matter of our first chapter, "MACHINERY, MATERIALS AND MEN" —the American designers' hope lies in the fact that as a consequence of the automaton, already machinery can do many desirable things, "by hand" prohibited or impossible. Now, mixed up with "MACHINERY, MATERIALS AND MEN," in our first chapter, was the word PLASTICITY used as Machine-aesthetic in modern designing for wood-working, stone-work, metal-casting and reproductive processes. Some practical suggestions were made to indicate how and wherein this new "aesthetic" which the machine has given to us may enable the Artist to make new use of old materials, and new use of new materials instead of making abuse of both.

"Plasticity" is of utmost importance. The word implies total absence of constructed effects as evident in the result. This important word, "Plastic," means that the quality and nature of materials are seen "flowing or growing" into form instead of seen as built up out of cut and joined pieces. "Composed" is the academic term for this academic process in furniture. "Plastic" forms, however, are *not* "composed" nor set up. They, happily, inasmuch as they are produced by a *"growing"* process, must be developed . . . *created*. And to shorten this discourse we may as well admit that if we go far enough to find cause in any single industry like furniture for this matter of STYLE, we will have the secret of origin and growth of STYLE in any or in all industries. After getting so far, there would come only specialization in differences of materials and machinery in operation.

Repeatedly and freely too we are to use this word STYLE—but if intelligently, what, then, is STYLE? Be sure of one thing in any answer made to the question —STYLE *has nothing to do with "the" Styles!* "The Great Styles" we call them. "Styles" have been tattered, torn and scattered to the four winds and all the breezes that blow between them as a form of mechanical corruption in industry, and yet, we have no STYLE. The more "Styles" in fact, the less STYLE, unless by accident—nor anything very much resembling the stimulating quality. Our designers for various industries—still busy, unfortunately, trying to imitate "STYLES" instead of *studying the principles* of STYLE intelligently— are at the moment jealously watching France as they see her products go from Wanamaker's on down the Avenue and out along the highways of these United States as far as the Pacific Ocean. And yet, if you will take pains to compare the best of French products, say in textiles, with the products of the ancient Momoyama of Japan you will see the industrial ideas of Old Japan at work in New French Industry as direct inspiration. The French product is not Japanese and nearly all of the textiles are within the capacity of the Machine; most of the product is good. But France, in all her moments of movement in Art and Craft, and no less at this "Modern" moment in this "modernistic" particular, helps herself liberally if not literally from Japanese sources, and creditably. She it was who discovered the Japanese Print by way of the De Goncourts. That discovery bore significant fruit in French Painting. And there are more valuable brochures in the French language on the Art of Japan in all its phases available for reference than in all other languages put together, the Japanese language included. France, the inveterate discoverer, must discover "l'esprit de l'art Japonais—à la Japon," to her great honor be it said. Holland arrived at Nagasaki first, but France is probably further along today in profitable industrial results in present arts and crafts from the revelations she found when she got to Yedo by way of Yokohama than is any other country, Austria excepted—unless our own country should soon prove formidable exception.

31

MODERN ARCHITECTURE

This does not mean that France or Austria copies Japan or that America may do so. It does mean that France is, only now, beginning to do approximately well what Japan did supremely well four centuries ago in the great Momoyama period of her development—yes, about four hundred years ago!

Any principle is fertile, perhaps it is fertility itself! If its application is once understood in any branch of design, it will go on blooming indefinitely, co-ordinately, in as many different schools and schemes as there are insects, or in forms as varied as the flowers themselves, or for that matter be as prolific of pattern as the fishes or the flora of the sea.

We should, were we going into the matter at length, get to Nature-forms later on as the best of all references for the working of the principles we are here seeking, and I should have preferred to go to them at once as is my habit. But for the purposes of this hour I have preferred Tradition because Japan has already done, in her own perfect way, what now lies for study before us. And I believe it well to know what humanity has accomplished in the direction we must take, if we are strong enough to profit by Tradition— the spirit or principle—and leave Traditions—the letter, or form—alone, as not our own. Even so, having finished with Tradition, we will still have before us and forever, as an open book of creation, that natural appeal to the Nature-court of Last Resort.

Remember, however, that long before France rationalized and vitalized her industries, during the period when she was still sickened and helpless in the serpentine coils of L'Art Nouveau, (derived from her own deadly Rococo), you may find in the "Secession" of Middle Europe an application earlier than the present application by France of the vital principles we are discussing on behalf of our subject.

I came upon the Secession during the winter of 1910. At that time Herr Professor Wagner, of Vienna, a great architect, the architect Olbrich, of Darmstadt, the remarkable painter Klimt of Austria and the sculptor Metzner of Berlin—great artists all—were the soul of that movement. And there was the work of Louis Sullivan and of myself in America. Many Europeans accounted for this Secession—their own early contribution to Modern Art— as a "Mohammedan Renaissance." (It was natural by that time to believe in nothing but some kind of Renaissance.) But later, when the Secession— though frowned upon by the Royal Academies—was in full swing in the

STYLE IN INDUSTRY

products of the Wiener Werkstätte, seen today similarly in the products of French Art and Craft, we find the Ancient Art and Craft of Japan's great Momoyama often approximated in effect.

Nothing at this "Modern" moment could be more ungracious nor arouse more contumacious "edge" than thus looking the "gift horse" or the "modernistic" in the teeth. Nevertheless, I believe it valuable to our future to raise this unpopular issue.

Artists, even great ones, are singularly ungrateful to sources of inspiration—among lesser artists ingratitude amounts to phobia. No sooner does the lesser artist receive a lesson or perceive an idea or even receive the Objects of Art from another source, than he soon becomes anxious to forget the suggestion, conceal the facts, or, if impossible to do this, to minimize, by detraction, the "gift." And as Culture expands, we soon, too soon, deny outright the original sources of our inspiration as a suspected reproach to our own superiority. This you may quite generally find in the Modern Art World. At this moment in our development Japan particularly is thus the "great insulted." Cowardly evasion seems unworthy of great artists or great causes, and certainly is no manner in which to approach great matter for the future. Ignorance of origins is no virtue—nor to keep fresh thought ill-advised concerning them. So let us pursue still further this quest as to what is STYLE by digging at the root of this ancient culture where I imagine there was more fertile ground and the workman had severer discipline than he ever had anywhere else in the world. Thus we may interpret a ready-made record that is unique. Let us study for a moment the Japanese dwelling, this humble dwelling that is a veritable sermon on our subject, "STYLE IN INDUSTRY."

It became what it is owing to a religious admonition. "Be Clean!" "Be Clean" was the soul of Shinto—JIMMU TENNO's own ancient form of worship. Shinto spoke not of a good man, nor spoke of a moral man, but spoke of a clean man. Shinto spoke not only of clean hands, but of a clean heart. "Be Clean" was the simple cry from the austere soul of Shinto. Japanese Art heard the cry, and therefore posterity has one primitive instance where a remarkably simple religious edict or ideal made Architecture, Art and Craftsmanship the cleanest, in every sense, of all clean workmanship the world over.

This simple ideal of cleanliness, held by a whole people, came to abhor waste as matter out of place, saw it as ugly—therefore as what we call "dirt."

MODERN ARCHITECTURE

Here you have a kind of spiritual ideal of natural and hence organic, simplicity. Consequently all Japanese Art with its imaginative exuberance and organic elegance (no fern-frond freshly born ever had more) was a practical study in elimination of the insignificant. All phases of Art Expression in the Momoyama period were organic. There was no great and no small Art. But there lived the profound Sotatzu, the incomparable Korin, the brilliant Kenzan and their vital schools, as, later in the Ukioyé, we find Kiyonobu, Toyonobu, Harunobu, Kiyonaga, Utamaro, Hokusai and Hiroshigé—a small student group gathered about each—all springing from the industrial soil thus fertilized by the school of the great Momoyama Masters. Instinctive sense of organic quality qualified them as Artists, *all*. Again, a kind of spiritual gift of significance. Here, as a saving grace in one civilization on Earth, feeling for significance, simplicity in Art was born, becoming soon an ideal naturally attained by organic means. Here, in this "Plastic-ideal" *attained by organic means*, we touch the secret of great STYLE. Wood they allowed to be wood, of course. Metal they allowed—even encouraged—to be metal. Stone was never asked to be less or more than stone. Nor did the designer of that day try to make any thing in materials or processes something other than itself. Here is a sound first principle that will go far to clear our encumbered ground for fresh growth in "Art in industry."

Also the modern process of standardizing, as we now face it on every side, sterilized by it, prostrate to it, was in Japan known and practised with artistic perfection by freedom of choice many centuries ago, in this dwelling we are considering. The removable (for cleaning) floor mats or "tatami" of Japanese buildings were all of one size, 3′ 0″ by 6′ 0″. The shape of all the houses was determined by the size and shape of assembled mats. The Japanese speak of a nine, eleven, sixteen or thirty-four mat house. All the sliding interior partitions occur on the joint lines of the mats. The "odeau"—polished wood posts that carry ceilings and roof—all stand at intersections of the mats. The light sliding paper shoji or outside wall-screens are likewise removable—for cleaning. The plan for any Japanese dwelling was an effective study in sublimated mathematics. And the house itself was used by those who themselves made it for themselves with the same naturalness with which a turtle uses his shell. Consider too that, "Be Clean"—"the simplest way without waste"—was dignified as *ceremonial* in Old Japan. The ceremonies of that ancient day were no more than the simple offices of daily life raised to the dignity of works of Art. True culture, therefore. Ceremonials, too, it seems, may be organic, integral though symbolic. For instance what is the important tea-ceremony of the Japanese but the most graciously perfect way, all considered, of serving a cup of tea to respected or beloved guests? Grace and elegance, as we may see—*of* the thing itself—organic elegance. Not *on* it Greek-wise as the "elegant solution." It was in easy, simple, spontaneous expression of Nature that the Japanese were so perfect—contenting themselves with humble obedience to Nature-law.

Naturally enough, Disorder, too, in this "clean" house built by JIMMU TENNO's people is in the same category as dirt. So everything large or little of everyday use, even the works of Art for humble and profound admiration, have appropriate place when in use and are carefully put away into safe keeping when not in use.

All designed for kneeling on soft mats on the floor you say? Yes—but the same ideal, in principle, would work out just as well on one's feet.

With this Shinto ideal of "Be Clean" in mind the Japanese dwelling in every structural member and fibre of its being means something fine, has genuine significance and straightway does that something with beautiful effect. Art, for once, is seen to be supremely natural.

Yes—here is definite root of STYLE in Industry. Also in every other country and period where STYLE developed as genuine consequence of natural or ethnic character, similar proofs may be found as to the origin of STYLE.

Today, it seems to me, we hear this cry "Be Clean" from the depths of our own need. It is almost as though the Machine itself had, by force, issued edict similar to Shinto—"Be Clean." Clean lines—clean surfaces—clean purposes. As swift as you like, but clean as the flight of an arrow. When this edict inspires organic results and not the mere picture-making that curses so-called "Modernism," we will here find the basic elements of STYLE in our own Industry to be the same by machine as they were by hand back there in the beginning of the history of a unique civilization. To give this edict of the Machine human significance there is the command of the creative Artist to keep a grip upon the earth in use of the architectural planes parallel to Earth, and to make new materials qualify the new forms of the new methods, so that all is warmly and significantly human in the result. The Human equation is the

Art equation in it all. "Clean," in human sense, does not mean "plain" but it does mean significant. Nor does it mean hard, nor mechanical nor mechanistic, nor that a man or a house or a chair or a child is a machine, except in the same sense that our own hearts are suction pumps.

Style in our industries will come out of similar, natural, "clean" use of machines upon "clean" material, with similar, unaffected, *heartfelt* simplicity instead of *head-made* simplicity. The nature of both machine and material for human use must be understood and mastered so they may be likewise in our case plastic interpretations by great Imagination. We will learn how to use both Machinery and Materials and perhaps Men as well in the coming century. But we must learn how to use them all not only for qualities they possess in themselves, but to use each so that they may be beautifully as well as scientifically related to human purpose in whatever form or function we humanly choose to put them. Then let us take all as much further along beyond the implications of "Be Clean," as our superior advantages in aesthetics permit.

To get nearer to the surface. We started to speak of textiles: having during the discourse of our first chapter touched upon woodworking, stonework and metalworking, let us now go back for a moment to the Rodier fabrics for an example of present-day, successful design for the loom. Textures, infinite in variety, are the natural product of the loom. Pattern is related to, and is the natural consequence of, the mechanics of these varying textures. Large, flat patterns involved with textures, textures qualifying them or qualified by them, picturesque but with no thought of a picture, as in this product, are entirely modern in the best sense. And I would emphasize for you, in this connection, the fact that the ancient Art we have just been interpreting was never, in any phase of its industries, ruined by childish love of the picture. The "picture" sense in Art and Craft came in with the Renaissance, as one consequence of the insubordination of the Arts that disintegrated Architecture as the great Art. And before we can progress in our own Machine products as Art, we, too, will have to dispose of the insufferable insubordination of the picture. Summarily, if need be. I should like to strike the pictorial death-blow in our Art and Craft. Of course I do not mean the picturesque.

Because of this insubordination of the picture few tapestries except the "Mille-fleurs" (and then very early ones) exist as good textile designs on account of the complex shading essential to the foolish picture as designed by the undisciplined painter. The insubordination of painting, setting up shop on its own account, divorced from Architecture, (Architecture being the natural framework and background of all ancient, as it will be of any future, civilization), has cursed every form of Art endeavor whatsoever with similar abuses of the *pictorial.* "Toujours la peinture," *ad libitum, ad nauseam*—the *picture.* We live in the Pictorial Age. We do not have childlike imagery in simplicity but are "childish" in Art, and whatever form our great Art and Craft in future may take, one thing it will not be, and that thing is "Pictorial." Even a Japanese Print, the popular form of imagery illustrating the popular life of Japan in all its phases, as the French well know, never degenerated to the mere picture. Let us be thankful that the Machine by way of the camera today takes the pictorial upon itself as a form of literature. This gratifying feat has, already, made great progress in the cinematograph. Let the Machine have it, I say, on those terms and keep it active there and serviceable in illustration as well, for what it may be worth—and it is worth much.But let us henceforth consider Literature and the Picture as one—eliminating both from the horizon of our Art and Craft—and for all time.

Let us now, in passing, glance at Glassmaking: the Leerdam glass products for which artists are employed to make designs upon a royalty basis, similar to authors writing for publishers, then the special Art of Lalique, and finally, the great, clear plates of our own commercial industry, the gift of the Machine, . . . great glass sheets to be cut up and used with no thought of beauty, valuable only because of their usefulness.

Here again let us insist that the same principle applies to glass as to wood, stone, metal or the textiles just mentioned. But how far variety may go can be seen in the range of the Holland product from the simple glass-blown forms of De Basle, Copius and Berlage at Leerdam to the virtuosity of French pieces by the genius Lalique. Certain characteristics of glass are properties of these designs: a piece by Lalique, being specialized handicraft, is useful as indicating the super-possibilities of glass as a beautiful material. Concerning our own "commercial" contribution (contributions so far are all "commercial") to glass—glass, once a precious substance, limited in quantity, costly in any size—the glass industry has grown so that a perfect clarity in any thickness, quality or dimension up to 250 square feet from 1/8″

37

in thickness to 1/2″ thick, is so cheap and desirable that our modern world is drifting towards structures of glass and steel.

The whole history of Architecture would have been radically different had the ancients enjoyed any such grand privileges in this connection as are ours. The growing demand for sunshine and visibility make walls—even posts—something to get rid of at any cost. Glass did this. Glass alone, with no help from any of us, would eventually have destroyed Classic Architecture, root and branch.

Glass has now a perfect visibility, thin sheets of air crystallized to keep air currents outside or inside. Glass surfaces, too, may be modified to let the vision sweep through to any extent up to perfection. Tradition left no orders concerning this material as a means of perfect visibility; hence the sense of glass as crystal has not, as poetry, entered yet into Architecture. All the dignity of color and material available in any other material may be discounted by glass in light, and discounted with permanence.

Shadows were the "brush-work" of the ancient Architect. Let the "Modern" now work with light, light diffused, light reflected, light refracted—light for its own sake, shadows gratuitous. It is the Machine that makes *modern* these rare new opportunities in Glass—new experience that Architects so recent as the great Italian forebears, plucked even of their shrouds, frowning upon our "Renaissance," would have considered magical. They would have thrown down their tools with the despair of the true Artist. Then they would have transformed their cabinets into a realm, their halls into bewildering vistas and avenues of light—their modest units into unlimited wealth of color patterns and delicate forms, rivalling the frostwork upon the window-panes, perhaps. They were creative enough to have found a world of illusion and brilliance, with jewels themselves only modest contributions to the splendor of their effects. And yet somehow Palladio, Vitruvius, Vignola, seem very dead, far away and silent in this connection, Bramante and Brunelleschi not so far, nor Sansovino, though we must not forget that the great Italians were busy working over ancient forms. There was Buonarroti. Where should he be in all this, I wonder?

The Prism has always fascinated man. We may now live in prismatic buildings, clean, beautiful and New. Here is one clear "material" proof of modern advantage, for Glass is uncompromisingly Modern. Yes—Architecture is soon to live anew because of Glass and Steel.

And so we might go on to speak truly of nearly all our typical modern industries at work upon materials with Machinery. We could go on and on until we were all worn out and the subject would be still bright and new, there are so many industrial fields—so much machinery, so many processes, such riches in new materials.

We began this discussion of Art in Industry by saying, "Toleration and Liberty are the foundations of a great Republic." Now let the Artist come. Well —let him come into this boundless new realm so he be a Liberal, hating only Intolerance and especially his own. As said at the beginning of this discourse, true Romanticism in Art is after all only Liberalism in Art. This quality in the Artist is the result of an inner experience and it is the essential poetry of the creative Artist that his exploring brother, tabulating the Sciences, seems never quite able to understand nor wholly respect. He distrusts that quality in life itself.

But the sense of Romance cannot die out of human hearts. Science itself is bringing us to greater need of it and unconsciously giving greater assurance of it at every step. Romance is shifting its center now, as it has done before and will do constantly—but it is immortal. Industry will only itself become and remain a Machine without it.

Our Architecture itself would become a poor, flat-faced thing of steel-bones, box-outlines, gas-pipe and hand-rail fittings—as sun-receptive as a concrete sidewalk or a glass tank without this essential *heart* beating in it. Architecture, without it, could inspire nothing, and would degenerate to a box merely to *contain* "Objets d'Art"—objects it should itself create and *maintain.* So beware! The Artist who condemns Romance is only a foolish reactionary. Such good sense as the Scientist or Philosopher in the disguise of "Artist" may have is not creative, although it may be corrective. Listen therefore and go back with what you may learn, to live and be true to Romance.

Again—there is no good reason why Objects of Art in Industry, because they are made by Machines in the Machine Age, should resemble the machines that made them, or any other machinery whatever. There might be excellent reason why they should *not* resemble machinery. There is no good reason why forms stripped clean of all considerations but function and utility should be

39

admirable beyond that point: they may be abominable from the human standpoint, but there is no need for them to be so in the Artist's hands.

The negation naturally made by the Machine, gracefully accepted now, may, for a time, relieve us of sentimental abortion and abuse, but it cannot inspire and recreate humanity beyond that point. Inevitably the negation proceeds upon its own account to other abuses and abortions, even worse than sentimentality. Again, let us have no fears of Liberalism in Art in our Industries, but encourage it with new understanding, knowing at last that the term Romanticism never did apply to make-believe or falsifying, except as it degenerated to the artificiality that maintained the Renaissance.

The facts confronting us are sufficiently bare and hard. The taste for mediocrity in our country grows by what it feeds on.

Therefore the public of this Republic will, more than ever now, find its love of commonplace elegance gratified either by the sentimentality of the "ornamental" or the sterility of ornaphobia. The Machine Age, it seems, is either to be damned by senseless sentimentality or to be sterilized by a factory aesthetic. Nevertheless, I believe that Romance—this quality of the *heart*, the essential joy we have in living—by human imagination of the right sort can be brought to life again in Modern Industry. Creative Imagination may yet convert our prosaic problems to poetry while modern Rome howls and the eyebrows of the Pharisees rise.

And probably not more than one-fifth of the American public will know what is meant by the accusation, so frequently made in so many different languages, that the American is uncreative, four-fifths of the accused pointing to magnificent machinery and stupendous scientific accomplishment to refute the impeachment. So while we are digesting the nationalities speaking those same languages within our borders, such Culture as we have in sight must assist itself with intelligence to materialize for Americans out of everyday common places—and transcend the commonplace.

• • •   • • •   • • •

So finally, a practical suggestion as to ways and means to grow our own STYLE in INDUSTRY.

The Machine, as it exists in every important trade, should without delay be put, by way of capable Artist interpreters, into student hands—for them, at first, to play with and, later, with which to work. Reluctantly I admit that to put the Machine, as the modern tool of a great civilization, to any extent into the hands of a body of young students, means some kind of school—and naturally such school would be called an Art School, but one in which the Fine Arts would be not only allied to the Industries they serve, but would stand there at the center of an industrial hive of characteristic industry as inspiration and influence in design-problems.

Sensitive, unspoiled students (and they may yet be found in this unqualified machine that America is becoming) should be put in touch with commercial industry in what we might call Industrial "Style" Centers, workshops equipped with modern machinery, connected perhaps with our universities, but endowed by the industries themselves, where the students would remain domiciled working part of the day in the shop itself.

Machinery-using crafts making useful things might through such Experiment Centers discover possibilities existing in the Nature of their craft—which the present industries know nothing about and might never discover for themselves. In such a school it would be the turn of the Fine Arts to serve Machinery in order that Machinery might better serve them and all together better serve a beauty-loving and appreciative United States.

Let us say that seven branches of Industrial Arts be taken for a beginning (a number should be grouped together for the reason that they react upon one another to the advantage of each). Let us name Glassmaking, Textiles, Pottery, Sheet Metals, Woodworking, Casting in Metal, Reproduction. Each Industry so represented should be willing to donate machinery and supply a competent machinist and to a certain extent endow its own craft, provided such industries were certain of proper management under safe auspices, and assured of a share in results which would be directly theirs—sharing either in benefit of designs or presently in designers themselves, both adapted to their particular field.

Such Experiment Centers intelligently conducted could do more to nationalize and vitalize our industries than all else, and soon would make them independent of France, Austria or any other country, except as instruction by international example from all countries would help work out our own forms. There is no reason why an Experiment Center of this character, each Center confined to forty students or less, should not make its own living and produce valuable articles to help in "carrying-on." As compared with the less favorably circumstanced factories, and owing to the Artists at the head of the group, each article would be of the quality of a work of Art and so be a genuine missionary wherever it went.

Such a school should be in the country, on sufficient land so that three hours a day of physical work on the soil would insure the living of the students and the resident group of seven artist workers, themselves the head of the student group. There would remain, say, seven hours of each day for forty-seven individuals in which to unite in production. A well directed force of this sort would very soon have considerable producing power. Thus belonging to the school each month there would be beautifully useful or usefully beautiful things ready for market and influence—stuffs, tapestries, table-linen, new cotton fabrics, table glassware, flower holders, lighting devices, window glass, mosaics, necklaces, screens, iron standards, fixtures, gates, fences, fire irons, enamelled metals for house or garden purposes, cast metal sculpture for gardens, building-hardware. All sorts of industrial art in aluminum, copper, lead, tin. Practical flower-pots, architectural flower containers on large scale, water jars, pots and sculpture. Paintings for decoration suitable for reproduction and designs for new media—for process-reproductions. Modern music, plays, rhythm, designs for farm buildings, the characteristic new problems like the gasoline station, the refreshment stand, food distribution, town and country cottages and objects for their furnishings, and factories, too, of various sorts.

The station might broadcast itself. Issue brochures, illustrated by itself, of pertinent phases of its work. Devote a branch to landscape studies on conservation and planting and town-planning. In short, the station would be a hive of inspired industry. Architecture, without hesitation, or equivocation, should be the broad essential background of the whole endeavor—again strong in Modern life as it ever was in Ancient times. It is logical to say that again it must be the background and framework of civilization. Such stations or centers could be alcoves in connection with standard University courses in the History of Art, Architecture and Archaeology. And it would not matter where the centers were located, were they sufficiently isolated in beautiful country. They should not be too easy of access.

STYLE IN INDUSTRY

No examinations, graduations or diplomas. But so soon as a student worker showed special competence in any branch of industry he would be available as teacher in the university or for a place in that industry, manufacturers who were contributors to the school having first right to use him or her. The body of inspirational talent and the trade machinists should be of such character that outside students would enjoy and seek points of contact with the work going on at the school—helpful to them and to the school as well.

I believe the time has come when Art must take the lead in Education because Creative Faculty is now, as ever, the birthright of Man—the quality that has enabled him to distinguish himself from the brute. Through tricks played upon himself by what he proudly styles his intellect, turning all experience into arrogant abstractions and applying them as such by systems of education, he has all but sterilized himself. Science has been tried and found to be only a body. Science, and Philosophy, too, have known but little of those inner experiences of the soul we call Art and Religion.

This creative faculty in man is that quality or faculty in him of getting himself born into whatever he does, and born again and again with fresh patterns as new problems arise. By means of this faculty he has the Gods if not God. A false premium has been placed by Education upon Will and Intellect. Imagination is the instrument by which the force in him works its miracles. Now—how to get back again to men and cultivate the creative quality in Man is the concern of such centers as here suggested. What more valuable step looking toward the future could any great institution take than to initiate such little Experiment Stations in out of the way places, where the creative endeavor of the whole youth is coordinate with the Machinery, and where the technique of his time is visible at work, so that youth may win back again the creative factor as the needed vitalizing force in Modern life?

We know, now, that creative Art cannot be taught. We know, too, that individual creative impulse is the salt and savour of the natural ego as well as the fruit and triumph of any struggle we call work. Civilization without it can only die a miserable death. To degrade and make hypocritical this quality of the individual by imposing mediocrity upon him in the name of misconceived and selfishly applied Democracy is the Modern Social Crime. Too plainly we already see the evil consequences of sentimentalized singing to Demos—foolishly ascribing to Demos the virtues of Deity. Concentration and sympathetic inspiration should be isolated and concentrated in experimental work of this kind in order to hasten the time when Art shall take the lead in Education, and character be a natural consequence. Were this to be put into effect on even a small scale in various units scattered over the surface of these United States, this indispensable ego might be strengthened and restored to a sanity compared to which "egotism," as we now know it in Education, would only be a sickly disease of Consciousness—highly improbable because manifestly absurd.

Thus given opportunity truly Liberal, American Youth might soon become the vital medium through which the Spirit of Man may so appear to men in their own work that they might again see and realize that great spirit as their own.

This Liberal opportunity to work and study is a practical suggestion for the growth of that quality of STYLE IN INDUSTRY we have been seeking this afternoon.

Behind personality Tradition should stand—behind Tradition stands the race.

We have put Tradition before personality—and made Tradition as a fatal hurdle for race.

3: THE PASSING OF THE CORNICE

UNITY TEMPLE
CONCRETE MONOLITH. GRAVEL SURFACE CAST IN
WOOD MOULDS. WATERPROOF WASHES AND
WATER TABLE. CANTILEVER SLAB ROOF.
INTERIOR SPACE SCREENED INSTEAD OF
WALLED.
1908

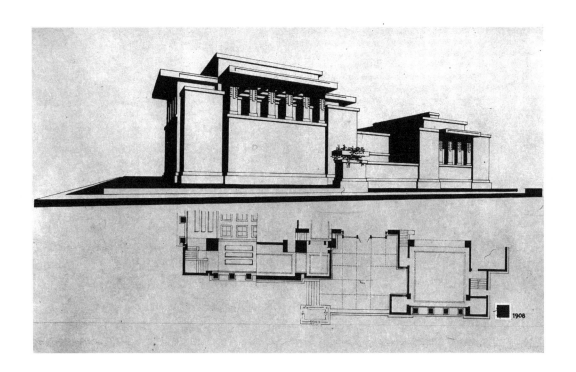

1908

3: THE PASSING OF THE CORNICE

INSTINCTIVELY, I think, I hated the empty, pretentious shapes of the Renaissance. When sixteen years old, I used to read the great "Modern" of his day—Victor Hugo. Reading his discursive novel, *Notre-Dame*, I came upon the chapter, "Ceci Tuera Cela." That story of the decline of Architecture made a lasting impression upon me. I saw the Renaissance as that setting sun all Europe mistook for dawn; I believed Gutenberg's invention of the shifting types would kill the great edifice as Architecture. In fact, as we all may now see, printing *was* the first great blow to Art by the Machine. I saw the life-blood of beloved Architecture slowly ebbing, inevitably to be taken entirely away from the building by the book, the book being a more liberal form of expression for human thought. This mechanical invention was to become the channel for thought—because more facile and more direct. In place of the Art of Architecture was to come Literature made ubiquitous.

I saw that Architecture, in its great antique form, was going to die. Ghastly tragedy—I could hardly bear the thought of the consequences.

About this time, too—catastrophe! As the new West Wing of the Old Wisconsin State Capitol at Madison fell, I happened to be passing in the shade of the trees that bordered the green Park in which the building stood. Suddenly I heard the roar of collapse—saw the clouds of white lime-dust rise high in the air—heard the groans and fearful cries of those injured and not killed—some forty workmen dead or seriously hurt. I remember clinging to the iron palings of the Park in full view of the scene, sick with horror as men plunged headlong from the basement openings—some seeming to be still madly fighting off falling bricks and timbers, only to fall dead in the grass outside, grass no longer green but whitened by the now falling clouds of lime.

The outer stone walls were still standing. Stone basement-piers carrying the iron interior supporting columns had given way and the roof took all the floors, sixty men at work on them, clear down to the basement. A great "classic" cornice had been projecting boldly out from the top of the building, against the sky. Its moorings partly torn away, this cornice now hung down in places, great hollow boxes of galvanized iron, hanging up there suspended on end. One great section of cornice I saw hanging above an upper window.

MODERN ARCHITECTURE

A workman hung, head downward, his foot caught, crushed on the sill of this window, by a falling beam. A red line streaked the stone wall below him and it seemed as though the hanging box of sheet-iron that a moment before had gloomed against the sky as the "classic" cornice, must tear loose by its own weight and cut him down before he could be rescued.

The spectacle of that sham feature hanging there, deadly menace to the pitifully moaning, topsy-turvy figure of a man—a working man—went far to deepen the dismay planted in a boy's heart by Victor Hugo's prophetic tale. This terrifying picture persisting in imagination gave rise to subsequent reflections. "This empty sheet-iron thing . . . a little while ago it was pretending to be stone, . . . and doing this, mind you, for the Capitol of the great State of Wisconsin, . . . what a shame!

"Somebody must have been imposed upon!

"Was it the State or perhaps the Architect himself?

"Had the Architect been cheated in that too, as well as in the collapsed piers that had let the structure down? Or was it all deliberate and everybody knew about it, but did nothing about it—did not care? Wasn't this the very thing Victor Hugo meant?"

I believed it was what he meant and began to examine cornices critically. "Why was it necessary to make them 'imitation'? If it was necessary to do that, why have them at all? Were they really beautiful or useful anyway? I couldn't see that they were particularly beautiful—except that a building looked 'strange' without one. But it looked more strange when the roof fell in and this thing called the cornice hung down endwise and was 'thin.' But that was it. . . . No matter how 'thin' it was, the cornice was put there regardless of Reality, to make the building familiar. It had no other meaning. Well, then, Victor Hugo saw this coming, did he, so long ago? . . . He foresaw that Architecture would become a sham? . . . Was it all now sham or was it just the cornice that was shamming? . . . And if they would lie about the cornice, or lie with it this way in matters of State, why wouldn't they lie about other parts of the building too . . . perhaps as a matter of taste?" And then came critical inquests held by the boy-coroner . . . the pilaster found to be another nauseating cheat. Others followed thick and fast, I remember.

48

THE PASSING OF THE CORNICE

It was early disillusionment and cruel, this vision of the life-blood of idolized architecture ebbing slowly away, vividly pointed and finally driven home by the horror of the falling building, showing the sham architecture, a preposterous bulk, threatening to take the very life of the workman himself, his life-blood already dripping away down the wall, just beneath. The poor workman became significant, himself a symbol. Both experiences, "Ceci Tuera Cela" and the wreck of the Capitol by internal collapse, did something to me for which I have never ceased to be grateful. If the old order is to be preserved—regardless—it is not well for boys to read the great poets nor see Classic buildings fall down.

Soon after this, Viollet-le-Duc's *Dictionnaire Raisonné de l'Architecture Française* fell into my hands by way of a beloved school-teacher aunt of mine and the work was finished, ready for the master to whom I came some four years later, Louis H. Sullivan—Beaux-Arts Rebel. I went to him, for one thing, because he did not believe in Cornices.

Now if the "pseudo-classic" forms of the Renaissance had had more life in them they would have died sooner and long ago have been decently buried—this in accord with Goethe's dictum that "Death is Nature's ruse in order that she may have more life." Renaissance Architecture, being but the dry bones of a life lived and dead, centuries before, the bones were left to bleach. For text, then, on this our third afternoon, our reference to authority is hereby inscribed to Moti, ancient Chinese Sage.

This inscription: "In twilight, light of the lantern, or in darkness, worship no old images nor run after new. They may arise to bind you, or, being false, betray you into bondage wherein your own shall wither." (Twilight probably meaning partial understanding; lantern-light, glamour; darkness, ignorance.)

Or another translation—Chinese is far from English:

"Except in full light of day bow down to no images, cast, graven, or builded by another, lest they, being false, betray and bind you powerless to Earth." Still another:

"Without full knowledge worship no images, lest being false they bind thee powerless to make thine own true."

And finally we have reached the title of the discourse—"The Passing of the Cornice," the image of a dead culture.

• • •   • • •   • • •

49

MODERN ARCHITECTURE

There was a Graeco-Roman feature advocated by the American Institute of Architects to finish a building at the top. This authentic feature was called the Cornice. Not so long ago no building, great or small, high or low, dignified and costly or cheap and vile, was complete without a Cornice of some sort. You may see accredited cornices still hanging on and well out over the busy streets in any American City for no good purpose whatsoever . . . really for no purpose at all. But to the elect no building looked like a building unless it had the brackets, modillions, and "fancy" fixings of this ornamental and ornamented pseudo-classic "feature." Cornices were even more significantly insignificant than it is the habit of many of the main features of our buildings to be. The Cornice was an attitude, the ornamental gesture that gave to the provincial American structure the element of hallowed "culture." That was all the significance Cornices ever had—the worship of a hypocritical theocratic "culture." Usually built up above the roof and projecting well out beyond it, hanging out from the top of the wall, they had nothing in reason to do with construction—but there the Cornice had to be. It was, somehow, become "manner"—something like lifting our hat to the ladies, or, in extreme cases, like the "leg" an acrobat makes as he kisses his hand to the audience after doing his "turn." The Cornice, in doing our "turn," became our commonplace concession to respectable "Form," thanks again to the Italians thus beset—and disturbed in their well earned Architectural slumber.

. . .   .

But, have you all noticed a change up there where the eye leaves our buildings for the sky—the "sky-line," architects call it? Observe! More sky! The Cornice has gone. Gone, we may hope, to join the procession of foolish "concessions" and vain professions that passed earlier. Gone to join the "corner-tower," the "hoop-skirt," the "bustle" and the "cupola."
Like them—gone! This shady-shabby architectural feature of our middle distance, the 'seventies, 'eighties and 'nineties, has been relegated to that mysterious scrap-heap supposedly reposing in the back-yard of oblivion. Look for a Cornice in vain anywhere on America's new buildings high or low, cheap or costly, public or private. You will hardly find one unless you are looking at some government "monument." Government, it seems, is a commitment, a rendezvous with Traditions that hang on.

50

THE PASSING OF THE CORNICE

But for a time no skyscraper—yes, it is all that recent—was complete without the Cornice. The Belmont Hotel and the Flatiron Building in New York City perhaps said the last word, took the last grand stand and made the final grand gesture in behalf of our subject. For about that time the hidden anchors that tied the pretentious feature back on some high Chicago buildings began to rust off and let this assumption-of-virtue down into the city streets to kill a few people on the sidewalks below. The people killed, happened to be "leading citizens." But for "accident" what would modern American cities be looking like, by now? Cornices cost outrageous sums, Cornices shut out the light below, but that didn't seem to hurt Cornices, much, with us. Not until Cornices became dangerous and "pseudo-classic" by way of the A.I.A. ("Arbitrary Institute of Appearances") began to crash down to city streets—did the city fathers talk "Ordinance" to the Institute. The learned architects listened, read the Ordinances, and though indignant, had no choice but to quit. Observe the relief!

Nor dare we imagine they would have dared to quit the Cornice on their own account!

• • •   • • •   • • •

Shall we see the stagey, empty frown of the Cornice glooming against the sky again? Has this cultured relic served its theatrical "turn" or are appearances for the moment *too* good to be true? Periodic "revivals" have enabled our aesthetic crimes to live so many lives that one may never be sure. But since we've learned to do without this particular "hangover" in this land of free progress and are getting used to bareheaded buildings, find the additional light agreeable, the money saved extremely useful, and as, especially, we are for "safety first," we are probably safe from the perennial Renaissance for some years to come. At any rate for the moment "the glory that was Greece, the grandeur that was Rome," ours by way of Italy, may cease turning in ancient and honorable graves. O Palladio! Vitruvius! Vignola!—be comforted —the twentieth century gives back to you your shrouds!

Ye Gods! And *that* was the American Architecture of Liberty! Yes, it was unwarranted liberty that American Architecture took.

• • •   • • •   • • •

MODERN ARCHITECTURE

We may well believe there is some subjective wave, that finally, perhaps blindly, gets buildings, costumes and customs all together in effect as civilization marches on. At least it would so seem as we look about us, for in the umbrageous Cornice-time immediately behind us, hats were extravagant cornices for human heads, just as the cornices were extravagant hats for buildings. And what about puffed sleeves, frizzes, furbelows and flounces? Didn't they go remarkably well with pilasters, architraves and rusticated walls? In fact, weren't they exactly the same thing? Even the skirts of the Cornice-period were extravagant cornices upside down over feet. And there was the "train" trailing the floor on occasion, the last word in cornices. Nor was "Dinner" in those days complete without its own peculiar "Cornice." They called it "Dessert." Many brave and agreeable men died of that less obvious "Cornice," but "Cornice" nevertheless.

And the manners of that period of grandomania! Were they not emulation of the "Cornice" when really manner? And top-heavy too, with chivalry and other thinly disguised brutalities? Now? No hat brim at all. Just a close sheath for the head. Skirts? None. Instead, a pair of silken legs sheer from rigid stilted heel to flexing knees; something scant and informal hung round the middle from above. What would have barely served as underwear in the late Cornice-days, now costume for the street. No "manner" in our best manners.

Study, by contrast, the flamboyant human and architectural silhouettes of the Cornice-period just past with the silhouettes of today. After the comparison, be as grateful as it is in your nature to be—for escape, for even the *appearance* of Simplicity.

Here comes "fashionable" penchant for the clean, significant lines of sculptural contours. Contrast these silhouettes in cars, buildings, clothing, hair dressing of today with those of the 'nineties. Even in the flower arrangements of the period of our "middle distance" and that of our immediate foreground you may see great difference. The "Bo-Kay" was what you remember it was. Now, a bouquet is a few long-stemmed flowers with artful carelessness slipped into a tall glass, or "au naturel," a single species grouped in close sculptural mass over a low bowl. Consider, too, that modern music no longer needs the Cornice. It, too, can stop without the crescendo or the grand finale, the flourish of our grandfathers, which was "classic." Yes, the Cornice was "flourish"

52

too. Curious! Jazz, all too consistently, belongs to this awakening period, to the "youth" that killed the Cornice, awakening to see that nothing ever was quite so pretentious, empty, and finally demoralizing as that pompous gesture we were taught to respect and to call the "Cornice." It had much—much too much—foreign baggage in its train, ever to be allowed to come back to America.

• • •   • • •   • • •

Should we now clearly perceive what the Cornice really meant in terms of human life, especially of our own life as dedicated to Liberty, we *would* be rid of Cornices forever. Turning instinctively from the Cornice shows our native instincts healthy enough. But we require *knowledge* of its fatality, where freedom is concerned, to insure protection from the periodic "aesthetic revival" that is successfully put over every few years just because of enterprising salesmanship and our own aimlessness. We must have a standard that will give us protection. If we know *why* we hate the Cornice now, it may never rise again to ride us or smite us some other day.

Suppose, for the sake of argument, once upon a time we *did* live in trees, lightly skipping from branch to branch, insured by our tails as we pelted each other with nuts. We dwelt sheltered from the sun and rain by the overhanging foliage of upper branches—grateful for both shelter and shade. Gratitude for that "overhead"—and the sense of it—has been with us all down the ages as the Cornice, finally become an emblem—a symbol —showed. Instinctive gratitude is of course fainter now. But whenever the Cornice, true to that primeval instinct, was *real shelter* or even the sense of it, and dropped roof-water free of the building walls—well, the Cornice was not a Cornice then but was an overhanging *roof*. Let the overhanging roof live as human shelter. It will never disappear from Architecture. The sense of Architecture as human shelter is a very fine sense—common sense, in fact.

But as soon as this good and innocent instinct became a habit, original meaning, as usual, lost by the time *usefulness* departed, the ancient and no less fashionable Doctor-of-Appearances took notice, adopted the "look" of the overhang, began to play with it, and soon the citizen began to view the overhang from the street, as *the* Cornice. If ever "the doctor" knew or ever cared what meaning the overhang ever had, the doctor soon forgot. He became "Cornice-conscious." The roof-water now ran back from the cornice on to the flat roof of the building and down inside down-spouts. But why should the doctor worry? Has the doctor of aesthetics ever worried about structural significances? No. So through him, although all had been reversed, this now obsession of the "overhead," for mere aesthetic effect, an aesthetic that had got itself into Greek and, therefore, into Roman life as Art for Art's sake, this arbitrary convention, became our accepted Academic pattern. It was all up with us then—until now.

The net result of it all is that no culture is recognizable to us as such without the Cornice. But just eliminate the troublesome and expensive feature from Greek and Roman buildings and see what happens by way of consequence. Then when you know what it meant in their buildings, just take that same concession to the academic artificiality of Tradition from their lives and see, as a consequence, what happens to "culture." You will see by what is lost, as well as by what is left, that the Cornice, as such, originally *was* Graeco-Roman culture and to such an extent that—"pasticcio-Italiano"—it has been our own "American pseudo-classic" *ever since*. Inasmuch as nearly everything institutional in our much over-instituted lives is either Roman or Graeco-Roman, we couldn't have had our chosen institutions without this cherished symbol. No, we had to do the precious Cornice too. So we did the Cornice-lie with the best of them, to the limit and far and away beyond any sense of limit at all.

Amazing! Utter artificiality become a more or less gracefully refined symbolic *lie*, the "culture" we Americans patterned and tried our best to make our own classic, too, and adored for a long, long time. Thomas Jefferson himself was blameworthy in that. George Washington no less so.

But pragmatic as the Romans were in all other matters, we may comfort ourselves a little, if there is any comfort in the fact that these same Romans, great Jurists and Executives, too, when it came to "culture," denied their own splendid engineering invention of the arch for centuries in order to hang on to the same Cornice—or more correctly speaking, to hang the Cornice on.

Not until the Roman Doctors-of-Appearances (their names are lost to us, so we cannot chastely and becomingly insult them) could conceal the Arch no longer, did they let the arch live as the Arch. Even then, in order to preserve "appearances," the doctors insisted upon running a cornice—in miniature—around over the arch itself and called the little cornice on the curve an

THE PASSING OF THE CORNICE

archivolt. They then let the matter go at that. Yes, the noble arches them-selves now had to have the cornices, and Renaissance Arches have all had cornices on their curves for several centuries or more, in fact had them on until today. Roofs were mostly now become flat or invisible. The roof-water ran back the other way. But here was the Cornice, derived from and still symbolic of the overhanging roof, continuing to hang over just the same. Yes, it was now great "Art." In other words, the cornice was secure as academic aesthetic. No one dared go behind the thing to see how and what it *really* was. It no longer mattered what it was.

Another human instinct had left home and gone wrong, but civilization sen-timentalized and made the degradation into prestige—irresistible. Professors taught the Cornice now as "good-school." Every building, more or less, had to defer to this corniced authority to be habitable or valuable. Only a radical or two in any generation dared fight such authority and usually the fight cost the radical his economic life.

But now you may look back, although the perspective is still insufficient, and see what a sham this undemocratic fetish really was, what an imposition it became, how pompously it lied to us about itself; realize how much social meanness of soul it hid and what poverty of invention on the part of great architects it cleverly concealed for many centuries. And you may now observe as you go downtown that the worst is over. Only very sophisticated Doctors-of-Appearances dare use the Cornice any more, and then the dead living dare use it only for national monuments to honor the living dead; especially have they done so for a monument to Abraham Lincoln who would have said, with Emerson, "I love and honor Epaminondas—but I do not wish to be Epaminondas. I hold it more just to love the world of this hour, than the world of *his* hour."

Here the Cornice, being by nature and derivation so inappropriate to the "great commoner," gave to the doctor his opportunity for final triumph. The doctor has now succeeded in using it where most awful—too insulting. When we see this, almost any of us—even the "Best" of us—may fully realize *why* cornices had to die, for at least "let us desire not to disgrace the Soul!"

Now, for some time to come, democratic governmental departments being what they are, it may be that America will continue to be-cornice her dead heroes, dishonor them by its impotence. But there is ample evidence at

55

MODERN ARCHITECTURE

hand on every side that the "quick," at least, have shed the Cornice. The sacred symbol is worn out—to be soon obliterated by free thought.

It is time man sealed this Tradition under a final monument. I suggest as admirable "project" for the students in Architecture at Princeton a design for this monument, and by way of epitaph:

"Here lies the most cherished liar of all the ages—Rest, that we may find Peace."

• • •   • • •   • • •

For the first six thousand years of the world, from the pagodas of Hindustan to the Cathedral of Cologne, Architecture was the great writing of mankind. Whoever then was born a poet became an Architect. All the other Arts were the workmen of the great work. The "symbol" unceasingly characterized, when it did not dogmatize, it all. Stability was an Ideal—hence a general horror of progress. What consecration there then was, was devoted to a conservation of previous primitive types.

According to the great Modern poet, neglected now, quoted at the outset of this discourse—In the Hindoo, Egyptian and Roman edifices it was always the priest . . . in the Phoenician, the merchant . . . in the Greek, the aristocratic republican . . . in the Gothic, the bourgeois. In the twentieth century—says our prophet—an Architect of genius may happen, as the accident of Dante happened in the thirteenth, although Architecture will no longer be the Social Art, the collective Art, the dominant Art. The great work of humanity it will be no longer.

But to Victor Hugo, when he spoke, Architecture was the grand residue of the great buildings that wrote the record of a theocratic, feudalistic humanity, theologic, philosophic, aristocratic. Concerning that Architecture his prophecy has come true. He foresaw Democracy as a consequence, but did not foresee the consequences of its engine—the Machine—except as that engine was symbolized by printing. He seems not to have foreseen that genius and imagination might find in the Machine mightier means than ever with which to create anew a more significant background and framework for twentieth century civilization than was ever known before. Nor foresee an Architect who might create anew in genuine Liberty—*for* great Liberty—on soil enriched by the very carcasses of the ancient Architectures. So let us take heart . . . we begin anew.

56

THE PASSING OF THE CORNICE

But instead of ourselves indulging in prophecy against prophecy, let us take hold of the Cornice at the source from which it came to us, and take it apart—in order to see what the feature actually was. It may give us something useful in our own hard case. Perhaps we may find in it something valuable to the "Modern"—in the sense that we ourselves are to be Modern or die disgraced. Of course I visited Athens—held up my hand in the clean Mediterranean air against the sun and saw the skeleton of my hand through its covering of pink flesh—saw the same translucence in the marble pillars of the aged Parthenon, and realized what "color" must have been in such light. I saw the yellow stained rocks of the barren terrain. I saw the ancient temples, barren, broken, yellow stained too, standing now magnificent in their crumbling state, more a part of that background than ever they were when born—more stoic now than allowed to be when those whose record they were had built them—more heroic, as is the Venus of Melos more beautiful without her arms. Like all who stand there, I tried to re-create the scene as it existed when pagan love of color made it come ablaze for the dark-skinned, kinky-haired, black-eyed Greeks to whom color must have been naturally the most becoming thing in life. I restored the arris of the mouldings, sharpened and perfected the detail of the cornices, obliterated the desolate grandeur of the scene with color, sound, and movement. And gradually I saw the whole as a great painted, wooden temple. Though now crumbling to original shapes of stone, so far as intelligence went at that time there were no stone forms whatever. The forms were only derived from wood! I could not make them stone, hard as I might try. Nor had the Greeks cared for that stone-quality in their buildings, for if traces found are to be trusted, and nature too, not only the forms but the marble surfaces themselves were all originally covered with decoration in gold and color. Marble sculpture was no less so covered than was the Architecture.

All sense of materials must have been lost or never have come alive to the Greeks. No such sympathy with environment as I now saw existed for them, nor had any other inspired them. No—not at all. These trabeated stone buildings harked back to what? A little study showed the horizontal lines of wooden beams, laid over vertical wooden posts, all delicately sculptured to refine and make elegant the resemblance. The pediments, especially the cornices, were the wooden projections of the timber roofs of earlier wooden tem-

57

ples, sculptured here in stone. Even the *method* of that ancient wood-construction was preserved in the more "modern" material, by way of the large, wooden beam ends that had originally rested on the wooden lintels, and by the smaller wooden beam ends that rested above those; even such details as the wooden pins that had fastened the beam structure together were here as sculptured stone ornament. Here then in all this fibrous trabeation was no organic stone building. Here was only a wooden temple as a "Tradition" embalmed—in noble material. Embalmed, it is true, with grace and refinement. But beyond that, and considering it all as something to be taken for itself, in itself, all was false—arbitrarily to preserve for posterity a tradition as arbitrary. Thought, then, in this life of the Greeks, was not so Free? The grand sculptured stone cornices of their greatest building had originally been but the timber edges and projections of an overhanging roof that was intended to drop roof-water free of the walls. Elegant refinements of proportion were not lost upon me, but there was small comfort to see recorded in them—for ever-more—that Liberty had not gone very far in thought in ancient Greece. Here at this remote day Architecture had been merely prostitution of the New as a servile concession to the high-priest of the Old Order. In the hands of the impeccable Greeks here was noble, beautiful stone insulted and forced to do duty as an imitation enslaved to wood. Well, at any rate, the beautiful marble was itself again falling back from the shame of an artificial glory upon its own, once more. Here too, then, in this triumph was tragedy!

Was all this symbolic—a mere symptom of an artificial quality of thought, an imposition of authority that condemned this high civilization of the Greeks to die? Their "elegant solutions" and philosophic abstractions beneath the beautiful surface—were they as sinister? Were they too as false to Nature as their Architecture was false? Then why had it all to be born, re-born and again and yet again—confusing, corrupting and destroying, more or less, all subsequent chance of true organic human culture? Here it seemed was subtle poison deadly to Freedom. Form and Idea or Form and Function had become separated for the Greeks, the real separation fixed upon a helpless, unthinking people, whose tool was the chattel slave. By what power did such authority exist? In any case what could there be for Democracy in this sophisticated abstraction, made by force, whether as intelligence or as power?

And then I thought of the beauty of Greek sculpture and the perfect *Vase* of the Greeks . . . . Keats' Ode to a Grecian Urn came to mind. How different the sculpture and the vase were from their architecture—and yet the same. But Phidias fortunately had the living human body for his Tradition. He was modern and his works eternal. The Vase was sculpture too, pure and simple, so it could be perfected by them. It would live and represent them at their best. And their great stone Architecture—it, too, was beautiful "sculpture" —but it had for its Architectural *Tradition* only a wooden Temple!

It should die: here today in our New Freedom, with the Machine as Liberator of the human mind, quickener of the Artist-Conscience—it is for us to bury Greek Architecture deep. For us it is pagan poison. We have greater buildings to build upon a more substantial base—an ideal of Organic Architecture, complying with the ideal of true Democracy.

Democracy is an expression of the dignity and worth of the individual; that ideal of Democracy is essentially the thought of the man of Galilee, himself an humble Architect, the Architect in those days called Carpenter. When this *unfolding* architecture as distinguished from *enfolding* architecture comes to America there will be Truth of feature, to Truth of being: individuality realized as a noble attribute of *being. That* is the character the architecture of Democracy will take and probably that architecture will be an expression of the highest form of aristocracy the world has conceived, when we analyze it. Now what Architecture? Clearly this new conception will realize Architecture as no longer the sculptured block of some building material or as any *en*folding imitation. Architecture must now *un*fold an inner content—express "life" from the "*within.*" Only a development according to Nature, an intelligently aimed at purpose, will materialize this ideal, so there is very little to help us in the old sculptural ideals of the Architecture Victor Hugo wrote about, so splendidly prophetic. And what little there is, is confined within the carved and colored corners of the world where and when it was allowed to be itself— and is underneath the surface, in far out-of-the-way places, hard to find.

But I imagine the great Romantic poet himself would be first to subscribe to this modern ideal of an organic architecture, a *creation* of industry wherein power unlimited lies ready for use by the *Modern Mind,* instead of the *creature* of chisel and hammer once held ready in the hands of the chattel slave. An Architecture no longer composed or arranged or pieced together as symbolic, but living as upstanding expression of reality. This Organic

59

architecture, too, would be so intimately a *growth*, all the while, as to make barbarous the continual destruction of the Old by the New. American Architecture, though both little and young, therefore conceives something deeper and at the same time more vital than the great Parthenon or even the beautiful Greek Vase: an Architecture no longer symbolic sculpture but a true culture that will *grow* greater buildings and *grow* more beautiful belongings true to the Nature of the thing and more at one with the Nature of Man. Radical, its roots where they belong—in the soil—this Architecture would be likely to live where all else has had to die or is dying.

Being integral this Art will not know contrasted and separate existence as Art, but will be as much "Nature" as we are ourselves natural. This should be the expression of any true Democracy. Such an ideal is nowise pagan, more nearly of the Crusades maybe—but racial or national no longer except in superficial sense. It is only the method, the proper technique in which to use our resources with new sense of materials, that remains to be realized. This realization may truly be said to be Modern: New in the thought of the coming world, in which the New and the Old shall be as one.

. . .   .

Now comes the usual feeling that this discourse has all been too free in idealization, not intimate enough realization of a very simple matter. The discourse simply means that "make-believe" is played out; that it has no longer nor ever had genuine significance as Art; that we are in a hard but hopeful case where any pretence fails to satisfy us. Something has happened in this new ideal of freedom we call America that is contagious and goes around the world. I don't even know that it belongs to us as a nation particularly, because we, being the thing itself, seem to realize it least. It is often so. Of that which a man is most, he usually speaks least unless he has to speak, and then he will tell you less than someone who is not so much the thing himself, but can see it a little apart, in perspective. We see then that in us is a deeper hunger— a hunger for integrity. For some such reason as this we are waking to see ourselves as the provincial dumping-ground for the cast-off regalia of civilization entire. We have been the village aristocracy of the great Art World—"putting on" the style we took "by taste" from the pattern-books, or saw at the movies, or admired on post-cards sent home by those who have "been abroad"

THE PASSING OF THE CORNICE

—don't you know? It never occurred to us that we had greater and more coming to us *as our own* than any of the aristocracy of art we aped and imitated ever had. But now we are beginning to see that even Colonial was a "hangover," was a cornice, a nice, neat one, but the machine soon made it nasty-nice. *Ad libitum*, intoxicated by facility of "reproduction," we ran the gamut of all the "Styles," the Machine right after us to spoil the party. What, I ask you, in all History haven't we as a "free" people made free with in the name of Art and Architecture? We have acted like hungry orphans turned loose in a bake-shop.

And like the poor orphans, too, we have a bad case of indigestion now that would kill a less young and robust adventurer in that tasty, pasty, sugary realm we have known as Art and Decoration. The confectionery we have consumed—yes, but not digested, mind you—would have mussed up the sources from which it came beyond hope of any mortal recovery.

We are sick with it and we are sick of it. Some of us for that reason, and some of us because we are growing up. It was all bad for us—the Machine made such "good taste" as we had, poisonous. Spanish was the latest acquired taste until "Modernistic" got itself here by way of the Paris market with Madame. We will soon be no better satisfied eating that layer-cake than with the other cake-eating. It is all too modish, too thin, too soon empty—too illiberal, too mean. Our dyspeptic American souls hunger for realization, for a substantial "inner experience." Something more than a mere matter of taste, a taste for cake! All we've had has been predilection in this matter of taste, and we've tasted until we're so taste full that it is only a question of "where do we go from here?"

No wonder sensible Henry says "Art is the bunk." He is right; all that *he* has known by that name is no more than what he says it is. And pretty much all that all America knows, too, is likewise. The corruption of our own sources of power and inspiration shames or amuses us when we try to go deeper. But we are going deeper now, just the same. When we get the *meaning* of our shame we are disgusted—likely we turn from it all, but we come back to it again.

We have realized that Life without Beauty accomplished is no Life; we grasp at anything that promises beauty and are somehow punished. We find that like the rose it has thorns; like the thistle, it has defenses not to be grasped that way. The old canons have lost fire and force. They no longer apply. We are lost in the face of a great adversary whose lineaments we begin to see. Destruction of the old standards we see on every side. This New thing becomes hateful—but fascinates us. As we struggle, we begin to realize that we live on it, and with it, but still we despise and fear it—nevertheless and all the more because it fascinates us.

Well—we begin to glimpse this great adversary as the instrument of a New Order. We are willing to believe there is a common sense. . . . A sense common to our time directed toward specific purpose. We see an aeroplane clean and light-winged—the lines expressing power and purpose; we see the ocean liner, stream-lined, clean and swift—expressing power and purpose. The locomotive, too—power and purpose. Some automobiles begin to look the part. Why are not buildings, too, indicative of their special purpose? The forms of things that are perfectly adapted to their function, we now observe, seem to have a superior beauty of their own. We like to look at them. Then, as it begins to dawn on us that Form follows Function—why not so in Architecture especially? We see that all features in a good building, too, should correspond to some necessity for being—the reason for them, as well as for other shapes, being found in their very purpose. Buildings are made of materials, too. Materials have a life of their own that may enter into the building to give it more life. Here certain principles show countenance. It is the countenance of Organic Simplicity. Order is coming out of Chaos. The word Organic now has a new meaning, a Spiritual one! Here is hope.

With this principle in mind we see new value in freedom because we see new value in individuality: And there is no individuality without Freedom. The plane is a plane; the steamship is a steamship; the motor-car is a motor-car, and the more they are and *look* just that thing the more beautiful we find them. Buildings, too—why not? Men too? Why not? And now we see Democracy itself in this fresh light from within as an Ideal that is consistent with all these new expressions of this new power in Freedom. We see this adversary to the Old Order, the Machine, as—at last—a sword to cut old bonds and provide escape to Freedom; we see it as the servant and saviour of the New Order—if only it be creatively used by man!

Now, how to use it?

Then—what Architecture?

62

4: THE CARDBOARD HOUSE

WOODLAWN AVENUE HOUSE
BRICK WALLS AND MULLIONS. STONE WASHES
AND WATER TABLE. FLAT TILE ROOF. COPPER
GUTTERS. PRAIRIE BASEMENT TYPE.
1906-1908

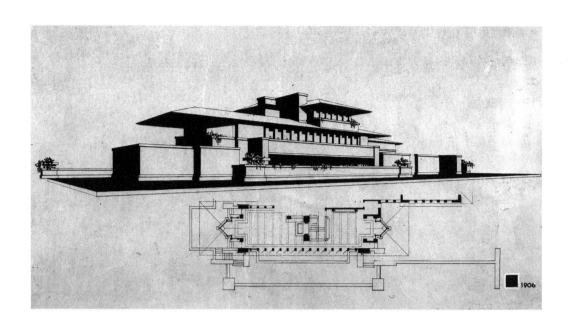

1906

4: THE CARDBOARD HOUSE

"INASMUCH as the rivalry of intelligences is the life of the beautiful—O Poet!—the first rank is ever free. Let us remove everything which may disconcert daring minds and break their wings! Art is a species of valor. To deny that men of genius to come may be the peers of the men of genius of the past would be to deny the everworking power of God!" . . .
Now what Architecture for America?

• • •   • • •   • • •

Any house is a far too complicated, clumsy, fussy, mechanical counterfeit of the human body. Electric wiring for nervous system, plumbing for bowels, heating system and fireplaces for arteries and heart, and windows for eyes, nose and lungs generally. The structure of the house, too, is a kind of cellular tissue stuck full of bones, complex now, as the confusion of Bedlam and all beside. The whole interior is a kind of stomach that attempts to digest objects—objects, "objets d'art" maybe, but objects always. There the affected affliction sits, ever hungry—for ever more objects—or plethoric with over plenty. The whole life of the average house, it seems, is a sort of indigestion. A body in ill repair, suffering indisposition—constant tinkering and doctoring to keep alive. It is a marvel, we its infestors do not go insane in it and with it. Perhaps it is a form of insanity we have put into it. Lucky we are able to get something else out of it, though we do seldom get out of it alive ourselves.

But the passing of the Cornice with its enormous "baggage" from foreign parts in its train clears the way for American homes that may be modern biography and poems instead of slanderous Liars and poetry-crushers.

A house, we like to believe, is *in statu quo* a noble consort to man and the trees; therefore the house should have repose and such texture as will quiet the whole and make it graciously at one with External Nature.

Human houses should not be like boxes, blazing in the sun, nor should we outrage the Machine by trying to make dwelling-places too complementary to Machinery. Any building for humane purposes should be an elemental, sympathetic feature of the ground, complementary to its nature-environment, belonging by kinship to the terrain. A House is not going anywhere, if we can help it. We hope it is going to stay right where it is for a long, long time. It is not yet anyway even a moving-van. Certain houses for Los Angeles may yet become vans and roll off most anywhere or everywhere, which is something else again and far from a bad idea for certain classes of our population.

But most new "modernistic" houses manage to look as though cut from cardboard with scissors, the sheets of cardboard folded or bent in rectangles with an occasional curved cardboard surface added to get relief. The cardboard forms thus made are glued together in box-like forms—in a childish attempt to make buildings resemble steamships, flying machines or locomotives. By way of a new sense of the character and power of this Machine Age, this house strips and stoops to conquer by emulating, if not imitating, machinery. But so far, I see in most of the cardboard houses of the "modernistic" movement small evidence that their designers have mastered either the machinery or the mechanical processes that build the house. I can find no evidence of integral method in their making. Of late, they are the superficial, badly built product of this superficial, New "Surface-and-Mass" Aesthetic falsely claiming French Painting as a parent. And the houses themselves are not the new working of a fundamental Architectural principle in any sense. They are little less reactionary than was the Cornice—unfortunately for Americans, looking forward, lest again they fall victim to the mode. There is, however, this much to be said for this house—by means of it imported Art and Decoration may, for a time, completely triumph over "Architecture." And such Architecture as it may triumph over—well, enough has already been said here, to show how infinitely the cardboard house is to be preferred to that form of bad surface-decoration. The Simplicity of Nature is not something which may easily be read—but is inexhaustible. Unfortunately the simplicity of these houses is too easily read—visibly an attitude, strained or forced. They are therefore decoration too. If we look into their construction we may see how construction itself has been complicated or confused, merely to arrive at exterior simplicity. Most of these houses at home and abroad are more or less badly built complements to the Machine Age, of whose principles or possibilities they show no understanding, or, if they do show such understanding to the degree of assimilating an aspect thereof, they utterly fail to make its virtues honorably or humanly effective in any final result. Forcing surface-effects upon mass-effects which try hard to resemble running or steaming or flying or fighting machines, is no radical effort in any direction. It is only more scene-painting and just another picture to prove Victor Hugo's thesis of Renaissance architecture as the setting sun—eventually passing with the Cornice.

The Machine—we are now agreed, are we not—should build the building, if the building is such that the Machine may build it naturally and therefore build it supremely well. But it is not necessary for that reason to build as though the building, too, were a Machine—because, except in a very low sense, indeed, it is not a Machine, nor at all like one. Nor in that sense of being a Machine, could it be Architecture at all! It would be difficult to make it even good decoration for any length of time. But I propose, for the purposes of popular negation of the Cornice-days that are passed and as their final kick into oblivion, we might now, for a time, make buildings resemble Modern bath-tubs and aluminum kitchen-utensils, or copy pieces of well designed machinery to live in, particularly the liner, the aeroplane, the street-car, and the motor-bus. We could trim up the trees, too, shape them into boxes—cheese or cracker—cut them to cubes and triangles or tetrahedron them and so make all kinds alike suitable consorts for such houses. And we are afraid we are eventually going to have as citizens Machine-made men, corollary to Machines, if we don't "look out"? They might be face-masqued, head-shaved, hypodermically rendered even less emotional than they are, with patent-leather put over their hair and aluminum clothes cast on their bodies, and Madam herself altogether stripped and decoratively painted to suit. This delicate harmony, characteristic of machinery, ultimately achieved, however, could not be truly affirmative, except insofar as the negation, attempted to be performed therein, is itself affirmative. It seems to me that while the engaging cardboard houses may be appropriate gestures in connection with "Now What Architecture," they are merely a negation, so not yet truly conservative in the great Cause which already runs well beyond them. *Organic simplicity* is the only simplicity that can answer for us here in America that pressing, perplexing question—Now What Architecture? This I firmly believe. It is vitally necessary to make the countenance of simplicity the affirmation of reality, lest any affectation of simplicity, should it become a mode or Fashion, may only leave this heady country refreshed for another foolish orgy in Surface decoration of the sort lasting thirty years "by authority and by order," and by means of which Democracy has already nearly ruined the look of itself for posterity, for a half-century to come, at least. Well then and again—"What Architecture?"

Let us take for text on this, our fourth afternoon, the greatest of all references to simplicity, the inspired admonition: "*Consider the lilies of the field—they toil not, neither do they spin, yet verily I say unto thee—Solomon in all his glory was not arrayed like one of these.*" An inspired saying—attributed to an humble Architect in ancient times, called Carpenter, who gave up Architecture nearly two thousand years ago to go to work upon its Source.

And if the text should seem to you too far away from our subject this afternoon—

"The Cardboard House"

—consider that for that very reason the text has been chosen. The cardboard house needs an antidote. The antidote is far more important than the house. As antidote—and as practical example, too, of the working out of an ideal of organic simplicity that has taken place here on American soil, step by step, under conditions that are your own—could I do better than to take apart for your benefit the buildings I have tried to build, to show you how they were, long ago, dedicated to the Ideal of Organic Simplicity? It seems to me that while another might do better than that, I certainly could not—for that is, truest and best, what I know about the Subject. What a man *does, that* he has.

When, "in the cause of Architecture," in 1893, I first began to build the houses, sometimes referred to by the thoughtless as "The New School of the Middle West," (some advertisers' slogan comes along to label everything in this our busy woman's country), the only way to simplify the awful building in vogue at the time was to conceive a finer entity—a better building—and get it built. The buildings standing then were all tall and all tight. Chimneys were lean and taller still, sooty fingers threatening the sky. And beside them, sticking up by way of dormers through the cruelly sharp, saw-tooth roofs, were the attics for "help" to swelter in. Dormers were elaborate devices, cunning little buildings complete in themselves, stuck to the main roof slopes to let "help" poke heads out of the attic for air.

THE CARDBOARD HOUSE

Invariably the damp sticky clay of the prairie was dug out for a basement under the whole house, and the rubble-stone walls of this dank basement always stuck up above the ground a foot or more and blinked, with half-windows. So the universal "cellar" showed itself as a bank of some kind of masonry running around the whole house, for the house to sit up on—like a chair. The lean, upper house-walls of the usual two floors above this stone or brick basement were wood, set on top of this masonry-chair, clapboarded and painted, or else shingled and stained, preferably shingled and mixed, up and down, all together with mouldings crosswise. These overdressed wood house-walls had, cut in them—or cut out of them, to be precise— big holes for the big cat and little holes for the little cat to get in and out or for ulterior purposes of light and air. The house-walls were be-corniced or bracketed up at the top into the tall, purposely profusely complicated roof, dormers plus. The whole roof, as well as the roof as a whole, was scalloped and ridged and tipped and swanked and gabled to madness before they would allow it to be either shingled or slated. The whole exterior was be-deviled— that is to say, mixed to puzzle-pieces, with corner-boards, panel-boards, window-frames, corner-blocks, plinth-blocks, rosettes, fantails, ingenious and jigger work in general. This was the only way they seemed to have, then, of "putting on style." The scroll-saw and turning-lathe were at the moment the honest means of this fashionable mongering by the wood-butcher and to this entirely "moral" end. Unless the householder of the period were poor indeed, usually an ingenious corner-tower on his house eventuated into a candle-snuffer dome, a spire, an inverted rutabaga or radish or onion or—what is your favorite vegetable? Always elaborate bay-windows and fancy porches played "ring around a rosy" on this "imaginative" corner feature. And all this the building of the period could do equally well in brick or stone. It was an impartial society. All material looked pretty much alike in that day. Simplicity was as far from all this scrap-pile as the pandemonium of the barn-yard is far from music. But it was easy for the Architect. All he had to do was to call: "Boy, take down No. 37, and put a bay-window on it for the lady!" So—the first thing to do was to get rid of the attic and, therefore, of the dormer and of the useless "heights" below it. And next, get rid of the un-wholesome basement, entirely—yes, absolutely—in any house built on the prairie. Instead of lean, brick chimneys, bristling up from steep roofs to hint at "judgment" everywhere, I could see necessity for one only, a broad generous one, or at most, for two, these kept low down on gently sloping roofs or perhaps flat roofs. The big fireplace below, inside, became now a place for a real fire, justified the great size of this chimney outside. A real fireplace at that time was extraordinary. There were then "mantels" instead. A mantel was a marble frame for a few coals, or a piece of wooden furniture with tiles stuck in it and a "grate," the whole set slam up against the wall. The "mantel" was an insult to comfort, but the *integral* fireplace became an important part of the building itself in the houses I was allowed to build out there on the prairie. It refreshed me to see the fire burning deep in the masonry of the house itself.

Taking a human being for my scale, I brought the whole house down in height to fit a normal man; believing in no other scale, I broadened the mass out, all I possibly could, as I brought it down into spaciousness. It has been said that were I three inches taller (I am 5' 8½" tall), all my houses would have been quite different in proportion. Perhaps.

House-walls were now to be started at the ground on a cement or stone watertable that looked like a low platform under the building, which it usually was, but the house-walls were stopped at the second story window-sill level, to let the rooms above come through in a continuous window-series, under the broad eaves of a gently sloping, overhanging roof. This made enclosing screens out of the lower walls as well as light screens out of the second story walls. Here was true *enclosure of interior space*. A new sense of building, it seems.

The climate, being what it was, a matter of violent extremes of heat and cold, damp and dry, dark and bright, I gave broad protecting roof-shelter to the whole, getting back to the original purpose of the "Cornice." The undersides of the roof projections were flat and light in color to create a glow of reflected light that made the upper rooms not dark, but delightful. The over-hangs had double value, shelter and preservation for the walls of the house as well as diffusion of reflected light for the upper story, through the "light screens" that took the place of the walls and were the windows.

At this time, a house to me was obvious primarily as interior space under fine *shelter*. I liked the sense of shelter in the "look of the building." I achieved it, I believe. I then went after the variegated bands of material in the old walls to eliminate odds and ends in favor of one material and a single surface from

70

THE CARDBOARD HOUSE

grade to eaves, or grade to second story sill-cope, treated as simple enclosing screens,—or else made a plain screen band around the second story above the window-sills, turned up over on to the ceiling beneath the eaves. This screen band was of the same material as the under side of the eaves themselves, or what architects call the "soffit." The planes of the building parallel to the ground were all stressed, to grip the whole to earth. Sometimes it was possible to make the enclosing wall below this upper band of the second story, from the second story window-sill clear down to the ground, a heavy "wainscot" of fine masonry material resting on the cement or stone platform laid on the foundation. I liked that wainscot to be of masonry material when my clients felt they could afford it.

As a matter of form, too, I liked to see the projecting base, or water-table, set out over the foundation walls themselves—as a substantial preparation for the building. This was managed by setting the studs of the walls to the inside of the foundation walls, instead of to the outside. All door and window tops were now brought into line with each other with only comfortable head-clearance for the average human being. Eliminating the sufferers from the "attic" enabled the roofs to lie low. The house began to associate with the ground and become natural to its prairie site. And would the young man in architecture ever believe that this was all "new" then? Not only new, but destructive heresy—or ridiculous eccentricity. So New that what little prospect I had of ever earning a livelihood by making houses was nearly wrecked. At first, "they" called the houses "dress-reform" houses, because Society was just then excited about that particular "reform." This simplification looked like some kind of "reform" to them. Oh, they called them all sorts of names that cannot be repeated, but "they" never found a better term for the work unless it was "Horizontal Gothic," "Temperance Architecture" (with a sneer), etc., etc. I don't know how I escaped the accusation of another "Renaissance."

What I have just described was all on the *outside* of the house and was there chiefly because of what had happened *inside*. Dwellings of that period were "cut-up," advisedly and completely, with the grim determination that should go with any cutting process. The "interiors" consisted of boxes beside or inside other boxes, called *rooms*. All boxes inside a complicated boxing. Each domestic "function" was properly box to box. I could see little sense in this inhibition, this cellular sequestration that implied ancestors familiar with the cells of penal institutions, except for the privacy of bed-rooms on the upper floor. They were perhaps all right as "sleeping boxes." So I declared the whole lower floor as one room, cutting off the kitchen as a laboratory, putting servants' sleeping and living quarters next to it, semi-detached, on the ground floor, screening various portions in the big room, for certain domestic purposes—like dining or reading, or receiving a formal caller. There were no plans like these in existence at the time and my clients were pushed toward these ideas as helpful to a solution of the vexed servant-problem. Scores of doors disappeared and no end of partition. They liked it, both clients and servants. The house became more free as "space" and more livable, too. Interior spaciousness began to dawn.

Having got what windows and doors there were left lined up and lowered to convenient human height, the ceilings of the rooms, too, could be brought over on to the walls, by way of the horizontal, broad bands of plaster on the walls above the windows, the plaster colored the same as the room ceilings. This would bring the ceiling-surface down to the very window tops. The ceilings thus expanded, by extending them downward as the wall band above the windows, gave a generous overhead to even small rooms. The sense of the whole was broadened and made plastic, too, by this expedient. The enclosing walls and ceilings were thus made to flow together.

Here entered the important element of Plasticity—indispensable to successful use of the Machine, the true expression of Modernity. The outswinging windows were fought for because the casement window associated the house with out-of-doors—gave free openings, outward. In other words the so-called "casement" was simple and more human. In use and effect, more natural. If it had not existed I should have invented it. It was not used at that time in America, so I lost many clients because I insisted upon it when they wanted the "guillotine" or "double-hung" window then in use. The guillotine was not simple nor human. It was only expedient. I used it once in the Winslow House—my first house—and rejected it thereafter—forever. Nor at that time did I entirely eliminate the wooden trim. I did make it "plastic," that is, light and continuously flowing instead of the heavy "cut and butt" of the usual carpenter work. No longer did the "trim," so called, look like carpenter work. The machine could do it perfectly well as I laid it out. It was all after "quiet."

72

THE CARDBOARD HOUSE

This plastic trim, too, with its running "back-hand" enabled poor workmanship to be concealed. It was necessary with the field resources at hand at that time to conceal much. Machinery versus the union had already demoralized the workmen. The Machine resources were so little understood that extensive drawings had to be made merely to show the "mill-man" what to leave off. But the "trim" finally became only a single, flat, narrow, horizontal wood-band running around the room, one at the top of the windows and doors and another next to the floors, both connected with narrow, vertical, thin wood-bands that were used to divide the wall-surfaces of the whole room smoothly and flatly into folded color planes. The trim merely completed the window and door openings in this same plastic sense. When the interior had thus become wholly plastic, instead of structural, a New element, as I have said, had entered Architecture. Strangely enough an element that had not existed in Architectural History before. Not alone in the trim, but in numerous ways too tedious to describe in words, this revolutionary sense of the plastic whole, an instinct with me at first, began to work more and more intelligently and have fascinating, unforeseen consequ ences. Here was something that began to organize itself. When several houses had been finished and compared with the house of the period, there was very little of that house left standing. Nearly every one had stood the house of the period as long as he could stand it, judging by appreciation of the change. Now all this probably tedious description is intended to indicate directly in bare outline how thus early there *was* an ideal of organic simplicity put to work, with historical consequences, here in your own country. The main motives and indications were (and I enjoyed them all):

First—   To reduce the number of necessary parts of the house and the separate rooms to a minimum, and make all come together as enclosed space—so divided that light, air and vista permeated the whole with a sense of unity.

Second— To associate the building as a whole with its site by extension and emphasis of the planes parallel to the ground, but keeping the floors off the best part of the site, thus leaving that better part for use in connection with the life of the house. Extended level planes were found useful in this connection.

Third— To eliminate the room as a box and the house as another by making all walls enclosing screens—the ceilings and floors and enclosing screens to flow into each other as one large enclosure of space, with minor subdivisions only.

Make all house proportions more liberally human, with less wasted space in structure, and structure more appropriate to material, and so the whole more livable. *Liberal* is the best word. Extended straight lines or stream-lines were useful in this.

Fourth— To get the unwholesome basement up out of the ground, entirely above it, as a low pedestal for the living-portion of the home, making the foundation itself visible as a low masonry platform on which the building should stand.

Fifth— To harmonize all necessary openings to "outside" or to "inside" with good human proportions and make them occur naturally— singly or as a series in the scheme of the whole building. Usually they appeared as "light-screens" instead of walls, because all the "Architecture" of the house was chiefly the way these openings came in such walls as were grouped about the rooms as enclosing screens. The *room* as such was now the essential architectural expression, and there were to be no holes cut in walls as holes are cut in a box, because this was not in keeping with the ideal of "plastic." Cutting holes was violent.

Sixth— To eliminate combinations of different materials in favor of mono-material so far as possible; to use no ornament that did not come out of the nature of materials to make the whole building clearer and more expressive as a place to live in, and give the conception of the building appropriate revealing emphasis. Geometrical or straight lines were natural to the machinery at work in the building trades then, so the interiors took on this character naturally.

Seventh—To incorporate all heating, lighting, plumbing so that these systems became constituent parts of the building itself. These service features became architectural and in this attempt the ideal of an organic architecture was at work.

74

THE CARDBOARD HOUSE

Eighth— To incorporate as organic Architecture—so far as possible—furnishings, making them all one with the building and designing them in simple terms for machine work. Again straight lines and rectilinear forms.

Ninth— Eliminate the Decorator. He was all curves and all efflorescence, if not all "period."

This was all rational enough so far as the thought of an organic architecture went. The particular forms this thought took in the feeling of it all could only be personal. There was nothing whatever at this time to help make them what they were. All seemed to be the most natural thing in the world and grew up out of the circumstances of the moment. Whatever they may be worth in the long run is all they are worth.

Now *simplicity* being the point in question in this early constructive effort, organic simplicity I soon found to be a matter of true coordination. And Beauty I soon felt to be a matter of the sympathy with which such coordination was effected. Plainness was not necessarily simplicity. Crude furniture of the Roycroft-Stickley-Mission Style, which came along later, was offensively plain, plain as a barn door—but never was simple in any true sense. Nor, I found, were merely machine-made things in themselves simple. To think "in simple," is to deal in simples, and that means with an eye single to the altogether. This, I believe, is the secret of simplicity. Perhaps we may truly regard nothing at all as simple in itself. I believe that no one thing in itself is ever so, but must achieve simplicity (as an Artist should use the term) as a perfectly realized part of some organic whole. Only as a feature or any part becomes an harmonious element in the harmonious whole does it arrive at the estate of simplicity. Any wild flower is truly simple, but double the same wild flower by cultivation, it ceases to be so. The *scheme* of the original is no longer clear. Clarity of design and perfect significance both are first essentials of the spontaneously born simplicity of the lilies of the field who neither toil nor spin, as contrasted with Solomon who had "toiled and spun"—that is to say, no doubt had put on himself and had put on his temple, properly "composed," everything in the category of good things but the cook-stove.

MODERN ARCHITECTURE

Five lines where three are enough is stupidity. Nine pounds where three are sufficient is stupidity. But to eliminate expressive words that intensify or vivify meaning in speaking or writing is not simplicity; nor is similar elimination in Architecture simplicity—it, too, may be stupidity. In Architecture, expressive changes of surface, emphasis of line and especially textures of material, may go to make facts eloquent, forms more significant. Elimination, therefore, may be just as meaningless as elaboration, perhaps more often is so. I offer any fool, for an example.

To know what to leave out and what to put in, just where and just how—Ah, *that* is to have been educated in knowledge of SIMPLICITY.

As for Objects of Art in the house even in that early day they were the "bête noir" of the new simplicity. If well chosen, well enough in the house, but only if each was properly digested by the whole. Antique or modern sculpture, paintings, pottery, might become objectives in the Architectural scheme and I accepted them, aimed at them, and assimilated them. Such things may take their places as elements in the design of any house. They are then precious things, gracious and good to live with. But it is difficult to do this well. Better, if it may be done, to design all features together. At that time, too, I tried to make my clients see that furniture and furnishings, not built in as integral features of the building, should be designed as attributes of whatever furniture was built in and should be seen as minor parts of the building itself, even if detached or kept aside to be employed on occasion. But when the building itself was finished, the old furniture the clients already possessed went in with them to await the time when the interior might be completed. Very few of the houses were, therefore, anything but painful to me after the clients moved in and, helplessly, dragged the horrors of the old order along after them.

But I soon found it difficult, anyway, to make some of the furniture in the "abstract"; that is, to design it as architecture and make it "human" at the same time—fit for human use. I have been black and blue in some spot, somewhere, almost all my life from too intimate contacts with my own furniture. Human beings must group, sit or recline—confound them—and they must dine, but dining is much easier to manage and always was a great artistic opportunity. Arrangements for the informality of sitting comfortably, singly or in groups, where it is desirable or natural to sit, and still to belong in disarray to the scheme as a whole—that is a matter difficult to accomplish. But it can be done now, and should be done, because only those attributes of human comfort and convenience, made to belong in this digested or integrated sense to the architecture of the home as a whole, should be there at all, in Modern Architecture. For that matter about four-fifths of the contents of nearly every home could be given away with good effect to that home. But the things given away might go on to poison some other home. So why not at once destroy undesirable things . . . make an end of them?

Here then, in foregoing outline, is the gist of America's contribution to Modern American Architecture as it was already under way in 1893. But the gospel of elimination is one never preached enough. No matter how much preached, Simplicity is a spiritual ideal seldom organically reached. Nevertheless, by assuming the virtue by imitation—or by increasing structural makeshifts to get superficial simplicity—the effects may cultivate a taste that will demand the reality in course of time, but it may also destroy all hope of the real thing.

Standing here, with the perspective of long persistent effort in the direction of an organic Architecture in view, I can again assure you out of this initial experience that Repose is the reward of true simplicity and that organic simplicity is sure of Repose. Repose is the highest quality in the Art of Architecture, next to integrity, and a reward for integrity. Simplicity may well be held to the fore as a spiritual ideal, but when actually achieved, as in the "lilies of the field," it is something that comes of itself, something spontaneously born out of the nature of the doing whatever it is that is to be done. Simplicity, too, is a reward for fine feeling and straight thinking in working a principle, well in hand, to a consistent end. Solomon knew nothing about it, for he was only wise. And this, I think, is what Jesus meant by the text we have chosen for this discourse—"Consider the lilies of the field," as contrasted, for beauty, with Solomon.

Now, a chair *is* a machine to sit in.

A home *is* a machine to live in.

The human body *is* a machine to be worked by will.

A tree *is* a machine to bear fruit.

A plant *is* a machine to bear flowers and seeds.

And, as I've admitted before somewhere, a heart *is* a suction-pump. Does that idea thrill you?

Trite as it is, it may be as well to think it over because the *least* any of these things may be, *is* just that. All of them are that before they are anything else. And to violate that mechanical requirement in any of them is to finish before anything of higher purpose can happen. To ignore the fact is either sentimentality or the prevalent insanity. Let us acknowledge in this respect, that this matter of mechanics is just as true of the work of Art as it is true of anything else. But, were we to stop with that trite acknowledgment, we should only be living in a low, rudimentary sense. This skeleton rudiment accepted, *understood*, is the first condition of any fruit or flower we may hope to get from ourselves. Let us continue to call this flower and fruit of ourselves, even in this Machine Age, ART. Some Architects, as we may see, now consciously acknowledge this "Machine" rudiment. Some will eventually get to it by circuitous mental labor. Some *are* the thing itself without question and already in need of "treatment." But "Americans" (I prefer to be more specific and say "Usonians") have been educated "blind" to the higher human uses of it all— while actually in sight of this higher human use all the while.

Therefore, now let the declaration that "all is machinery" stand nobly forth for what it is worth. But why not more profoundly declare that "Form follows Function" and let it go at that? Saying, "Form follows Function," is not only deeper, it is clearer, and it goes further in a more comprehensive way to say the thing to be said, because the implication of this saying includes the heart of the whole matter. It may be that Function follows Form, as, or if, you prefer, but it is easier thinking with the first proposition just as it is easier to stand on your feet and nod your head than it would be to stand on your head and nod your feet. Let us not forget that the Simplicity of the Universe is very different from the Simplicity of a Machine.

New significance in Architecture implies new materials qualifying form and textures, requires fresh feeling, which will eventually qualify both as "ornament." But "Decoration" must be sent on its way or now be given the meaning that it has lost, if it is to stay. Since "Decoration" became acknowledged as such, and ambitiously set up for itself as Decoration, it has been a makeshift, in the light of this ideal of Organic Architecture. Any House Decoration, as such, is an architectural makeshift, however well it may be done, unless the decoration, so called, is part of the Architect's design in both concept and execution.

Since Architecture in the old sense died and Decoration has had to shift for itself more and more, all so-called Decoration is become *ornamental*, therefore no longer *integral*. There can be no true simplicity in either Architecture or Decoration under any such condition. Let Decoration, therefore, die for Architecture, and the Decorator become an Architect, but not an "Interior Architect."

Ornament can never be applied to Architecture any more than Architecture should ever be applied to Decoration. All ornament, if not developed within the nature of Architecture and as organic part of such expression, vitiates the whole fabric no matter how clever or beautiful it may be as something in itself.

Yes—for a century or more Decoration has been setting up for itself, and in our prosperous country has come pretty near to doing very well, thank you. I think we may say that it is pretty much all we have now to show as Domestic Architecture, as Domestic Architecture still goes with us at the present time. But we may as well face it. The Interior Decorator thrives with us because we have no Architecture. Any Decorator is the natural enemy of organic simplicity in Architecture. He, persuasive Doctor-of-Appearances that he *must* be when he becomes Architectural substitute, will give you an imitation of anything, even an imitation of imitative simplicity. Just at the moment, May 1930, he is expert in this imitation. France, the born Decorator, is now engaged with "Madame," owing to the good fortune of the French market, in selling us this ready-made or made-to-order simplicity. Yes, Imitation Simplicity is the latest addition to imported "stock." The Decorators of America are now equipped to furnish *especially* this. Observe. And how very charming the suggestions conveyed by these imitations sometimes are!

Would you have again the general principles of the spiritual-ideal of organic simplicity at work in our Culture? If so, then let us reiterate: First, Simplicity is Constitutional Order. And it is worthy of note in this connection that 9 x 9 equals 81 is just as simple as 2 plus 2 equals 4. Nor is the obvious more simple necessarily than the occult. The obvious is obvious simply because it falls within our special horizon, is therefore easier for us to *see;* that is all. Yet all simplicity near or far has a countenance, a visage, that is characteristic. But this countenance is visible only to those who can grasp the whole and enjoy the significance of the minor part, as such, in relation to the whole when in flower. This is for the critics.

This characteristic visage may be simulated—the real complication glossed over, the internal conflict hidden by surface and belied by mass. The internal complication may be and usually is increased to create the semblance of and get credit for—simplicity. This is the Simplicity-lie usually achieved by most of the "surface and mass" architects. This is for the young architect.

Truly ordered simplicity in the hands of the great artist may flower into a bewildering profusion, exquisitely exuberant, and render all more clear than ever. Good William Blake says exuberance is *beauty*, meaning that it is so in this very sense. This is for the Modern Artist with the Machine in his hands.

False Simplicity—Simplicity as an affectation, that is, Simplicity constructed as a Decorator's *outside* put upon a complicated, wasteful engineer's or carpenter's "Structure," outside or inside—is not good enough Simplicity. It cannot be simple at all. But that is what passes for Simplicity, now that startling Simplicity-effects are becoming the *fashion*. That kind of Simplicity is *violent*. This is for "Art and Decoration."

Soon we shall want Simplicity inviolate. There is one way to get that Simplicity. My guess is, there is *only* one way really to get it. And that way is, on principle, by way of *Construction* developed as Architecture. That is for us, one and all.

5: THE TYRANNY OF THE SKYSCRAPER

BOCK ATELIERS
CONCRETE. SLAB ROOF. STONE WASHES
AND WATER TABLE. WINDOWS WRAPPING
CORNERS TO EXPRESS INTERIOR SPACE.
1902.

1902

5: THE TYRANNY OF THE SKYSCRAPER

MICHELANGELO built the first skyscraper, I suppose, when he hurled the Pantheon on top of the Parthenon. The Pope named it St. Peter's and the world called it a day, celebrating the great act ever since in the sincerest form of human flattery possible. As is well known, that form is imitation.

Buonarroti, being a sculptor himself (he was painter also but, unluckily, painted pictures of sculpture), probably thought Architecture, too, ought to be Sculpture. So he made the grandest statue he could conceive out of Italian Renaissance Architecture. The new church dome that was the consequence was empty of meaning or of any significance whatever except as the Pope's mitre has it. But, in fact, the great dome was just the sort of thing authority had been looking for as a symbol. The world saw it, accepted and adopted it as the great symbol of great Authority. And so it has flourished as this symbol ever since, not only in the great capitals of the great countries of the world, but, alas, in every division of *this* country, in every State, in every county, in every municipality thereof.

From general to particular the imitation proceeds, from the dome of the National Capitol itself to the dome of the State Capitol. From the State Capitol to the dome of the County Court House, and then from the County Court House on down to the dome of the City Hall. Everywhere the symbol leaves us, for our authority, in debt to Michelangelo for life. Great success the world calls this and Arthur Brisbane calls it Great Art. Many institutions of learning also adopted the dome. Universities themselves affected it until they preferred Gothic. Big business, I suspect, covets it and would like to take it. But to its honor be it said that it has not yet done so. Yes—this is success. Probably every other sculptor who ever lived would like to have done or to do the thing that Michelangelo did.

Yet, as consequence of a great sculptor's sense of grandeur in an Art that was not quite his own, we may see a tyranny that might well make the tyrannical skyscraper of the present day sway in its socket sick with envy, although the tyrannical dome is by no means so cruel as the tyrannical skyscraper. But the tyrannical dome *is* more magniloquent waste. How tragic

83

it all is! It is not only as though Buonarroti himself had never seen the Grand Canyon, which of course he never could have seen, but it is as though no one else had ever seen it either, and monumental buildings therefore kept right on being domeous, domicular or dome-istic—on stilts because they knew no better.

Domed or damned was and is the status of official buildings in all countries, especially in ours, as a consequence of the great Italian's impulsive indiscretion. But no other individual sculptor, painter or architect, let us hope, may ever achieve such success again, or Architecture at the end of its resources may pass out in favor of something else.

It would be interesting to me to know what Buonarroti would think of it now. But it is too late. We shall never know except as we imagine it for ourselves.

We should have to ignore the cradle-of-the-race, Persia, even Rome itself, to say that the sculptor did more than appropriate the dome. The earlier Romans had already made flat ones thrusting against the building walls, and the domes of Persia, relatively modest, though seated deep in the building, were tall and very beautiful. Stamboul and Hagia Sophia of course make St. Peter's look like the scrap-pile of reborn posts, pilasters and mouldings of the Graeco-Roman sort that it is.

But Buonarroti got his dome up higher than all others—got it out of the building itself up onto stilts! Ah! that was better. History relates, however, that a hurry-up call had to be sent in at the last moment for the blacksmith. A grand chain was needed, and needed in a hurry, too, to keep this monumental grandeur, up there where it was, long enough for it to do its deadly work. While they were getting this grand chain fastened around the haunches of the grand dome, in jeopardy on its stilts, our hero, the truly great sculptor, deeply, or rather highly, in trouble with Architecture, must have known some hours of anguish such as only Architects can ever know.

I can imagine the relief with which he crawled into bed when all was secure, and slept for thirty-six hours without turning over. This contribution "by the greatest artist who ever lived"—Arthur Brisbane says that is what he is —was our grandest heritage from the rebirth of Architecture in Italy, called the Renaissance, and countless billions it has cost us to brag like that.

84

THE TYRANNY OF THE SKYSCRAPER

But all triumph, humanly speaking, is short-lived and we ourselves have found a new way to play hobby-horse with the Renaissance—a way particularly our own, and now we, in our time, astonish the world similarly. We are not putting a dome up on stilts—no, but we are carrying the stilts themselves on up higher than the dome ever stood and hanging reborn Architecture, or Architecture-soon-to-be-born, all over the steel, chasing up and down between the steel-stilts in automatic machines at the rate of a mile a minute, until the world gasps, votes our innovation a success, and imitates. Another worldly success, but not this time empty in the name of grandeur. By no means, we are no longer like that. We are doing it for money, mind you—charging off whatever deficit may arise in connection therewith to Advertising Account.

We are now, ourselves, running races up into the sky for advertising purposes, not necessarily advertising authority now but still nobly experimenting with human lives, meantime carrying the herd-instinct to its logical conclusion. Eventually, I fervently hope, carrying the aforesaid instinct to its destruction by giving it all that is coming to it so that it will have to get out into the country where it belongs—and stay there, for the city will be no more, having been "done to death."

Our peculiar invention, the skyscraper, began on our soil when Louis H. Sullivan came through the door that connected my little cubicle with his room in the Auditorium Tower, pushed a drawing-board with a stretch of manila paper upon it over onto my draughting-table, and, without a word, went back again into his own room and closed the door behind him.

There it was, in delicately pencilled elevation. I stared at it and sensed what had happened. It was the Wainwright Building—and there was the very first human expression of a tall steel office-building as Architecture. It was tall and consistently so—a unit, where all before had been one cornice building on top of another cornice building. This was a greater achievement than the Papal Dome, I believe, because here was utility become beauty by sheer truimph of imaginative vision.

Here out of chaos came one harmonious thing in service of human need where artist-ingenuity had struggled with discord in vain. The vertical walls were vertical screens, the whole emphatically topped by a broad band of ornament fencing the top story, resting above the screens and thrown into shade

MODERN ARCHITECTURE

by an extension of the roof-slab that said, emphatically, *"finished."* The extension of the slab had no business to say "finished," or anything else, so emphatically above the city streets, but that was a minor matter soon corrected. The Skyscraper as a piece of Architecture had arrived.

About the same time John Wellborn Root conceived a tall building that was a unit—The Monadnock. But it was a solid-walled brick building with openings cut out of the walls. The brick, however, was carried across openings on concealed steel angles and the flowing contours, or profile, unnatural to brick work was got by forcing the material—hundreds of special moulds for special bricks being made—to work out the curves and slopes. Both these buildings therefore had their faults. But the Wainwright Building has characterized all skyscrapers since, as St. Peter's characterized all domes, with this difference: there was synthetic Architectural stuff in the Wainwright Building, it was in the line of organic Architecture—St. Peter's was only grandiose Sculpture.

• • •   • • •   • • •

A man in a congested downtown New York street, not long ago, pointed to a vacant city lot where steam shovels were excavating. "I own it," he said, in answer to a question from a man next to him (the man happened to be me), "and I own it clear all the way up," making an upward gesture with his hand. Yes—he did own it, "all the way up," and he might have added, too, "all the way down through to the other side of the world." But then he might have thoughtfully qualified it by, "at least through to the center of the earth." Yes, there stood His Majesty, legal ownership. Not only was he legally free to sell his lucky lot in the landlord lottery to increase this congestion of his neighbors "all the way up," but he was blindly encouraged by the great city itself to do so, in favor of super-concentration. The city, then, gets a thrill out of "going tall"? Architects, advertising as wholesale "manufacturers of space for rent," are advocating tall, taller and tallest, in behalf of their hardy clients. Inventive genius, too, properly invited, aids and abets them all together, until this glorious patriotic enterprise, space-making for rent, is looked upon as bona-fide proof of American progress and greatness. The space-makers-for-rent say skyscrapers solve the problem of congestion, and might honestly add, create congestion, in order to solve it some more some other day, until it will all probably dissolve out into the country, as in-

86

evitable reaction. Meantime, these Machine-made solutions with an ancient architectural look about them all, like the Buonarroti dome, are foolishly imitated out on the western prairies and in the desolate mountain States. In large or even in smaller and perhaps even in very small towns, you may now see both together.

Our modern steel Goliath has strayed as far away from native moorings as Tokio, Japan, where it is almost as appropriate to that country as the Cornice is appropriate to Abraham Lincoln, in our own.

This apotheosis of the landlord may be seen now as another tyranny—The Tyranny of the Skyscraper. It is true, so it seems, that "it is only on extremes that the indolent popular mind can rest."

Having established an approximate form for these lectures—a preliminary amble in the direction of the subject, then a reference to authority as text, then the discourse and a conclusion to lay it finally before you, all in the good old manner of my father's sermons—let us keep the form, choosing as text this time: "Do unto others as ye would that others should do unto you." The attribution is universally known. But not so well known perhaps is the command by MOTI, the CHINESE SAGE: "Do yourselves that which you would have others do themselves."

THE TYRANNY OF THE SKYSCRAPER

It has only just begun, but we may observe that Father Knickerbocker's Village, to choose our most conspicuous instance, is already gone so far out of drawing, beyond human scale, that—become the great Metropolis—it is no good place in which to live, to do good work in, or wherein even to go to market. This, notwithstanding the stimulus or excitation of the herd-instinct that curses the whole performance. "The only way to cross the street in New York City now is to be born on the other side," one of her own has recently said.

None the less—in fact just because of this—the price of ground that happens to be caught in the urban drift as it runs uptown in a narrow streak—no doubt to rush back again—soars just because the lucky areas may be multiplied by as many times as it is possible to sell over and over again the original ground area—thanks to the mechanical device of the skyscraper. The ground area used to be multiplied by ten, it was soon multiplied by fifty, and it may now be multiplied by one hundred or more. Meantime, we patiently pass over wide, relatively empty spaces in the city to get from one such congested area to another such congested area, waiting patiently, I suppose, until the very congestion, which is the source of inflated values, overreaches itself by solution and the very congestion it was built to serve severely interferes with and finally curses its own sacred sales-privilege. New York, even at this very early stage of the high and narrow, speaks of the traffic problem, openly confessing such congestion—though guardedly. And as congestion must rapidly increase, metropolitan misery has merely begun. Yes—merely begun—for should every owner of a lot contiguous to or even already within the commercially exploited areas, not to mention those hopefully lying empty in between, actually take advantage of this opportunity to soar, all upward flights of ownership would soon become useless and worthless. This must be obvious to any one. Moreover the occupants of the tall buildings are yet only about one-third the motor-car men that all will eventually emerge if their devotion to machine-made concentration means anything profitable to them.

So only those congestion-promoters with their space-manufacturers and congestion-solvers who came first, or who will now make haste, with their extended telescopes, uplifted elephant-trunks, Bedford-stone rockets, Gothic toothpicks, modern fountain pens, and "Eversharps" shrieking verticality, selling perpendicularity to the earthworms in the village lane below, can ever be served. Nevertheless property owners lost between the luck, continue to capitalize their undeveloped ground on the same basis as the man lucky enough to have got up first into the air. So fictitious land-values are created on paper. Owing to the vogue of the skyscraper, real estate values boom on a false basis, and to hold and handle these unreal values, now aggravated by the machine-made, standard solution, subways—sub-subways—are proposed, and super sidewalks, or super, super sidewalks or double-decked or triple-decked streets. Proposals are made to set all the fair forest of buildings up out of reach of the traffic on their own fair stilts as a concession to the crowd. The human life flowing in and out of all this crowded perpendicularity is to accommodate itself to growth as of potato sprouts in a cellar. Yes—these super-most solutions are seriously proposed to hold and handle landlord *profits* in a dull craze for verticality and vertigo that concentrates the citizen in an exaggerated super-concentration that would have shocked Babylon—and have made the tower of Babel itself fall down to the ground and worship.

"To have and to hold," that is now the dire problem of the skyscraper minded. Just why it should be unethical or a weakness to allow this terrific concentration to relieve itself by spreading out is quite clear. Anyone can see why. And to show to what lengths the landlord is willing and prepared to go to prevent it: as superior and philanthropic a landlord as Gordon Strong of Chicago recently argued—as the Germans originally suggested—the uselessness of the freedom of sun and air, claiming artificial ventilation and lighting now preferable, demanding that walls be built without windows, rooms be hermetically sealed, distribution and communication be had by artificially lighted and ventilated tunnels, subways and super-ways. Here, on behalf of the landlord, by way of the time-serving space-maker-for-rent, we arrive at the "City of Night": Man at last and all so soon enslaved by, and his very life at the mercy of, his own appliances.

A logical conclusion, this one of Gordon Strong's, too, with its strong points— if the profits of exciting and encouraging the concentration of citizens are to be kept up to profitable pitch and the citizen be further educated and reconciled to such increased congestion as this would eventually put up to him. This patient citizen—*so much more valuable, it seems, if and when congested!* Must the patient animal be further congested or further trained to congest himself until he has utterly relinquished his birthright? Congested yet some more and taught—he can learn—to take his time (his *own* time especially, mind you), and watch his step more carefully than ever? Is he, the pickle in this brine, to be further reconciled or harder pushed to keep on insanely crowding himself into vertical grooves in order that he may be stalled in horizontal ones?

Probably—but in the name of common sense and an Organic Architecture, why should the attempt be made to so reconcile him, by the Architects themselves, at least? Architects are yet something more than hired men, I hope. Else why should they not quit and get an honest living by honest labor in the country, preparing for the eventual urban exodus?

May we rightfully assume Architecture to be in the service of humanity?

MODERN ARCHITECTURE

Do we not know that if Architecture is not reared and maintained in such service it will eventually be damned?

The city, too, for another century, may we not still believe, was intended to add to the happiness, security and beauty of the life of the individual considered as a human being? Both assumptions, however, are denied by the un-American false premium put upon congestion by the skyscraper minded: un-American, I say, because for many years past rapid mobilizing, flying, motoring, teletransmission, steadily proceeding, have given back to man the sense of space, free space, in the sense that a great, free, new country ought to know it—given it back again to a free people. Steam took it away. Electricity and the Machine are giving it back again to man and have not only made super-concentration in a tight, narrow tallness unnecessary, but vicious, as the human motions of the city-habitant became daily more and more compact and violent. All appropriate sense of the space-values the American citizen is entitled to now in environment are gone in the great American City, as freedom is gone in a collision. Why are we as architects, as citizens, and as a nation, so slow to grasp the nature of this thing? Why do we continue to allow a blind instinct driven by greed to make the fashion and kill, for a free people in a new land, so many fine possibilities in spacious city planning? The human benefits of modern automobilization and teletransmission—where are they? Here we may see them all going by default, going by the board, betrayed—to preserve a stupid, selfish tradition of proprietorship. Is it because we are all, more or less, by Nature and opportunity, proprietors? Are we proprietors first and free-men afterward—if there is any afterward? At any rate, all these lately increased capacities of men for a wide range of lateral movement due to mechanicization are becoming useless to the citizen, because we happen to be sympathetic to the cupidity of proprietorship and see it not only as commercially profitable but as sensational.

Now, as a matter of course and in common with all Usonian villages that grow up into great cities and then grow on into the great metropolis, Father Knickerbocker's Village grew up to its present jammed estate; the great metropolis grew up on the original village-gridiron. New York, even without skyscrapers and automobiles, would have been crucified long ago by the gridiron. Barely tolerable for a village, the grid becomes a dangerous criss-cross check to all forward movements even in a large town where horses are motive power. But with the automobile and skyscraper that opposes and kills the automobile's contribution to the city, stop-and-go attempts to get across to somewhere or to anywhere, for that matter, in the great Metropolis, are inevitable waste—dangerous and maddening to a degree where sacrificial loss, in every sense but one, is for everyone.

Erstwhile village streets become grinding pits of metropolitan misery. Frustration of all life, in the-village-that-became-a-city, is imminent in this, the great unforeseen Metropolis; the Machine that built it and furnishes it forth also was equally unforeseen. Therefore it may not be due, alone, to this ever-to-be-regretted but inherited animal tendency of his race to herd, that the citizen has landed in all this urban jam. But that animal tendency to herd is all that keeps him jammed now against his larger and more important interests as a thinking being. He is tragically, sometimes comically, jammed. True, properly fenced, he jams himself. Properly fenced he may continue to jam himself for another decade or so, and cheerfully take the consequences. Strangely helpless for long periods of time is this Usonian, human social unit! But let us try to believe that—as Lincoln observed—not all of him for all of the time.

Now what does the human unit, so far in contempt in all this commercial Bedlam, receive as recompense for the pains of stricture and demoralizing loss of freedom, for the insulting degradation of his appropriate sense of space? What does he receive beside a foolish pride in the loss of himself to his time, increase in his taxes and increase in the number of handsome policemen at crossings?

A little study shows that the skyscraper in the rank and file of the "big show" is becoming something more than the rank abuse of a commercial expedient. *I see it as really a mechanical conflict of machine resources. An internal collision!* Even the landlord must soon realize that, as profitable landlordism, the success of verticality is but temporary, both in kind and character, because the citizen of the near future preferring horizontality—the gift of his motor-car, and telephonic or telegraphic inventions—will turn and reject verticality as the body of any American City. The citizen himself will turn upon it in self-defense. He will gradually abandon the city. It is now quite easy and safe for him to do so. Already the better part of him can do better than remain.

MODERN ARCHITECTURE

The landlord knows to his dismay that to sell the first ten floors of New York City is his new problem. The city fathers, too, now see that, except on certain open spaces, and under changed conditions where beautiful tall buildings might well rise as high as the city liked, the haphazard skyscraper in the rank and file of city streets is doomed—doomed by its own competition. In certain strategic locations in every village, town or city, tall buildings, and as tall as may be, should be permissible. But even in such locations very tall buildings should be restricted to only such area of the lot on which they stand as can be lighted from the outside and be directly reached from a single interior vertical groove of direct entrance to such space. Normal freedom of movement may thus be obtained below on the lot-area that is proprietary to the building itself. Thus all tall building would be restricted to the central portion thus usable of each private lot area, adding the balance of that area, as park space, to the city streets. There would then be no longer interior courts in any building.

All real estate in the rank and file and upon which the tall buildings will cast their shadows, and from which they must partly borrow their light, should in building stay down to the point where the streets will be relieved of motor-car congestion, whether that point be three, five, seven or nine stories, this to be determined according to the width of the streets on which the buildings stand.

As for the widening of streets, the present sidewalk and curb might be thrown into the street as transportation area, and the future sidewalks raised to head room above the present street level, becoming in skilful hands well designed architectural features of the city. And these elevated sidewalks should be connected across, each way, at the street intersections and down, by incline, to the streets below at the same four points of street intersections. This would make all pedestrian movement free of automobilization and—crossing in any direction above the traffic—safe. Motor cars might be temporarily parked just beneath these elevated sidewalks, the sidewalks, perhaps, cantilevered from the buildings.

Parking space in front of all present shop-windows would thus be provided and protected overhead by the elevated sidewalks. Show-windows would become double-decked by this scheme. Show-windows above for the sidewalks and show-windows below for the road-bed. This practical expedient, for of course it is no more than an expedient—only expedients are possible—would put a show-window emphasis on the second-story sidewalk level, which might become a mezzanine for entrances to the different shops also.

Entrances could be had to stores from the road-bed by recessions built in the lower store-front or by loggias that might be cut back into them. Such restraint and ordered release for tall buildings as here proposed might enhance the aspect of picturesque tallness and not leave further chaotic unfinished masses jamming into the blue. Such well designed separation of transportation and pedestrians as this might save the wear and tear of citizens doing daily the stations of the cross on their way to work.

Since in the Metropolis the gridiron is organic disaster, and to modify it much is impossible, why not, therefore, accept and respect it as definite limitation and ease it by some such practical expedient? Working toward such modifications as suggested would vastly benefit all concerned:

> First—By limiting construction.
> Second—By taking pedestrians off the road-bed and so widening it.

The upper sidewalks might be made sightly architectural features of the city. While all this means millions expended, it might be done; whereas to abandon the old cities may be done but to build new ones will not be done.

Various other expedients are now practicable, too, if they were to be insisted upon, as they might well be, in the public welfare—such as allowing no coal to be burned in the city, all being converted into electricity outside at the mines, and cutting down the now absurd automobile sizes of distinctly city carriers. All these things would palliate the evil of the skyscraper situation. But the danger of the city to humanity lies deeper, in the fact that human sensibilities naturally become callous or utterly damned by the constantly increasing futile sacrifices of time and space and patience, when condemned by stricture to their narrow grooves and crucified by their painful mechanical privileges. Condemned by their own senseless excess? Yes, and worse soon.

It seems that it has always been impossible to foresee the great city; not until it has grown up and won an individuality of its own is it aware of its needs. Its greatest asset is this individuality so hard won. The city begins as a village, is sometimes soon a town and then a city. Finally, perhaps, it becomes a Metropolis; more often the city remains just another hamlet. But every village could start out with the plans and specifications for a Metropolis, I suppose. Some few, Washington among them, did so and partially arrived after exciting misadventures.

But the necessity for the City wanes because of the larger human interest. That larger human interest? Is it not always on the side of *being*, considering the individual as related, even in his work—why not especially in his work?— to health and to the freedom in spacing, mobile in a free new country; living in and related to sun and air; living in and related to growing greenery about him as he moves and has his little being here in his brief sojourn on an Earth that should be inexpressibly beautiful to him!

What is he here for anyway? *Life* is the one thing of value to him, is it not? But the Machine-made in a Machine Age, here in the greatest of Machines, a great City, conspires to take that freedom away from him before he can fairly start to civilize himself. We know why it does. And let us at this moment try to be honest with ourselves on another point, this "thrill"—the vaunted *beauty* of the skyscraper as an individual performance. At first, as we have seen, the skyscraper was a pile of cornice-buildings in reborn style, one cornice-building riding the top of another cornice-building. Then a great Architect saw it as a unit, and as beautiful Architecture. Pretty soon, certain other architects, so educated—probably by the Beaux-Arts—as to see that way, *saw it as a column*, with base, shaft and capital. Then other architects with other tastes seemed to see it as Gothic—commercial competitor to the Cathedral. Now the wholesale manufacturers of space-for-rent are seeing it as a commercial tower-building with plain masonry surfaces and restrained ornament upon which New York's set-back laws have forced a certain picturesque outline, an outline pretty much all alike. A picturesqueness at first welcome as a superficial relief, but already visible as the same monotony-in-variety that has been the fate of all such attempts to beautify our country. Standardization defeats these attempts—the Machine triumphs over them all, because they are all false. Principle is not at work in them.

The Skyscraper of today is only the prostitute semblance of the architecture it professes to be. The heavy brick and stone that falsely represents walls is, by the very set-back laws, unnaturally forced onto the interior steel stilts to be carried down by them through twenty, fifty or more stories to the ground. The picture is improved, but the picturesque element in it all is false work

94

built over a hollow box. These new tops are shams, too—box-balloons. The usual service of the Doctor-of-Appearances has here again been rendered to modern Society.

New York, so far as material wealth goes, piled high and piling higher into the air, is a commercial Machine falsely qualified by a thin disguise. The disguise is a collection of brick and masonry façades, glaring signs and staring dead walls, peak beside peak, rising from canyon cutting across canyon. Everything in the narrowing lanes below is "on the hard," groaning, rattling, shrieking! In reality the great machine-made Machine is a forest of riveted steel posts, riveted girder-beams, riveted brackets and concrete slabs, steel reinforced, closed in by heavy brick and stone walls, all carried by the steel framing itself—finally topped by water-tanks, set-backs, and spires, dead walls decorated by exaggerated advertising or chastely painted in panels with colored brick-work.

What beauty the whole has is haphazard, notwithstanding the book-architecture which space-makers-for-rent have ingeniously tied onto the splendid steel sinews that strain from story to story beneath all this weight of make-believe. But the Lintels, Architraves, Pilasters and Cornices of the pseudo-classicist are now giving way to the better plainness of surface-and-mass effects. This is making, now, the picturesque external New York, while the steel, behind it all, still nobly stands up to its more serious responsibilities. Some of the more recent skyscraper decoration may be said to be very handsomely suggestive of an Architecture to come. But how far away, yet, are appearances from reality!

The true nature of this thing is prostitute to the shallow picturesque, in attempt to render a wholly insignificant, therefore inconsequential, beauty. In any depth of human experience it is an ignoble sacrifice. No factitious sham like this should be accepted as "Culture."

As seen in "THE PASSING OF THE CORNICE," we are the modern Romans.

Reflect that the ancient Romans at the height of their prosperity lied likewise to themselves no less shamefully, when they pasted Greek architecture onto their magnificent engineering invention of the masonry arch to cover it decently. The Romans, too, were trying to make the kind of picture or the grand gesture demanded by Culture. The Roman arch was, in that age, comparable to the greatest of all scientific or engineering inventions

95

in our own Machine Age, comparable especially to our invention of steel. So likewise, what integrity any solution of the skyscraper problem might have in itself as good steel-and-glass construction has been stupidly thrown away. The native forests of steel, concrete and glass, the new materials of our time, have great possibilities. But in the hands of the modern Doctor-of-Appearances they have been made to *seem* rather than allowed to *be*. Sophisticated polishing by the accredited Doctor only puts a glare upon its shame. It cannot be possible that sham like this is really our own civilized choice?

But owing to the neglect of any noble standard, such as that of an organic architecture, it is all going by default. All—sold.

Were it only strictly business there would be hope. But even that is not the case except as competitive advertising in any form is good business. Business ethics make a good platform for true Aesthetics in this Machine Age or in any other.

No—what makes this pretentious ignorance so tragic is that there is a conscious yearn, a generosity, a prodigality in the name of taste and refinement in nearly all of it. Were only mummery dropped, temporary expedient though it may be in itself, space-manufacturing-for-rent, so far as that goes in the skyscraper, might become genuine architecture and be beautiful as standardization in steel, metals and glass.

We now have reasonably safe mechanical means to build buildings as tall as we want to see them, and there are many places and uses for them in any village, town, or city, but especially in the country. Were we to learn to limit such buildings to their proper places and give them the integrity as standardized steel and glass and copper they deserve, we would be justly entitled to a spiritual pride in them; our submission to them would not then be servile in any sense. We might take genuine pride in them with civic integrity. The skyscraper might find infinite expression in variety—as beauty.

But today the great city as an edifice mocks any such integrity. Artists idealize the edifice in graphic dreams of gigantic tombs into which all life has fled—or must flee—or in which humanity remains to perish. Uninhabitable monstrosities? An insanity we are invited to admire?

From any humane standpoint the super-concentration of the skyscraper is super-imposition not worth its human price.

It is impossible not to believe that, of necessity, horizontality and the freedom of new beauty will eventually take the place of opportune verticality and senseless stricture. And if these desiderata cannot be realized *in* the city, if they have no place there, they will take *the place of the city*. Breadth is now possible and preferable to verticality and vertigo, from any sensible human standpoint. Transportation and electrical transmission have made breadth of space more a human asset than ever, else what does our great machine-power mean to human beings? In all the history of human life upon earth, breadth, the consciousness of freedom, the sense of space appropriate to Freedom, is more desirable than height to live with in the use and beauty that it yields mankind.

Why then, has Commerce, the soul of this great, crude and youthful Nation, any pressing need further to capitalize and exploit the rudimentary animal instincts of the race it thrives on, or need to masquerade in the path picturesque, like the proverbial wolf in sheep's clothing, in New York City or anywhere else?

As for Beauty—Standardization and its cruel but honest tool, the Machine, given understanding and accomplished technique, might make our own civilization beautiful in a new and noble sense. These inept, impotent, mechanistic elements, so cruel in themselves, have untold possibilities of beauty. In spite of prevalent and profitable abuses Standardization and the Machine are here to serve humanity. However much they may be out of drawing, human imagination may use them as a means to more life, and greater life, for the Commonwealth. So why should the Architect as Artist shirk or ignore humane possibilities to become anybody's hired man—for profit? Or if he is on his own why should he be willing to pay tribute to false gods merely to please the unsure taste of a transitory period, or even his own "superior" taste?

* * *   * * *   * * *

Today all skyscrapers have been whittled to a point, and a smoking chimney is usually the point. They whistle, they steam, they moor dirigibles, they wave flags, or they merely aspire, and nevertheless very much resemble each other at all points. They compete—they pictorialize—and are all the same.

But they do not materialize as Architecture. Empty of all other significance, seen from a distance something like paralysis seems to stultify them. They

97

are monotonous. They no longer startle or amuse. Verticality is already stale; vertigo has given way to nausea; perpendicularity is changed by corrugation of various sorts, some wholly crosswise, some crosswise at the sides with perpendicularity at the center, yet all remaining "envelopes." The types of envelope wearily reiterate the artificial set-back, or are forced back for effect, with only now and then a flight that has no meaning, like the Chrysler Building.

The light that shone in the Wainwright Building as a promise, flickered feebly and is fading away. Skyscraper Architecture is a mere matter of a clumsy imitation masonry envelope for a steel skeleton. They have no life of their own—no life to give, receiving none from the nature of construction. No, none. And they have no relation to their surroundings. Utterly barbaric, they rise regardless of special consideration for environment or for each other, except to win the race or get the tenant. Space as a becoming psychic element of the American city is gone. Instead of this fine sense is come the tall and narrow stricture. The skyscraper envelope is not ethical, beautiful, or permanent. It is a commercial exploit or a mere expedient. It has no higher ideal of unity than commercial success.

6: THE CITY

SMALL TOWN HALL
PLASTERED FRAME.
1912-1913

6: THE CITY

IS THE city a natural triumph of the herd instinct over humanity, and therefore a temporal necessity as a hang-over from the infancy of the race, to be outgrown as humanity grows?

Or is the city only a persistent form of social disease eventuating in the fate all cities have met?

Civilization always seemed to need the city. The city expressed, contained, and tried to conserve what the flower of the civilization that built it most cherished, although it was always infested with the worst elements of society as a wharf is infested with rats. So the city may be said to have served civilization. But the civilizations that built the city invariably died with it. Did the civilizations themselves die *of it?*

Acceleration invariably preceded such decay.

Acceleration in some form usually occurs just before decline and while this acceleration may not be the cause of death it is a dangerous symptom. A temperature of 104 in the veins and arteries of any human being would be regarded as acceleration dangerous to life.

In the streets and avenues of the city acceleration due to the skyscraper is similarly dangerous to any life the city may have left, even though we yet fail to see the danger.

I believe the city, as we know it today, is to die.

We are witnessing the acceleration that precedes dissolution.

Our modern civilization, however, may not only survive the city but may profit by it; probably the death of the city is to be the greatest service the Machine will ultimately render the human being if, by means of it, Man conquers. If the Machine conquers, it is conceivable that Man will again remain to perish with his city, because the city, like all minions of the Machine, has grown up in man's image—minus only the living impetus that is Man. The city is itself only Man-the-Machine—the deadly shadow of Sentient Man.

But now comes a shallow philosophy accepting Machinery, in itself, as prophetic. Philosophers draw plans, picture, and prophesy a future city, more desirable, they say, than the pig-pile now in travail, their pictures reducing everything to a mean height—geometrically spaced.

101

MODERN ARCHITECTURE

In order to preserve air and passage, this future city relegates the human individual as a unit or factor to pigeonhole 337611, block F, avenue A, street No. 127. And there is nothing at which to wink an eye that could distinguish No. 337611 from No. 337610 or 27643, bureau D, intersection 118 and 119.

Thus is the sentient individual factor—the citizen—appropriately disposed of in the cavernous recesses of a mechanistic system appropriate to man's ultimate extinction.

This future city may be valuable and utilitarian along a line of march toward the ultimate triumph of the Machine over Man and may be accomplished before the turn finally comes.

To me it is dire prophecy. Skull and cross-bones symbolize a similar fate. Let us prefer to prophesy, finally, the triumph of Man over the Machine.

• • •   • • •   • • •

For final text, then, for our final discourse:

"Except as you, Sons-of-Earth, honor your birthright, and cherish it well by human endeavor, you shall be cut down, and perish in darkness, or go up in high towers—a sacrifice to the most high God. Look you well, therefore, to yourselves in your posterity. Keep all close to Earth, your feet upon the Earth, your hands employed in the fruitfulness thereof be your vision never so far, and on high."

—*Attributed to some unheeded Babylonian prophet.*

What built the cities that, invariably, have died? Necessity.

With that necessity gone, only dogged Tradition that is another name for *habit* can keep the city alive, Tradition that has the vitality of inertia and the power of the ball and chain.

Necessity built the city when we had no swift, universal means of transportation and had no means of communication except by various direct personal contacts. Then the city became naturally the great meeting-place, the grand concourse, the immediate source of wealth and power in human intercourse. Only by congregating thus, the vaster the congregation the better, could the better fruits of human living then be had.

In that day the real life of the city lay in the stress of individual ties and the

102

variety of contacts. The electric spark of curiosity and surprise was alive in the street, in public buildings, in the home.

Government the city had—Fashions and Fads. But the salt and savour of individual wit, taste and character made the city a festival of life: a carnival as compared with any city today.

And Architecture then reflected this livelier human condition as it now reflects the Machine. Nor had the common denominator then arrived in the reckoning.

The common denominator has arrived with the Machine in *Usonia*. Machine prophecy such as we have just referred to shows, if nothing else, that we are to deal with machinery considered as common-denominator salvation and in its most dangerous form here among us and deal with it soon, before it has finally to deal with our posterity as dominator. To deny virtue to the common denominator or to deny virtue to its eventual emancipator the Machine would be absurd. But the eventual city the common denominator will build with its machines will not only be greatly different from the olden city or the city of today; it will be vastly different from the new Machine-city of Machine-prophecy as we see it outlined by Le Corbusier and his school.

What once made the city the great and powerful human interest that it was is now preparing the reaction that will drive the city somewhere, into something else. The human element in the civic equation may already be seen drifting or pushed—going in several different directions.

Congestion was no unmixed human evil until electricity, electrical intercommunication, motor cars, the telephone and publicity came; add to these the airship when it lays away its wings and becomes a self-contained mechanical unit.

Accepting all these, everything changes.

Organic consequences of these changes, unperceived at first, now appear. Freedom of human reach and movement, therefore the human *horizon* as a sphere of *action* is, in a single decade, immeasurably widened by new service rendered by the Machine. Horizontality has received an impetus that widens human activities immeasurably.

Therefore such need for concentration as originally built the city is really nearing an end. But these new facilities—of movement—gifts to us of the Machine, have, for a time, only intensified the old activity.

MODERN ARCHITECTURE

We are really witnessing an inevitable collision between mechanistic factors. The struggle is on. Additional human pressure, thus caused, thoughtlessly finds release by piling high into the air. The thoughtless human tendency in any emergency is to stand still, or to run away. We do—stay right there and pile up, or run away from the collision, to live to fight again some other day. To meet this human trait of staying right where we are, the skyscraper was born and, as we have seen, has become a tyranny. But the skyscraper will serve, equally well, those who are to run away, because probably the tall building has its real future in the country. But the skyscraper is now the landlord's ruse to hold the profits not only of concentration but of super-concentration: in the skyscraper itself we see the commercial expedient that enables the landlord to exploit the city to the limit, and exploit it by ordinance.

So Greater Freedom to spread out without inconvenience, the most valuable gift brought by these new servants—electrical intercommunication, the automobile, telephone, airship and radio—has been perverted for the moment into the skyscraper, and the gifts of the Machine diverted to profit lucky realty.

Let us admit popular thrill in the acceleration, the excitement, directly due to these *new* mechanistic facilities. Temperatures run high. No one seems to know whether the excess is healthy excitement of growth or the fever of disease; whether it means progress or is only some new form of exploitation.

Forces are themselves blind. In all history we may see that the human beings involved with elemental forces remain blind also for long periods of time. But —saving clause—along with the forces released by our new mechanistic servants, there comes in our day an *ubiquitous publicity*, a valuable publicity that often succeeds in getting done in a month what formerly may have drifted a decade. We have already cut elapsed time in all forms of human intercommunication, a hundred to one. To be conservative, what took a century in human affairs now takes ten years.

Fifteen years, an epoch.

Thirty years, an age.

So the reactions to any human activity, idea or movement may control this great agency, and even in one lifetime show the people the wisdom or folly of the nature of any particular activity and call for correction before the affair is too far gone. Thus the fate of earlier civilization may be avoided by the dissemination of knowledge in ours. Educational influences thus brought to bear may avert disaster.

• • •　　• • •　　• • •

The traffic problem, as we have already seen in the "TYRANNY OF THE SKY-SCRAPER," forces attention to tyrannical verticality. The traffic problem is new but increasingly difficult—if not impossible—of solution.

Other problems will call soon and call louder.

As we have seen, the gridiron, originally laid out for the village now grown to the metropolis, already is cause for sufficient economic waste and human pain to wreck the structure of the city. High blood pressure, in the congested veins and arteries that were once the peaceful village gridiron, is becoming intolerable.

The pretended means of relief provided by space-makers-for-rent—the sky-scraper itself—is now rendering distress more acute. The same means of relief carried somewhat further, and long before the solution reaches its logical conclusion, will have killed the patient—the overgrown city. Witness the splitting up of Los Angeles and Chicago into several centers, again to be split into many more.

And yet in new Machine-prophecy, the tyranny of the skyscraper now finds a philosophy to fortify itself as an *ideal!*

We see, by the prophetic pictures of the city of the future, how the humanity involved therein is to be dealt with in order to render the human benefits of electricity, the automobile, the telephone, the airship and radio into herd-exploitation instead of into individual human lives.

And alongside these specific skyscraper solutions-by-picture of downtown difficulties there usually goes the problem of the tenement, the none-too-pretty picture of wholesale housing of the poor.

The poor, it seems, are still to be with us and multiplied, in this grand new era of the Machine. At any rate they are to be accepted, confirmed and especially provided for therein as we may see in the plans.

Catastrophe is to be made organic—built in.

That the poor will benefit by increased sanitation may be seen and granted at first glance. But not only are the living quarters of the poor to be made germproof, but life itself, wherever individual choice is concerned, is to be made just as antiseptic, if we trust our own eyes.

The poor man is to become just as is the rich man—No. 367222, block 99, shelf 17, entrance K.

But the surface-and-mass architecture that now proposes to extinguish the poor man as human, has already proposed to do the same for his landlord. Therefore why should the poor man complain? Has he not, still, his labor for his pains?

There he is, the poor man! No longer in a rubbish heap. No. He is a mechanized unit in a mechanical system, but, so far as he goes, he still is but two by twice. He has been cleaned up but toned down.

Nor can the poor in the modernistic picture choose anything aesthetically alive to live with, at least so far as neighbors or landlord can see it. Dirty rags have been covered with a clean cardboard smock.

The poor man is exhibit C—cog 309,761,128 in the machine, in this new model for the greater machine the city is to become.

Observe the simplified aspect!

This indeed, is the *Ne Plus Ultra* of the *E Pluribus Unum* of Machinery. This new scheme for the city is delightfully impartial, extinguishes everyone, distinguishes nothing except by way of the upper stories, unless it be certain routine economies sacred to a business man's civilization, certain routine economies to be shared by the innovators with the ubiquitous numericals who are the "common denominator," shared with them by the nominators of the system as seen perfected in the picture. Shared fifty-fifty? Half to the initial nominator, half to the numericals? Fair enough—or—who can say?

The indistinguishable division of the benefits must in any case be left to the generosity of the initial nominators themselves, whoever they are. And who may say who they are?

But Humanity here is orderly. Human beings are again rank and file in the great war—this time industrial—a peaceful war. The rank and file of the common denominator this time is gratuitously officered by architecture, standardized like any army, marched not only to and fro but up and down. Up and down—even more—much more and more to come. The common denominator on these up-and-down terms would be no more alive without the initial nominator than the machine will be without the human brain.

106

THE CITY

The common denominator itself has become the Machine, come into its very own at last before the war is fairly begun.

"The Noble Duke of York, he had ten thousand men"—he made them all go ten floors up and ten floors up again. And none may know just why they now go narrowly up, up, up, to come narrowly down, down, down—instead of freely going in and out and comfortably around about among the beautiful things to which their lives are related on this earth. Is this not to reduce everyone but the mechanistic devisors and those who may secure the privileges of the top stories, to the ranks—of the poor?

$$\cdots \quad \cdots \quad \cdots$$

Well—the poor?

Why are they the poor? Is there mechanical cure, then, for shiftlessness—machine-made? Or are the thriftless those whom the Machine Age is to herd beneficially in the mass and cover becomingly with a semblance of decency in a machine-made Utopia? Or are the poor now to be the thrifty—themselves thus turned poor in all senses but one?

The lame, halt, blind and the sick are the only poor. As for the other poor—the discouraged, the unhappy—fresh air, free space, green grass growing all around, fruits, flowers, vegetables in return for the little work on the ground they require, would do more to abolish their poverty than any benefice mechanistic devisors can ever confer.

At present the urban whirl *is* common-denominator recreation; the urban crowd *is* common-denominator consolation; the dark corners of movie halls *are* the common-denominator retreats for recreation when those retreats are not far worse.

And the herd-instinct that moves in the crowd and curses it is only the more developed by the mechanistic conditions in which the crowd swarms and lives. Millions are already sunk so low as to know no other preferment, to desire none. The common denominator—so profitable when congested—being further educated to congest, *taught* to be lost when not excited by the pressure and warmth of the crowd, turns argus-eyed toward what—more whirl?

Yet many of the individuals composing the crowd, the best among them, know well that an ounce of independence and freedom in spacing under natural circumstances, is worth a ton of machine patronage, however disguised or distributed as sanitation or as "Art."

107

MODERN ARCHITECTURE

A free America, democratic in the sense that our forefathers intended it to be, means just this *individual* freedom for all, rich or poor, or else this system of government we call democracy is only an expedient to enslave man to the Machine and make him like it.

But Democracy will, by means of the Machine, demonstrate that the city is no place for the poor, because even the poor are human.

· · ·   · · ·   · · ·

The Machine, once our formidable adversary, is ready and competent to undertake the drudgeries of living on this Earth. The margin of leisure even now widens as the Machine succeeds. This margin of leisure should be spent, with the fields, in the gardens and in travel. The margin should be expanded and devoted to making beautiful the environment in which human beings are born to live—into which one brings the children who will be the Usonia of tomorrow.

And the Machine, I believe—absurd as it may seem now, absurd even to those who are to be the first to leave—will enable all that was human in the city to go to the country and grow up with it: enable human life to be based squarely and fairly on the ground. The sense of freedom in space is an abiding human desire, because the horizontal line is the line of domesticity —the Earthline of human life. The City has taken this freedom away.

A market, a counting-house and a factory is what the city has already become: the personal element in it all—the individual—withdrawing more and more as time goes on.

Only when the city becomes purely and simply utilitarian, will it have the order that is beauty, and the simplicity which the Machine, in competent hands, may very well render as human benefit. That event may well be left to the Machine.

This, *the only possible ideal machine* seen as a *city*, will be invaded at ten o'clock, abandoned at four, for three days of the week. The other four days of the week will be devoted to the more or less joyful matter of living elsewhere under conditions natural to man. The dividing lines between town and country are even now gradually disappearing as conditions are reversing themselves. The country absorbs the life of the city as the city shrinks to the utilitarian purpose that now alone justifies its existence. Even that concentration for utilitarian purposes we have just admitted may be first to go, as the result of impending decentralization of industry. It will soon become unnecessary to concentrate in masses for any purpose whatsoever. The individual unit, in more sympathetic grouping on the ground, will grow stronger in the hard earned freedom gained at first by that element of the city not prostitute to the Machine. Henry Ford stated this idea in his plan for the development of Muscle Shoals.

Even the small town is too large. It will gradually merge into the general non-urban development. Ruralism as distinguished from Urbanism is American, and truly Democratic.

The country already affords great road systems—splendid highways. They, too, leading toward the city at first, will eventually hasten reaction away from it. Natural parks in our country are becoming everywhere available. And millions of individual building sites, large and small, good for little else, are everywhere neglected. Why, where there is so much idle land, should it be parcelled out by realtors to families, in strips 25', 50' or even 100' wide? This imposition is a survival of feudal thinking, of the social economies practised by and upon the serf. An acre to the family should be the democratic minimum if this Machine of ours *is a success!*

What stands in the way?

It is only necessary to compact the standardized efficiency of the Machine, confine the concentration of its operation to where it belongs and distribute the benefits at large. The benefits are human benefits or they are bitter fruit. Much bitter fruit already hangs on the city-tree beside the good, to rot the whole.

An important feature of the coming disintegration of the Usonian city may be seen in any and every service station along the highway. The service station is future city service in embryo. Each station that happens to be naturally located will as naturally grow into a neighborhood distribution center, meeting-place, restaurant, rest room or whatever else is needed. A thousand centers as city equivalents to every town or city center we now have, will be the result of this advance agent of decentralization.

To many such traffic stations, destined to become neighborhood centers, will be added, perhaps, features for special entertainment not yet available by a man's own fireside. But soon there will be little not reaching him at his own fireside by broadcasting, television and publication. In cultural means, the Machine is improving rapidly and constantly.

Perfect distribution like ubiquitous publicity is a common capacity of the Machine. This single capacity, when it really begins to operate, will revolutionize our present arrangement for concentration in cities. Stores, linked to decentralized chain service stations, will give more perfect machinery of distribution than could ever be had by centralization in cities.

Complete mobilization of the people is another result fast approaching. Therefore the opportunity will come soon for the individual to pick up by the wayside anything in the way of food and supplies he may require, as well as to find a satisfactory temporary lodging.

The great highways are in process of becoming the decentralized metropolis. Wayside interests of all kinds will be commonplace. The luxurious motor-bus, travelling over magnificent road-systems, will make intercommunication universal and interesting. The railway is already only for the "long haul" in many parts of the country.

A day's journey anywhere will soon be something to be enjoyed in itself, enlivened, serviced and perfectly accommodated anywhere en route. No need to tangle up in spasmodic stop-and-go traffic in a trip to town or to any city at all.

Cities are great mouths. New York the greatest mouth in the world. With generally perfect distribution of food and supplies over the entire area of the countryside, one of the vital elements helping to build the city has left it forever, to spread out on the soil from which it came: local products finding a short haul direct, where an expensive long haul and then back again was once necessary.

Within easy distance of any man's dwelling will be everything needed in the category of foodstuffs or supplies which the city itself can now supply. The "movies," "talkies" and all, will soon be seen and heard better at home than in any hall. Symphony concerts, operas and lectures will eventually be taken more easily to the home than the people there can be taken to the great halls in old style, and be heard more satisfactorily in congenial company. The home of the individual social unit will contain in itself in this respect all the city heretofore could afford, plus intimate comfort and free individual choice.

110

THE CITY

Schools will be made delightful, beautiful places, much smaller, and more specialized. Of various types, they will be enlivening, charming features along the byways of every *countryside*. Our popular games will be features in the school parks, which will be really sylvan parks available far and near to everyone.

To gratify what is natural and desirable in the get-together instinct of the community natural places of great beauty—in our mountains, seasides, prairies and forests—will be developed as automobile objectives, and at such recreation grounds would center the planetarium, the race-track, the great concert hall, the various units of the national theater, museums, and art galleries. Similar common interests of the many will be centered there naturally, ten such places to one we have now.

There will be no privately owned theaters, although there will be places for them along the highways. But good plays and other entertainments might be seen at these automobile objectives from end to end of the country in various national circuits—wherever a play showed itself popular or desired.

Such objectives would naturally compete with each other in interest and beauty, stimulate travel, and make mobilization a pleasure, not a nuisance— affording somewhere worth while to go. The entire countryside would then be a well developed park—buildings standing in it, tall or wide, with beauty and privacy for everyone.

There will soon remain the necessity for only shorter and shorter periods of concentration in the offices directly concerned with invention, standardization and production. The *city of the near future* will be a depot for the factory— perhaps. Whatever it is, it will be only a degraded mechanistic servant of the Machine, because Man himself will have escaped to find all the city ever offered him, plus the privacy the city never had and is trying to teach him that he does not want. Man will find the *manlike Freedom* for himself and his that Democracy must mean.

Very well—how to mitigate, meantime, the horror of human life caught helpless or unaware in the machinery that is the city? How easiest and soonest to assist the social unit in escaping the gradual paralysis of individual independence that is characteristic of the Machine-made moron, a paralysis of the emotional nature necessary to the triumph of the Machine over Man, instead of the quickening of his humanity necessary to Man's triumph over the Machine?

That is the Architect's immediate problem, as I see it.

Measured over great free areas, the living interest should be educated to lie in the contact of free individualities in the freedom of sun, light and air, breadth of spacing—*with* the ground. Again we need the stress of encountering varieties on a scale and in circumstances worthy the ideal of democracy and more a part of External Nature than ever before seen—more so because of internal harmony. We want the electric spark of popular curiosity and surprise to come to life again, along the highways and byways and over every acre of the land. In charming homes and schools and significant public gathering places . . . architectural beauty related to natural beauty. Art should be natural and be itself the joy of creating perfect harmony between ourselves and the birthright we have all but sold.

We may now dream of the time when there will be less government, yet more ordered freedom. More generous human spacing, we may be sure, will see to that.

When the salt and savour of individual wit, taste and character in modern life will have come into its own and the countryside far and near will be a festival of life—great life—then only will Man have succeeded with his Machine. The Machine will then have become the Liberator of Human Life.

And our Architecture will reflect this.

• • •   • • •   • • •

Shirking this reality, vaunted "modernity" is still making another "picture," everywhere clinging to the pictorial—missing joy in merely seeking pleasure. "Modernistic" is attempting by fresh attitudinizing to improve the "picture." The "new movement" still seeks to recreate joy by making shift to improve the imitation, neglectful of all but appropriate gestures.

But even an improved imitation as a picture will soon be trampled down and out—because of the Machine. No amount of picture making will ever save America now!

The Artifex alone in search of Beauty can give back the significance we have lost—and enable the Republic to arrive at that Great Art, in the inevitably Man-made concerns of life, which will be to the human spirit what clear

112

THE CITY

springs of water, blue sky, green grass and noble trees are to parched animal senses. For where the work of the artificer is a necessity, there the Artist must be creatively at work on *significance* as a higher *form* of life, or the life of the human spirit will perish in this fresh endeavor that as yet is only a promise in this twentieth century.

The Necessity for Artistry, that is laid upon us by the desire to be civilized, is not a matter only of appearances. Human *necessity*, however Machine-made or mechanically met, carries within itself the secret of the beauty we must have to keep us fit to live or to live with. We need it to live in or to live on. That new beauty should be something to live *for*. The "picture," never fear, will take care of itself. In any organic architecture the Picture will be a natural result, a significant consequence, not a perverse *cause* of pose and sham.

Eventually we must live for the Beautiful whether we want to or not. Our industrial champion, Henry Ford, was forced to recognize this—probably not connecting the beautiful with Art, "the Bunk." Just as he did in his industry, so America will be compelled to allow necessity its own honest beauty, or die a death nowise different from those nations whose traditions we accepted and idolized.

Unless what we now miscall culture becomes natively fit and is no longer allowed to remain superficial, this Picture, which America is so extravagantly busy "pictorializing," can only hasten the end. The buttons, stuffs, dictums, wheels and things we are now using for the purpose of the picture will smother the essential—the life they were falsely made to falsely conceal instead of to express. And this experiment in civilization we call Democracy will find its way to a scrap-heap into which no subsequent race may paw with much success for proofs of quality.

Suppose some catastrophe suddenly wiped out what we have done to these United States at this moment. And suppose, ten centuries thereafter, antiquarians came to seek the significance of what *we* were in the veins of us—in the ruins that remained, what would they find? Just what would they find to be the nature of this picture-minded "pictorialization" of life and its contribution to the wisdom or the beauty of the ages past or to come?

Would the future find we were a jackdaw-people with a monkey-psychology given over to the vice of devices—looking to devices for salvation—and discovering this very salvation to be only another and final device?

No? Just the same, they *would* find broken bits of every civilization that ever took its place in the sun hoarded in all sorts of irrevelant places in ours.

They would dig up traces of sacred Greek monuments for banking houses. The papal dome in cast iron fragments would litter the ancient site of every seat of authority, together with fragments in stone and terra-cotta of twelfth century cathedrals where offices and shops were indicated by mangled machinery—relics of dwellings in fifty-seven varieties and fragments of stone in heaps, none genuine in character, all absurdly mixed. They would find the toilet appurtenances of former ages preserved as classic parlor ornaments in ours. They would find a wilderness of wiring, wheels and complex devices of curious ingenuity, and—ye gods—what a collection of buttons! They might unearth traces of devices that enabled men to take to the air like birds or to go into the water like fishes, and they might find relics of our competent schemes of transportation and a network or web of tangled wires stringing across the country, the relic of all our remarkable teletransmissions. But I think the most characteristic relic of all would be our plumbing. Everywhere a vast collection of enamelled or porcelain waterclosets, baths and washbowls, white tiles and brass piping. Next would be the vast confusion of riveted steelwork in various states of collapse and disintegration where it had been imbedded in concrete. Where the steel was not so buried all would be gone except here and there where whole machines—a loom, a linotype, a cash register, a tractor, a dynamo, a passenger elevator—might be entombed in concrete chambers and so preserved to arouse speculation and curiosity, or to cause amusement as they were taken for relics of a faith in devices—a faith that failed! Of the cherished PICTURE we are making nothing of any significance would remain. The ruin would defy restoration by the historian; it would represent a total loss in human Culture, except as a possible warning. A few books might be preserved to assist restoration, although the chemicalized paper now in use would probably have destroyed most of them utterly. Such glass and pottery as we make could tell but little except curious falsehoods. Certain fragments of stone building on the city sites would remain to puzzle the savant, for they would be quite Greek or quite Roman or quite Medieval Gothic, unless they were Egyptian or Byzantine. But mainly they would find heaps of a Pseudo-Renaissance,—something that never told, nor ever could tell, anything at all. Only our industrial buildings could tell anything worth knowing about us. But few of these buildings would survive that long —electrolysis and rust would have eaten them utterly, excepting those where steel was buried in concrete. Glass fragments would be found in great quantity, but the frames, unless they happened to be bronze, and all else would be gone. They would have no skyscraper to gauge us by. Not one of those we have built would be there.

How and where, then, were it suddenly interrupted, would our progressive democratizing based upon picturizing the appliance, take its place in the procession of civilizations that rose and fell at appointed times and places? What Architecture would appear in the ruins?

· · ·   · · ·   · · ·

And yet—in all this attempt behind the significantly insignificant picture, may we not see culture itself becoming year by year more plastic? Are not some of our modern ideas less obviously constructed and more potent from within wherever we are beginning to emerge from the first intoxication of liberty? The eventual consequence of Individual Freedom is surely the elimination by free thought of the insignificant and false. Imprisoning forms and fascinating philosophic abstractions grow weaker as character grows stronger and more enlightened according to Nature; this they will do in Freedom such as we profess—*if only we will practise* that Freedom. And, in spite of our small hypocrisy and adventitious reactions, let no one doubt that we really do yearn to practise genuine Freedom to a far greater extent than we do, all inhibitions and prohibitions notwithstanding. Yes, we may see a new sense of manlike Freedom growing up to end all this cruel make-believe. Freedom, in reality, is already impatient of pseudo-classic posture and will soon be sick of all picturizing whatsoever.

A common sense is on the rise that will sweep our borrowed finery, and the scene-painting that always goes with it, to the museums, and encourage good life so to live that America may honorably pay her debt to manhood by keeping her promises to her own Ideal.